New Faces of Canadian Catholics

The Asians

Terence J. Fay SJ

NOVALIS

© 2009 Novalis Publishing Inc.

Cover design: Blair Turner
Layout: Audrey Wells
Interior photographs: courtesy of Terence J. Fay SJ, except for the photograph on page 92, Crestock, artist: donsimon, Angeles Philippines, and the photograph on page 113, which is courtesy of Manila Metropolitan Cathedral-Basilica, Philippines

Published by Novalis
10 Lower Spadina Avenue, Suite 400
Toronto, Ontario, Canada
M5V 2Z2
www.novalis.ca

Library and Archives Canada Cataloguing in Publication

Fay, Terence J. (Terence James), 1932-
    New faces of Canadian Catholics : the Asians / Terence J. Fay.

Includes bibliographical references and index. ISBN 978-2-89646-148-6

    1. Asian Canadians--Religion. 2. Catholic Church--Canada. I. Title.

BX1421.3.F39 2009   282'.71   C2009-903930-3

Printed in Canada.

We acknowledge the financial support of the Government of Canada through the Book Publishing Industry Development Program (BPIDP) for our publishing activities.

5   4   3   2   1   13   12   11   10   09

New Faces of Canadian Catholics

The Asians

Acknowledgments

Since 2002, numerous Asian Canadian readers have purchased copies of my *A History of Canadian Catholics*. Since that volume deals with events up to the years immediately following the Second Vatican Council, which ended in 1965, it contains little content about the contribution of Asian Canadians to the Catholic Church. After Vatican II, Asians migrated to Canada in large numbers and since then have made important contributions to the Church. Thus, it became apparent to me that a full history of the Catholic Church in Canada required a supplementary volume on the migration and integration of Asian Catholics into the Canadian Church.

I assembled the materials for this study of Asian Catholics with the help of many people from various places across Canada and elsewhere. First, I would like to thank my colleagues at the Toronto School of Theology and the members of my religious community at Our Lady of Lourdes parish in downtown Toronto for their support during this enterprise. I am most grateful to Mark McGowan, Principal of the University of St. Michael's College, Peter Meehan of Seneca College and York University, and Elizabeth McGahan of the University of New Brunswick, Saint John, who read parts or all of the manuscript and made incisive comments. I acknowledge the expert help of Stanley Amaladas of Royal Roads University at Victoria for helping me understand the subtle wisdom and methods of qualitative analysis. I appreciate the assistance from Archivist Marc Lerman and the Director of the Personnel Office, Msgr. Marco Laurencic, of the Archdiocese of Toronto. Some sections of the manuscript were published in another form in *Historical Studies*, the journal of the Canadian Catholic Historical Association, and in *Budhi: A Journal of Ideas and Culture*, published by Ateneo de Manila University in the Philippines. I am pleased with the enthusiastic support I received from editor Anne Louise Mahoney and Novalis in preparing the manuscript for publication.

I wish to express my gratitude to Archbishop Adam Exner OMI and to Asian Canadian pastors in various cities across Canada, who helped me select parishioners to interview: Fathers Peter Chiang, Dennis Polanco SA, Paul Chu, and Aloysius Lou (Chinese), Father Donald Larson (Filipino), and Father Peter Kiang (Korean) in Vancouver; Fathers Vincent Tungolh and Diosdado Parrenas (Filipino), and Father John Nguyen (Vietnamese) in Winnipeg; Fathers Peter Leung, Dominic Kong, and Peter Chin (Chinese), Fathers Gregory Choi, Peter Choi, and Min Kyu Park (Korean), Fathers Dominic Bui and Joseph Tap Tran (Vietnamese), and Father Peter Gitendran (Tamil) in Toronto; and Fathers Thomas Tou and J.B. Thanh Son Dinh (Chinese), Father Frank Alvarez (Filipino), Father Pierre Ki Tek Sung (Korean), and Jesuit Fathers Jacques Bruyère and Paul Deslierres in Montreal.

I am very grateful to those interviewed who shared their life stories with me. Over the course of five years, I interviewed 126 Asian Canadians and 48 Asians in the Philippines and Bangkok.

With fondness, I remember the warm welcome I received from the Jesuits at Ateneo de Manila University, including John Schumacher SJ, Thomas Steinbugler SJ, and Luis David SJ, who were very generous in sharing their time and thoughts with me. I especially appreciate the concern and help of Irene and Cesar

Peralejo, who helped me locate people to interview in the metropolitan centre of Manila, and J.J. Jesena SJ, who introduced me to Filipinos in other parts of the country. I would like to thank Professor Imtiyaz Yusuf of Assumption University of Thailand and Professor Jean Barry SJ of Bangkok, who facilitated my lecture on Asian spirituality and its publication at that university. I am most grateful to all those who, through their sharing, made this volume possible.

Contents

Introduction

Asians are arriving in Canada in record numbers. The *Toronto Star* predicts that by 2017, over 50 per cent of the populations of Vancouver and Toronto will be composed of minority groups. The Canadian Census of 2001 confirmed that an increasing number of Asians, including East Indians, Koreans, and Arabs, are taking up residence in Canada.[1] It is often said that "Asians are necessarily non-Christians,"[2] or "Asians are Buddhists, not Catholics." Although only 2 per cent of Asians are Catholic,[3] the Census shows that 40 per cent of Asian newcomers to Canada are Christians; of these Asian Christians, 73 per cent are Catholics and 23 per cent are Protestants.[4]

This is good news for Canadian Christians, and especially good news for Canadian Catholics. Since 1970, Asian Catholics have been a boon to the Canadian Catholic Church and have made a significant impact. They bring with them a rich religious heritage and are highly individualistic.

Asian watcher and journalist Thomas C. Fox writes that "spirituality is the rhythm of Asia .... Personal pieties and family rituals shape the flow of life throughout Asia. Asian Catholics pass on devotions from generation to generation in the same way that they pass on stories and proverbs intended to teach values and enhance family ties."[5] In North America, Professor Jonathan

Tan contends, Asians "choose to establish and maintain their own churches,"[6] and these national parishes are thriving. Their congregations provide important social functions that assist Asian communities in sustaining their unique cultural traditions. Assimilation to other congregations does not seem to be a viable option. Asian Catholics like participating in and operating their own parishes. Canadian dioceses have ordained many Asian born Catholics to lead Canadian parishes, and Asian Canadian prayer groups in the parishes are well subscribed.[7] For example, the Archdiocese of Toronto, over 20 years (1990–2009), has ordained as Catholic priests Canadians (31 per cent), European Canadians (25 per cent), Asian Canadians (24 per cent), African Canadians (8 per cent), Latin American Canadians (8 per cent), and Canadians from the United States (4 per cent).[8] More young men and women are being prepared to serve the Canadian Church by making this multicultural Church less Euro-centric.

In the study of Asian Catholics that I conducted, the techniques of narrative analysis were employed along with the traditional methods of history to incorporate the contemporary experiences of living human beings into the historical analysis. People love to tell their stories, and stories are everywhere. In her volume *Narrative Analysis*, Catherine Kohler Riessman states that narrative inquiry guides historians to gather contemporary stories to record, assess, analyze, and interpret them.[9] As memories are always selective reconstructions and contain plots of their own, historical analysis asks why these stories are being told in one way rather than another. Narrative analysis attempts to unpack the loaded words and weighty meanings behind the storyteller's account. Beginning in the early 1970s, North American post-modern history quickly moved away from general historiography to give attention to the particular histories of women, family, Amerindians, ethnic groups, rural activities, and other neglected areas of investigation.[10]

The narrative inquiry approach reconstructs the environment in which these events happened, checks them against historical sources, and places them in a meaningful context. Jean Clandinin and Michael Connelly explain in their book *Narrative Inquiry* that the techniques of qualitative analysis are heuristic and are not necessarily seeking "certainty." Through careful attention to the importance of dialogue, this kind of analysis seeks a clearer understanding in the midst of human ambiguity and complexity.[11] Juanita Johnson-Bailey explains the delicacy of narrative analysis as "a joyous balancing act among the data, the methodology, the story, the participant, and the researcher."[12] A leader in postmodern approaches to ethnography, Norman K. Denzin, assures researchers that their balancing act will ultimately produce an ethnographic report that will present "an integrated synthesis of experience and theory."[13] Thus the techniques of narrative analysis look at the specific and are part of postmodern history, and, when they are verified and extended by the historical methods of library and archival research, become doubly effective. We will see that the techniques of both narrative analysis and historiography are employed in tandem throughout this study.

Once the techniques of narrative analysis are admitted in the service of historiography, the written style and format change, and the style becomes postmodern. Rather than offering a traditional historical survey, the techniques of qualitative analysis allow the specific information of particular individuals to be recorded. Instead of the antiseptic nature of quantitative information, qualitative analysis supplies the warmth and informality of real people subjectively telling their stories. Instead of the sterile consistency of a seamless narrative, contradictions, gaps, and uncertainties of the subjects are allowed to surface in the text.

To prepare our subjects for qualitative inquiry, I telephoned the volunteer interviewees, sent them a project description, and made an appointment for the interview. At the beginning of the interview, I explained to participants their right to answer the questions they chose. As this is a historical study, I asked them to give me permission to use their names in the text. I created a consent form, under the watchful eye of the University of Toronto Research Ethics Unit and guided by the Tri-Council Policy Statement, which I asked them to sign.[14] An interview guide (see Appendix) included questions about family members, education, passage to Canada, employment before and after immigration, linguistic difficulties and discrimination encountered, how family decisions were made, generational conflict, cultural retention among first, second, and third generations, inter-ethnic and interfaith marriages, connections to Canadian events, sojourning or permanent residency, prayer life and religious devotions, prayer groups, outreach to community groups, and their ethnic charism brought to Canada. For the purpose of this study, those born and educated in Asia and who came as adults to Canada are referred to as second-generation newcomers. Their parents, or the grandparents, who were brought over to Canada to look after the children and teach the language and culture, are considered to be first-generation newcomers. Those born in Asia but educated in Canada are second-generation, and those who are Canadian born are considered third-generation Canadians.

Although Chinese have been present in Canada since the nineteenth century, it was only in the 20th century that Chinese Canadians began to form their own Chinese Christian communities. Presbyterians, Anglicans, and Catholics offered support for the formation of these communities. The first Catholic Chinese mission was formed in Montreal in the 1910s, and a second in Vancouver in the 1920s. Yet it was only in the 1970s that newcomers from Catholic schools in China arrived in sufficient numbers to form Catholic parishes in the principal Canadian cities. For instance, in Toronto, Chinese Catholics gathered at Markham in 1987 to found the second Chinese parish, and within seven years they had a large church up and running. Since then, Chinese Martyrs parish has never looked back, baptizing between 300 and 600 parishioners annually, while the average

Toronto parish baptizes 84.[15] An exciting time for Chinese Canadian Catholics!

Chinese Catholic newcomers to Canada have persevered to meet the high expectations demanded of them. They found they had to accept the least desirable jobs and endure employer exploitation and discrimination. They integrated Eastern and Western values in their lives and changed their familial structure to adjust. To bear the cultural shock of crossing the Pacific Ocean, they retained their religious and cultural traditions. They joined organizations that would sustain their mental, physical, and spiritual health, and they communicated their sturdy faith to Canadian churchgoers.

The strengths of Filipino newcomers coming to Canada include their knowledge of English and their familiarity with Western culture. Filipino spirituality is rooted in the intensity of Spanish Catholicism. The secularism of the French Enlightenment hardly touched the Philippines, and the people there remained remote from the upheavals of metropolitan France. A people of positive spirituality, Filipinos remain grateful to the Spanish for bringing their language and religion, and to the Americans for English and the public school system. The numerous shrines of Mother Mary dot the Filipino countryside, and women have become the driving force of Filipino spirituality. The spirituality of Filipino men is more subdued, and they have few shrines to inspire them. Filipino men in the postmodern tradition have an individualistic spirituality: they reflect, pray alone, and find God in the isolated chambers of their minds and hearts.

Driven by prayer groups, Filipino professional organizations have initiated enormous projects for the betterment of their fellow citizens. Volunteers construct homes and build villages for the homeless. The villages include schools, churches, job training, health care, and community participation. Volunteers work to eliminate the shantytowns and alleviate malnutrition in their region. Volunteers who are self-directed are moving Filipino spirituality toward the postmodern world.

Many Filipino newcomers bring their concern and skills as caregivers to Canada. Since the 1990s, Filipinos have dominated the field of domestic help and have had a formidable influence in the Canadian medical and nursing systems. Caregiving seems natural to Filipinos, goes way beyond a people trained to colonial service, and is more genuinely rooted in the generosity of a gift-giving people. Coming to Canada as temporary workers, Filipinos decide to remain and give their labour and skills to their new land. They learn to overcome initial discrimination and exploitation, resolve cultural conflict and, after a time, join the Filipino Canadian establishment.

Korean immigrants came to Canada with the disadvantage of having only slight contact with English language and culture. Upon arrival in a Canadian city, Koreans must learn English and quickly adjust to the culture. They discover that their business credentials are not recognized, and they must lower their job expectations and sometimes even endure deception in the workplace. Through religious exercises, they learn it is better to forgive and transcend cultural difficulties. In their struggle to retain their faith, they combine the best of Eastern and Western traditions. Their religious communities give them strength, energy, and moral support; through these same communities, they look after their sick and aged and assist their newly arrived neighbours.

While integrating into Canadian life, Koreans hope to retain their language and culture. Some mobilize the Internet and printed resources to keep their culture cohesive and alive. But generally, the third generation is less interested in retaining the Korean language and Catholic religion and more interested in fitting into Canadian secular culture. Korean youth excel in academic activities at Canadian universities and prepare themselves for integration into North America.

The hearts and minds of Tamil Catholics remain fixed on the island of Sri Lanka, which continues to undergo intense political turmoil. Whereas Tamil language skills in English are adequate, their accommodation to Canadian mores happens more slowly. In Canada, Tamils have a deep desire to maintain Tamil culture, such as courting customs and arranged marriages, and to protect these activities for the Tamil Canadian community. They celebrate the Tamil religious festivals of Christmas, Easter, and St. Anthony. They make use of the pharmaceutical drugs of Western medicine, but also choose traditional medicine and faith healers. Tamils are educated, have a strong sense of their own religious and cultural identity, and enjoy a stable family life.

Many Vietnamese were forced to leave their homeland in 1975 when the Communists took over South Vietnam. These emigrants endured the very painful boat passage to refugee camps in Malaysia and the Philippines, and from these locations applied for admission to Canada. Arriving in Canada, they faced the problems of learning the language, adjusting to the culture, finding employment, and getting accustomed to lower job expectations. Their families were challenged by the Canadian lifestyle, and had to accept the pressures that threatened family life.

This study of Asian Catholics will present the reader with a survey compiled from interviews with Chinese, Filipino, Korean, Tamil, and Vietnamese Canadians, which reveal what it means to be newcomers in Canada, where the culture and religious observance is very different from their home country. The presence of these groups from Asia is having a lasting influence on Canadian Catholics.

Secular scholars provide little information on the religious activities of Asian Catholics. The emphasis in this study was to record these experiences of acclimatization before they are lost and to provide an initial analysis to discern their meaning for Canadian Christianity and Canadian life. It is hoped that the reader will enjoy the warmth of those interviewed and ponder the Asian experience of learning about Canada, and that further studies will document and analyze this cultural transformation while it is still fresh.

Chinese Our Lady, St. Francis Xavier church, Vancouver

1

Chinese Parishes Across Canada: Persistent Achievers

The first Chinese immigrants to arrive in Canada in 1858 were drawn by the Fraser River gold boom and came from California. Other Chinese arrived from Hong Kong and China, joining the 4,000 already living in British Columbia by 1860.[1] At a time when natural disasters, a depressed economy, and local warfare were plaguing the countryside, some inhabitants—coming from "the oldest continuous civilization in the world"—in pursuit of employment to support their families, committed themselves to overseas migration.[2] As contract labourers, they travelled abroad to work for set periods and then returned home to their families. Many who arrived in Canada came from Canton in southern China.[3]

Chinese Christians

In the nineteenth and early 20th centuries, few Christians were among the Chinese arrivals to Canada. The single men who disembarked in British Columbia had limited English language skills and were inured to long hours of hard work. They carried with them the traditional beliefs of their ancestors.[4] "At the most 10 per cent of the Chinese in Canada were Christians by 1923."[5]

But during the 1920s, the women and children who began to arrive were impressed with the preaching and assistance of the Methodists, Presbyterians, Anglicans, and Catholics. These new arrivals joined these churches and became enthusiastic members.

Data from Vancouver suggested that those born and, especially, raised outside China were likely to be frequent churchgoers. Indeed, churches appealed to both the young and the elderly. Student Christian Fellowship groups were organized in colleges and universities throughout Canada. Chinese Canadians with a high level of educational achievement and a prestigious occupation were more likely to be members of church groups than were the less well educated.[6] Chinese Canadians through the 20th century have proved to be appreciative churchgoers.

Many Chinese newcomers joined Christian churches during the 1920s and 1930s. "Large segments of each of these [church] communities were Canadian-born or naturalized and large proportions were, or claimed to be, Christian."[7] For instance, Canadian-born Andrew Lam was appointed an Anglican pastor in Vancouver in 1941. As a community leader, he published articles in the *Chinatown News*. He recommended that Chinese Canadians seek to integrate into Canadian society, but not assimilate—that is, that they not lose their identity as Chinese Canadians. He urged them to "participate whole-heartedly as Canadian citizens in the life of Canada .... At the same time, let us be proud of our ethnic origin and identity." As diverse ethnic groups, such as French Canadians and Ukrainians, had contributed the riches of their unique cultures to Canadian society, so would the Chinese, scholar Wing Chung Ng predicted, in due time.[8]

The number of Chinese Christians in Canada rose from 7,600 in 1931, or 16 per cent of the Chinese Canadian community, to 10,000 in 1941, or 30 per cent. The majority of Chinese in Atlantic Canada were Christians. In contrast, only about 20 per cent of Chinese in Vancouver were Christians in 1941. The United Church, particularly in urban Ontario, was successful in enrolling about one half of Chinese Christians. The Presbyterians claimed another 25 per cent, with the Catholics and Anglicans each enrolling 10 per cent. "Quebec was exceptional in the extent of Roman Catholic influence [on the Chinese]. Nearly 50 per cent of the Chinese Christians there were Catholics."[9]

In the 1960s, after Canada dropped its immigration restrictions, Chinese Catholics began to arrive in greater numbers, yet the roots of modern Chinese Catholicism go back to seventeenth-century Catholic communities in China founded by Matteo Ricci and his Jesuit companions. The planting of these Catholic roots was similar in many ways to the seventeenth-century labours of Jean de Brébeuf and his Jesuit companions among Aboriginals in the land that would become Canada. The renewal of Catholicism in China at the end of the nineteenth century extended itself to Canada by the middle of the 20th century. Numerous Chinese Christians who had attended Catholic or Protestant schools learned English and became familiar with North American culture.[10] For example, the French-Canadian Jesuits, who had been in China since 1918, operated Hsin-Hsin Chung Hsueh High School in Suchow, a language school in Beijing, Aurora University in Shanghai, Kung Shanh University in Tientsin, and other schools and universities in Hong Kong. The Missionary Sisters of the Immaculate Conception from Montreal opened schools in various Chinese cities.[11] Fu Jen Catholic University was founded by the Benedictine order in Beijing in 1925, but was moved to Taiwan and reopened in Taipei in 1961 under the Taipei archdiocese, the Divine Word Fathers, and the Jesuits.[12]

The latest Canadian census (2001) dealing with religion revealed that 21 per cent of Chinese Canadians identified themselves as Christians; of these, 57 per cent were Catholic and 43 per cent Protestant.[13] It is also significant that 59 per cent listed themselves as having no religious affiliation. David Chuenyan Lai and his colleagues state that the Canadian census recognizes Chinese ethnicity and culture, but not the non-denominational religion that is part of them.[14] Twelve per cent of Chinese are listed as Buddhist.[15]

Catholic Hostels and Hospitals for Chinese Canadians

Chinese Catholics arriving in Canada from Asian Catholic schools in the 1920s, along with other Chinese, were considered by many Canadians to be the vanguard of "the Yellow Peril," and were not welcomed into Canadian schools or hospitals.[16] Thus, Chinese Canadians sought help in Christian communities, among them the Catholic communities in Vancouver, Toronto and Montreal. At the request of Bishop Timothy Casey, four Missionary Sisters of the Immaculate Conception travelled from Montreal to Vancouver in 1921 to open a school for Chinese children. They visited the hovels of the sick and the destitute, discovering that "poor old men of sixty and more, their clothing in shreds, passed the night lying on a hard floor or curled up on chairs, without pillow or blanket, in February weather." Moved by such hardship, the sisters purchased a house in 1924 and opened a dispensary on the first floor and a refuge on the second and third floors. Immediately, four octogenarians moved into the house; in a short time, the refuge was filled with fifteen residents. Benefactors contributed so that some health care was provided for Chinese workers. For instance, a Vancouver doctor donated his services for the needy. The sisters begged help in Chinatown by going from house to house. Donors supplied food, the Sisters of Providence at St. Paul's Hospital cooked meals, and charitable women delivered them.[17]

The Chinese community of Vancouver supported the sisters' refuge and dispensary. For instance, the Chinatown Lions Club supported the work of the Missionary Sisters because they focused their care on chronically ill single men. Three years later, the sisters began construction of St. Joseph's Oriental Home, near the refuge; St. Joseph's opened in 1928. The health-care facility was rebuilt in a new location in 1941 and renamed

Mount St. Joseph Hospital. The Chinese Lions Club backed this charitable enterprise and funded health care there for Chinese Canadians.[18]

Besides administrating the Chinese hospital, the Missionary Sisters operated Sunday schools to instruct Chinese Catholics and organized classes in English, French, and Chinese for adults and youngsters. From these good works, the sisters had 50 conversions and baptisms each year. The sisters served the Chinese community across Canada, and the Chinese community in turn raised funds for the sisters' hospitals in Vancouver and Montreal, and for the Chinese centres in Ottawa and Quebec City.[19]

Catholic Parishes in Vancouver: St. Francis Xavier, Corpus Christi and St. Theresa

In Vancouver, Chinese Catholics mainly from Hong Kong found welcome at St. Francis Xavier church, which currently offers four weekend masses: two in Cantonese, one in Mandarin, and one in English. The parish's 2,000 members are principally Chinese, and language classes are held in Mandarin, Cantonese and English. The former pastor, Father Aloysius Lou, arrived from Hong Kong in 1972. In an interview in 2003, as a history enthusiast, he told me with relish that the Scarboro Fathers, under the leadership of Father Hugh Sharkey, opened a chapel in 1933 in downtown Vancouver for Chinese to visit. At the same time, three Grey Sisters arrived from Pembroke, Ontario, to conduct the Chinese Mission kindergarten. Five years later, three more Grey Sisters arrived to open a Chinese grammar school for grades 1 to 8 on the third floor of the Bank of Commerce building. The school began with 55 students. The rented classrooms were replaced in 1940 by a school built for the purpose: St. Francis Xavier School. Archbishop William M. Duke blessed St. Francis Xavier church the same year, and parish organizations such as the Legion of Mary and the Catholic Women's League were launched.[20]

After the Communist takeover of China in 1949, Chinese seamen fleeing their country landed in Vancouver and visited St. Francis Xavier church looking for help. One such man was a mechanic who worked in a shop across the street. When he visited the church, he was struck by seeing Jesus on the cross, suffering more than he was. He asked a Grey Sister who Jesus was, and this interest led to his conversion to Christianity. The Grey Sisters hired him as their janitor.

In 1953, Archbishop Duke requested that Father Peter Chow, completing his doctorate in Canon Law in Rome, be sent to St. Francis Xavier. Chow was the first Chinese born priest to minister in Canada; when he arrived, he was pleased to meet the mechanic-turned-janitor, and they became good friends. Having compassion for the mechanic, who was lonely, Father Chow put him in touch with a pen pal, a schoolgirl in Hong Kong. After a lengthy correspondence, she came to Vancouver to marry the mechanic-janitor.[21]

Wing Chung Ng's study of Vancouver Chinese found that Father Chow had much contact with Chinese Canadian youth. Chow saw that generational conflict within Chinese families had its roots in "the lack of 'acquired intimacy ...,' which was caused by prolonged separation between the sojourning father and his children at home." Chow became associated with the struggle of youth to survive pressures from their elders, who were trying to preserve Chinese heritage, live in Christian harmony, and act with filial piety. The youth perceived their parents to be oppressive, backward and fuddy-duddy.[22]

The Scarboro Fathers withdrew from St. Francis Xavier in 1961 to allow Chow to be the first Chinese pastor of the Vancouver church. Chow added two classrooms to the school, introduced a pastoral council, and encouraged the students to participate in the Chinese Youth Festival. The parish choir sang Christmas carols at St. Vincent's Home, St. Joseph's Oriental Home, Mount St. Joseph Hospital, and the Bayshore Inn. In 1966, Chow established the Chinese Catholic Youth Organization. Two years later, he purchased a former Ukrainian church, originally a Swedish Lutheran church built in 1903. His work in Vancouver done, he dramatically announced from the pulpit his intentions to return to Hong Kong. After a sincere farewell, he returned to Hong Kong, leaving Father Aloysius Lou as his replacement as pastor.[23]

From early on, Chinese parishioners showed great generosity to the parish. During the 1970s, Sister Margaret of the Grey Sisters of the Immaculate Conception was the choirmaster at St. Francis Xavier. She wished to get a powered organ to replace the 20-year-old manual organ to make the weekly singing a pleasure for both the singers and the congregation. Her research revealed that a new organ would cost the parish at least $7,000. Overhearing complaints about the existing instrument, parishioner Buck Wong offered to underwrite expenses for a new one. A hardworking truck driver, Buck wanted to improve music in the church. When Father Lou learned of Buck's generous offer, he suggested that first the parishioners be consulted and donations solicited. Lou went to the parishioners and exhorted them that listening to the improved organ would be listening to their own donations singing the praises of God. The parish collection brought in $3,500, but the same amount again was still needed. Father Lou asked Buck and nine other parishioners to contribute a total of $3,500 to make up the balance. The full amount was raised and the organ was purchased in 1977. This fundraising experience demonstrated the determination of the Chinese Canadian parishioners, who contributed what they could to improve church music at St. Francis Xavier. Later, Father Lou suggested that parishioners contribute one half-hour's wage per week to the church and the same amount to another charity. Wealthier parishioners contributed even larger amounts. This approach provided donations in the 1990s to raise $14 million for a new location and new school.

Another Chinese boy, Fred Wong, born in 1930, would become an associate pastor in 1980. As a neighbourhood boy,

Fred visited the parish, and the sisters admitted him to kinder-garten at the school. Fred had been baptized into the Anglican tradition. In this time before ecumenism, Fred's Anglican pastor told Fred's older sister to remove her five-year-old brother from the Catholic school to be sure he would not become a Catholic. However, Fred liked the sisters, continued to visit them, and received catechetical instruction from them. As an adult, he became a printer and printed *Holy Childhood*, a publication of the Scarboro Foreign Mission Society. He liked the Scarboro Fathers, and joined their seminary program in 1959. He was ordained to the priesthood at Holy Rosary Cathedral in Vancouver in 1965. The following year, Father Wong was sent to Our Lady of Fatima church in Georgetown, Guyana. After years of mission work, he returned home to Vancouver for his father's funeral in 1980 and was appointed to St. Francis Xavier Chinese church. A decade later, at age 60, Father Wong died in the Vancouver neighbourhood where his faith was first awakened.[24]

The growth of a second Chinese community at Corpus Christi church in Vancouver was guided by a series of Irish pastors. In the 1970s, English-speaking Asians in increasing numbers began to attend Corpus Christi. A Cantonese Mass was celebrated on Sunday, 100 neophytes were baptized yearly, and Chinese parishioners came to represent 50 per cent of the parish's 3,200 members.

A third community sprang up at St. Theresa's church in Burnaby, BC when Father Francis Chang was pastor. Seven hundred and fifty parishioners from various ethnic backgrounds attend Sunday Mass in Mandarin.

A Catholic Parish in Richmond: Canadian Martyrs

Richmond is the hub of Chinese Canadian economic activity on Canada's west coast, and has become an expanding centre for residential homes and family life. Richmond businesses have adjusted and become more cosmopolitan to cater to the needs of middle-class immigrants from Hong Kong. New office buildings provide space for professional services. But a number of Chinese "astronauts" continue to shuttle back and forth between their Hong Kong businesses and their family homes in Richmond.[25]

Canadian Martyrs' church, Richmond, British Columbia; opened in 2002

Canadian Martyrs parish was formed in Richmond in 1995 by the Chinese parishioners from St. Paul's parish, under the direction of Father Robert Wong SJ. Father Paul Chu replaced Wong and in 2002 completed construction of a spacious new church. Ninety per cent of the 1,000 families who belong to the parish are Chinese Canadian, with the remainder being Filipino and of other Asian backgrounds. The four weekend masses are celebrated in Cantonese, Mandarin, and English. The Rite of Christian Initiation of Adults (RCIA), conducted in Mandarin and Cantonese, has 40 participants annually. Baptisms average about 60 per year. The Legion of Mary has four presidia (groups): one Mandarin, two Cantonese, and another for Cantonese youth. The Catholic Women's League and the Knights of Columbus meetings are conducted in Cantonese. Two Canossian Sisters,

Sister Beatrice Mak and Sister Cecilia Cham, are attached to the parish; they visit the sick at Mount St. Joseph's and Vancouver General hospitals.

Father Peter Chiang was the pastor of St. Paul's parish when Chinese people were the majority, but has since moved to the English-speaking St. Stephen's parish in North Vancouver. While Filipinos are now the largest ethnic group at St. Paul's, many Chinese remain, along with Vietnamese, Iranian, and Tamil parishioners. The six weekly masses are now celebrated in English.

A Multicultural Parish in Vancouver: Joseph and Doreen Chau's Experience at St. Joseph the Worker

Canadian Chinese also attend the multicultural parish of St. Joseph the Worker. Typical are parishioners Joseph and Doreen Chau, who are bilingual and active in the parish. At age 20, Joe came from Hong Kong to Winnipeg in 1971 to take business management courses. He was accepted at the University of Manitoba and earned an honours degree with a specialty in commerce. He later moved to Vancouver to launch his career as an accountant. Joe was articling, but in 1977, before he passed the qualifying examination, had a serious car accident and suffered a head injury. After convalescing, he married a Canadian-born medical secretary of Chinese descent, Doreen Mah, in 1978, and hoped to return to his firm. In the courting stage, Doreen had resolved to become a Catholic; she made her profession of faith a month before the wedding.

That year, Joe was hospitalized four times, and Doreen was very angry with God. She "felt life was so unfair." But Joe never gave up and was more concerned about Doreen than about his own problems. He assured that things would work out. When Robert and Aurora Yu invited them to take part in an Alpha course at their parish, Doreen looked at the topics of the talks listed in the brochure and thought it was just right for her. She was also "impressed by the commitment" of the Alpha committee members.

> On the first night of Alpha, the Holy Spirit embraced me the moment I entered the room. I was touched by the warmth of the reception committee, impressed by how well organized the evening was. The roast beef dinner was delicious (it's my favourite, as I always overcook it) and I was assigned to Group 7. Number 7 is my favourite number.[26]

Doreen went through the ten talks and found that by reading Nicky Gumbel's book *Questions of Life*, which provides the course outline, ahead of time, she would receive much inspiration from the talks. The Alpha talks enriched Joe and Doreen's relationship, and they agreed to go on the weekend retreat as a follow-up. Contrary to what Doreen expected, "The Holy Spirit embraced me the whole day .... I was absolutely moved by the very powerful, caring, thoughtful prayers of the animators, Joanna and Valerie. Their words seemed to flow with such great love. I felt as though I had been saved and was born again."

As a result of the weekend, the Lord's Prayer became meaningful to Doreen, and popular songs, such as Céline Dion's *A New Day Has Come*, had fresh significance. Unlike in the past, when Doreen attended church mainly for the music and the homily, she now looked forward to participating in the parts of the Mass, from the entrance song right through to the offering of peace and the final blessing. She enjoyed reading the Bible and associating with people "who have a close relationship with Jesus." She admitted that she now had a close relationship with Jesus, and discovered him in the events of her day. She realized that she has "a loving, good, kind son," Jonathan, at home; "many caring colleagues at work"; and "some very loving friends and wonderful neighbours." And when things do not go as planned, "I now pray to Jesus that he will help me to understand, be open and to accept God's will."

After their wedding in 1978, Joe was still having difficulty concentrating. Seven years after his car accident, he was diagnosed with bipolar disorder. A fervent Catholic and committed member of the Legion of Mary, he became self-employed and intensified his spiritual life by prayer and good works. Twice a week, he visited seniors at Lyon's Manor and was a minister of Holy Communion at the parish.

Doreen continued working as a medical secretary. Although she was a Catholic when she married, Doreen admitted, "I was ignorant of my faith [and] accepted most things unquestioningly." She went on to say that "I felt God loves us all and when we are faced with frustration, disappointment, and hurtful times, it was just too bad for us." She admired Joe because "he was a very prayerful, spiritual person. He reads his Bible daily, says his rosary, and does behind-the-scenes volunteer work for St. Joe's. He's a kind, caring, compassionate person with a quiet, unassuming manner." Through the "valleys and mountains" of their relationship, Joe's strong faith never allowed him to give up. Doreen taught catechism at St. Joseph's. They were trying to get their son Jonathan into Catholic school, and Joe counselled, "If it's God's will, he will be accepted." Doreen expressed her delight when Jonathan was accepted, saying, "I think it was the best two years of his school life, and also of mine as a school volunteer." (Jonathan has since completed his training to become a radiation therapist.)[27]

The lives of Doreen and Joe, despite the valleys and mountains, have been greatly enriched by their Catholic community. They now share their lives with others of all ethnic cultures at St. Joseph the Worker parish.

A Catholic Parish in Calgary: Our Lady of Perpetual Help

In Calgary, Chinese speakers at Our Lady of Perpetual Help may choose between Mandarin, Cantonese, or English masses.

Father C. K. Mak founded the Chinese mission in Calgary in 1981. Renting space for a time to hold its eucharistic gatherings, the community moved in 1983 to St. Paul's church, which they bought outright in 1989. This 200-seat structure soon became too small for the growing Chinese community; Bishop Paul O'Byrne suggested in 1996 that the community move to Our Lady of Perpetual Help, which has a 600-seat capacity. The Chinese Catholic community became established at this Calgary location and now has 4,000 parishioners. The parish brings spiritual directors from across Canada to guide Advent and Lenten retreats, and holds seminars on Christian faith, liturgy, catechism, and morality. Volunteer catechists educate about 60 neophytes yearly in the RCIA program and welcome them at Easter through the sacrament of baptism for a yearly average of 120 new Christians.[28]

A Catholic Parish in Edmonton: Mary Help of Christians

Chinese Catholics at Mary Help of Christians Chinese parish in Edmonton attend one of the two Cantonese masses or the English mass. In the late 1970s, Chinese Catholics gathered around a Sister of Charity, Gertrude Kwan, to form a Chinese Catholic community, which initially celebrated the Eucharist at St. Joseph's church at the University of Alberta. The Scripture readings and the prayers of the faithful were read in Chinese, and the hymns were sung in Chinese. The Archdiocese of Hong Kong sent Father Francisco Lau SDB to Edmonton in 1982 to preside at the Eucharist for the Chinese community. St. Patrick's church welcomed the community for a Cantonese Sunday mass, and prepared an office for Father Lau. He formed a pastoral council and facilitated Bible study, catechetical instruction, an annual retreat, and the Apostleship of Prayer group. He visited families and organized social activities for Christmas and Chinese New Year, then started a summer camp for Chinese children.

In 1984, the Chinese community of Edmonton organized the Salesian Chinese School to provide cultural education for Chinese children on Saturdays. Catholic religious and the diocesan clergy formed a Chinese centre to preserve Chinese language, culture, and community; the Alberta government provided funds for this endeavour. A building committee was established in 1985 to receive monthly donations and to organize bazaars, garage sales, lucky draws, and variety shows. Donations also came from Hong Kong and from various Canadian provinces. The following year, the Chinese Catholic community purchased St. Emeric's church from the Hungarian community for $160,000 and renamed it Mary Help of Christians parish. In 1987, Archbishop Joseph MacNeil, presiding at mass there, proclaimed that Mary Help of Christians was to be the Chinese Catholic parish in Edmonton. On weekends, three Chinese masses and one English mass are celebrated.

The parish pastoral council was formed in 1989; Vincent Liu was elected chair. The basement was renovated to become a Chinese centre. The Chinese Salesian Society rented accommodations for overseas students, and named the residence the Dominic Savio Students' Hostel. Father Joseph Ho SDB succeeded Father Lau as pastor in 1990. The Lenten parish retreat was preached by Father John Lung of San Francisco, and 250 parishioners attended. The daily rosary was said during May; these devotions were accompanied by seminars reflecting on the life of Christ at the parish and in the homes of parishioners. In August, a parish pilgrimage visited St. John the Baptist church in Morinville, the former missionary centre of Lac la Biche, and the Skaro Shrine. In Edmonton in November, a Family Fun Nite was held to play games, sing songs, and affirm family life. At Christmas, donations were collected for Catholic social services, and dinner was served to the needy in the church hall. Mary Help of Christians is now an active Catholic parish of about 500 families. It instructs five or six neophytes yearly and baptizes 20 new Christians. In 1996, Father Ho and the pastoral council purchased the empty Knights of Columbus hall for $820,000 to build a new church on this site. The location was desirable, the hall could be renovated for a community centre, and its large parking lot provided 60 spaces. In November 1998, the construction of a church at this site was completed.[29]

The Chinese Catholic Community in Winnipeg

Winnipeg has a sizable Chinese community, the Catholic members of which attend various local parishes rather than gathering at one particular church. Arriving from Hong Kong, Philip Lee came to Winnipeg through the help of his sister, Angelina, who was the family pathfinder. The first member of the family to arrive, Angelina earned a bachelor of education at the University of Manitoba. Philip arrived in 1962 to enroll at the same university. In Hong Kong, he had learned basic English at a school operated by the Missionary Sisters of the Immaculate Conception, and learned about Western culture through the prism of the Montreal sisters. They also taught their students Western hygiene, prayer, and socializing. In Winnipeg, undeterred by the limits of his English, Philip began classes at St. Paul's College at the University of Manitoba. He received help from the Jesuit professors, who drilled him in English until he responded as quickly as Manitoba-born students. He also learned the importance of associating with the non-Chinese community to improve his facility in English.

Philip Lee and Anita Lau married in 1968 at St. Vital church in Winnipeg. The Lee family, which now included his mother, attended Sunday mass at St. Paul's College Chapel at the University of Manitoba campus from 1968 to 1984, and rallied the Chinese Catholics on Christmas and Chinese New Year. Philip's parents lived with the family, and Philip and Anita's three daughters grew up eating Chinese food, speaking Chinese at home, and learning about Chinese culture. Philip worked as a chemist for the city of Winnipeg in industrial waste control and eventually became the branch head. At the same time, he was involved in the political, social, and religious dimensions of the Chinese community. One of the civic responsibilities he welcomed was his appointment as the human rights commissioner of Manitoba. Later, he became president of the Winnipeg Chinatown Non-Profit Housing Corporation, a political candidate in provincial elections, and in 2009 was appointed the Lieutenant Governor of Manitoba.

Philip's home life did not go as smoothly as his public life. From his father, Philip learned the importance of personal and familial discipline. Yet his daughters let him know that they did not automatically appreciate or accept these values. Thinking they were doing the right thing, Philip and Anita tried to guide their oldest daughter's choice of boyfriends, but, through this experience, learned that it was sometimes better to agree to disagree with their daughters. The second daughter responded positively to this approach, bringing home a young man more in line with family expectations. The fact that the grandparents also lived in the family home heightened both traditional ex-pectations and conflict. For example, Philip's brother married a Caucasian woman; his mother did not accept her because she was neither Chinese nor Catholic. Accommodating other cultures and other views as part of Canadian multiculturalism was a learning experience for this family.

Chinese Catholics in Winnipeg, according to Lee, have yet to produce creative leaders who are involved in Catholic com-munity life. The United Church Chinese have three churches, whereas Winnipeg Chinese Catholics do not have their own parish; instead, they attend English-speaking parishes.

In Canada, Chinese women prove to be more religious than the men. Education is a primary value for the Chinese Canadian community, since it is through education that a family establishes itself, gains status, and creates wealth. Winnipeg's Chinatown is no longer a place where Winnipeg Chinese live, but rather a political centre where they do business. Chinatown has become a tourist attraction with its Chinese food, furnishing, clothing, and artifacts. The Chinese cultural centre, meanwhile, helps Chinese Canadians find suitable housing.[30] McGill professor John Zucchi writes that the move to the suburbs is ambiguous for Chinese newcomers, since it is a sign of "integration [but] with the persistence of ethnicity." As Chinese move into suburban neighbourhoods, they create their ethnic community, now called an "ethnoburb."[31] For instance, many Chinese Canadians gravitate toward the suburbs of Winnipeg, while others move out of Manitoba to Richmond, BC, or Scarborough, Ontario.

Explosion of Four Chinese Parishes in Toronto: Our Lady of Mount Carmel, Chinese Martyrs, St. Agnes Kouying Tsao, and Saviour of the World

In downtown Toronto, at Our Lady of Mount Carmel church, and at Chinese Martyrs church in Markham, northeast of Toronto, Catholic services are celebrated in Cantonese, Mandarin, and English. At St. Agnes Kouying Tsao church in Richmond Hill, north of Toronto, and at Saviour of the World Chinese Catholic church in Mississauga, west of Toronto, Mass is celebrated in Cantonese and English.[32] In the Chinese tradition of Christianity, these parishes are well attended and have a large number of baptisms and confirmations each year.[33] According to Father Peter Leung of Chinese Martyrs, one incentive for adult baptisms for new Chinese Canadians is the good reputation of Catholic schools, especially in Hong Kong, but also in Macau, Malaysia, and Taiwan.[34] Many families who arrive in Ontario from overseas wish to have their children attend Catholic schools, so they and their children are baptized.[35]

Our Lady of Mount Carmel

The oldest Chinese church in Toronto is Our Lady of Mount Carmel. Originally a wooden structure built in 1861, it was rebuilt in 1867 in yellow brick in the Gothic style. Over the years, it passed from Irish Canadian Catholics to German, Italian, Portuguese and Korean Canadian Catholics, and finally, in 1970, to Chinese Canadian Catholics. The first Chinese Catholics to arrive in the downtown area in the late 1960s were Hakkas (a subgroup of Han Chinese who speak the Hakka language), followed by Vietnamese and Hong Kong Chinese. Lacking a Chinese speaking priest to administer the sacrament of reconciliation (then called "confession") in Toronto, Chinese Catholics travelled to Holy Spirit church in Montreal to unburden their souls to Father Thomas Tou, the second Chinese priest ministering in Canada. Father Tou went to Toronto to ask Archbishop Philip Pocock to appoint a Chinese pastor for the Chinese community of Toronto.[36] Later that year, the archbishop appointed the pioneer priest Father Louis Tchang to preside at a Chinese Eucharist for 80 Catholics. According to Leo Ng, archivist of Our Lady of Mount Carmel church, those who attended were mainly Chinese students from the University of Toronto. Most were former graduates of Aberdeen Technical (Salesian) School in Hong Kong, members of the Chinese High School Student Association, or members of the Legion of Mary. The Chinese Catholic Centre was built next to Our Lady of Mount Carmel church in 1985 as a gathering place for parishioners to share Christian fellowship. The Chinese community raised the sum of $1.5 million towards the cost of the centre.[37]

Our Lady of Mount Carmel offered one Mandarin and two Cantonese masses each weekend and one English mass on the first and third Sunday. In 1992, the archdiocese officially declared Our Lady of Mount Carmel Chinese church a parish, and daily masses in Chinese have been celebrated there ever since. In 1972, Father J. B. Mak took over leadership of the community, assisted by Sister M. A. Ouang. The pastoral council established many organizations, including altar servers, a choir, three Bible study groups, three presidia for the Legion of Mary, and the Apostleship of Prayer, Catholic Women's League, and Chinese Catholic Youth Organization. A Chinese school for children was established, as was an English school for adults. The teachers were young volunteers. Immigration assistance was offered, the Chinese Catholic Students Association was formed, and the St. Joseph's Society for the elderly was founded. By 1977, the community numbered 3,000. By 1987, it had expanded to 6,000.[38]

Following the death of Father Mak in 2001, Father Peter Chin, a Redemptorist psychotherapist from Malaysia, Australia, and Edmonton, was appointed as pastor. He welcomed new Canadians in four languages: Hakka, Cantonese, Mandarin, and English. Since that time, Chinese from Malaysia, Taiwan, Mauritius, Southeast Asia, India, the Caribbean, and Mainland China have joined the downtown Catholic community. Chinese parishioners from Brampton, Mississauga, and other Toronto suburbs drive to Our Lady of Mount Carmel for Sunday liturgy and the familial community.

The Asian culture, with its connections to Confucianism, Buddhism, and Chinese natural religion is deeply spiritual and helps Chinese to cope with life and death, with joy and pain in their lives. Although rooted in this Asian culture, many Chinese Canadians look to Christianity for a transcendent and eternal goal.[39] The Rite of Christian Initiation of Adults (RCIA) at Mount Carmel parish offers four classes for 120 neophytes each year. Two classes are in Cantonese and two are in Mandarin.

Many of the original Cantonese parishioners living downtown were getting older. The new arrivals, on the other hand, are Mandarin speakers from Taiwan and the Mainland in their 20s and 30s. They were resolved to change things.

Young Chinese Catholics arrive in Canada bruised from their harsh treatment in Communist China. New parishioners in Toronto come from both the official and the unofficial Catholic churches in China. In the Canadian Catholic parishes, they seek to join a Christian community in which they can enjoy Chinese Catholic liturgy, reconnect with Chinese culture, and find a second home. Young non-Christian Chinese also arrive in

Canada disillusioned by communism; they are intrigued by the international belief system of Catholicism. At Mount Carmel, they are instructed in the Gospel, English, and computer skills. They are given help in finding work and integrating into Canadian society.

Chinese Martyrs

Mount Carmel was catering to downtown Chinese Canadians, but with the arrival of the new professionals in the 1980s, Chinese Canadians began to buy homes in the Toronto suburbs of Scarborough, Markham, and Richmond Hill.[40] In early 1986, 60 Chinese Catholics invited the pastor of Our Lady of Mount Carmel, Father J. B. Mak, to preside at mass in Cantonese at Prince of Peace church in Markham once a month. Father Thomas Harding, the pastor of Prince of Peace, supported the initiative and provided some start-up funding. Inspired by an enthusiastic beginning, 100 families who had been in Canada for ten to 20 years gathered in Markham and decided to form a Chinese Catholic parish. Chinese Catholics from cities across Canada who had relocated their families to Markham for personal and professional reasons became involved in the formation of a Catholic community. These included Cantonese speakers from Hong Kong and Mandarin speakers from Taiwan and Mainland China. Other families in the vicinity drove weekly from Brampton, Oakville, Pickering, Newmarket, and downtown Toronto to attend the Catholic Eucharists celebrated in Cantonese and Mandarin. These Catholic families assembled in Markham in 1987 to form a Chinese Catholic community.

The community requested a Chinese pastor from the Catholic Archdiocese of Toronto. Bishop Aloysius Ambrozic appointed Father Paul Tang as pastor of Chinese Martyrs parish in October 1987. Parish activities were quickly organized, including Christmas and Chinese New Year liturgies, retreats, youth camps, Bible studies, pilgrimages, and prayer services. A pastoral council was formed, and Dr. Theresa Chiu was chosen as chair. A committee began meeting in 1989 to plan the purchase of property and the construction of the church. Their plans to build a church and community centre were presented to the diocesan building committee. The diocesan committee in its turn questioned whether the Chinese community had enough resources and faith commitment to see the church building project to completion.[41] The response of the Chinese Canadian community was a thunderous "yes!"

Fundraising began in earnest. The faith and zeal of the parishioners was soon evident in their fundraising ability. Over three years, sing-a-thons raised $136,000 and bazaars raised $72,500. Chinese opera performances were given, and parishioners were asked to make pledges. Dinner dances and craft sales provided additional revenue. Within five years, more than $1 million was raised for the construction of the church.[42]

Parishioners organized a liturgy group, parish choir, altar servers, and a finance committee. They also formed the RCIA to instruct new Christians. Each of the above groups elected a leader to represent them on the pastoral council. The pastoral council organized parish activities, allotted resources, prepared a yearly budget, and made decisions on building and environmental issues. The council became the centre of community harmony and good fellowship. Under its chair, Joe Chan, the council planned the construction of the church and in record time guided its completion.[43]

The RCIA program at Chinese Martyrs, according to parish elders Tony Ma and Joe Chan, was begun in 1988 under the direction of Father Paul Tang, Paul Chan, and Edwin Lee. The catechists were recruited from among the parishioners. Thirty or 40 catechists were needed for the different languages and follow up. At times, classes were filled to capacity, with as many as 90 neophytes. In September and January of each year, neophytes were prepared for the rite of acceptance. In 1989, the tragic year of the Tiananmen Square massacre, many people from Hong Kong scurried to the safe haven of Canada. Some of them settled in Toronto. That year, 396 neophytes were baptized at Chinese Martyrs, and baptisms at the parish continued to rise throughout the 1990s. When the average number of baptisms in Toronto parishes was 84, the number of baptisms at Chinese Martyrs rose from 510 in 1991 to a peak of 634 in 1992, and continues in high numbers to this day. In 1997, when Communist China took control of the administration of Hong Kong, another wave of neophytes arrived at Chinese Martyrs, which ended the decade by baptizing 598 people in 1999 – outstanding figures for any parish!

The driving force behind the formation of a Catholic community in Markham and the building of the parish church was the strong desire of Chinese Catholics to guide their families in a Chinese Christian way. Chinese Canadians recognized the importance of home and church as the first schools of faith, hope, and love for their children. Some catechists formed six or seven families into groups that met monthly in homes for prayer and Bible sharing.[44] Parents believed that the support of the Church would help them protect, nourish, and guide their children when coping with this world. Young children attending church with their family learn to love Jesus Christ and accept the duties of a Christian. Education specialist and parishioner Dr. Doris Au wrote, "Perhaps the importance of a family unit in the Chinese culture and the faith of those who are parents have much to do with the visible presence and involvement of our youth in parish liturgies and activities." These new Canadians sought baptism in their quest for truth and their desire to participate in the Chinese Canadian community. Most Chinese parents wanted their children to attend Catholic schools and encouraged them to attend church on Sunday. "The parish community must be conscientious in its obligation to teach, support and comfort its members. Child or adult, male or female, each should find acceptance and understanding, each should feel known and wanted, loved and respected in the community."[45] The Chinese

Martyrs community in Markham prayed for strong families who would fully live the Gospel of Jesus Christ.

In the summer of 1991, the Archdiocese of Toronto purchased a building site at Denison and Featherstone streets for the Chinese community to construct its church. The church building committee, under chair Tony Ma, sprang into action in 1992, inviting architectural designs, requesting a low-interest loan of $2.5 million from the archdiocese, and choosing Fahuki Construction Ltd. to be the builders. Plans were submitted and quickly approved by the Archdiocesan Church Building Committee. Bishop Robert Clune officiated at the ground-breaking ceremony on November 10, 1992, and construction continued through the following year. Appropriately for Chinese Martyrs, a community that has performed so many baptisms, the first mass in the church was celebrated on January 9, 1994, the Feast of the Baptism of the Lord. During the first half of this new year, the marble altars, sanctuary lectern, baptismal font, tabernacle, stained-glass windows, and other furnishings were installed. Bishop Attila Miklósházy blessed the completed church on October 15, 1994, and brought this miraculous saga of church construction to an end.[46] The response of the Chinese community was powerful: 11,500 parishioners registered to attend the seven weekend Masses, and 200 to 500 neophytes joined the congregation each year.

St. Agnes Kouying Tsao

The third of the Chinese churches in the Toronto area is St. Agnes Kouying Tsao parish in Markham, whose church building was completed in 2002. In 1992, 30 Chinese Catholic families in Markham asked Archbishop Ambrozic to find them a Chinese speaking priest to guide the founding of a third Chinese Catholic community, with St. Agnes Kouying Tsao as its patron. Agnes Kouying (her name means "laurel flower") Tsao was a poor widow who taught Christianity for twelve years in the mid-nineteenth century to minority groups in the remote regions of southern China. Persecuted for her Catholic faith, Agnes was martyred in 1853, at age 32. She was beatified in 1900 and canonized in 2000. An experienced missionary from the Archdiocese of Hong Kong, Father Nicola Ruggiero PIME, volunteered in 1992 to come to Toronto to shepherd this Chinese Canadian community. He presided at the Eucharist at Christ the King school, and the Chinese congregation swelled in numbers. There were four masses in Chinese at St. Agnes and an additional English mass to welcome Chinese Canadian young people and Catholics from the neighbourhood. His successor, Father Dominic Kong OFM, on loan from the Archdiocese of Hong Kong, arrived in Canada in 1998 to direct a growing community of 1,500 Chinese Catholic families. Father Kong and the pastoral council appointed architect David Sin to design and supervise the construction of the large church and community centre.

The parish leaders included Dominic Lau, Francis Chow, K. C. Woo, Philomena Lo, Anita Ko, Frank Yue, and Felix Leung. Each mass had its own choir, named variously the St. Cecilia Senior Choir, St. Francis of Assisi Choir, and English Mass Choir. The parishioners formed the Recreation Group to organize pilgrimages, walk-a-thons, dances, and the children's Christmas party. Buses were chartered for pilgrimages to Our Lady of Fatima in Lewistown, New York, and to the Martyrs' Shrine in Midland, Ontario. Walk-a-thons, which always concluded with a barbeque, raised charitable funds and strengthened family ties. Three hundred parishioners turned out for the annual dance.

Young people at the parish attend Sunday school for instruction in Christian life and values. A large staff of teachers and assistants volunteers its services to instruct the youth. Mass servers were formed into a group, and 40 girls and boys were instructed to serve at the altar for the five weekend Masses. The altar servers' organization was a catalyst for the youth to share their linguistic and social skills with one another at barbeques and potluck suppers. A Scout troop was formed in 1995. Its outdoor activities have attracted 18 leaders and 68 youngsters.

The fourth Chinese Canadian church in the Toronto area is Saviour of the World Chinese Catholic church in Mississauga, which is celebrating its fourteenth year of formation. Father John Lung was appointed in 1995 to organize the Chinese Catholic community to the west of Toronto. Fundraising began in 1998; $2 million was gathered towards the construction of a $6 million church. Construction began in 2002, and the church, which seats 650, opened in the summer of 2004. The Chinese community has daily mass in Cantonese and five weekend masses in Cantonese, Pu-tong-hua, and English. The pastoral and finance councils direct the ministries for youth and seniors.

A Chinese Catholic Community in Ottawa

In the bilingual capital city of Ottawa, 400 kilometres from Toronto, Chinese Canadians hear Mass in their own language at the Ottawa Chinese Catholic Community. Chinese Canadian Catholics currently meet at the Archdiocesan Centre on Kilborn Place. The Missionary Sisters of the Immaculate Conception first opened the Chinese Centre in Ottawa on Gilmour Street in 1955. The highly motivated and well-organized Sister Nina Ennis MIC was assigned in 1961 to the Chinese Centre, which provided Sunday Mass for Chinese university students. A chaplaincy team of sisters, along with catechist Alice Wong from Canton, offered a home and services for Chinese students at Ottawa universities. During the mid-1980s, Sister Cecilia Hong MIC also assisted the students.

Father Bosco Wong, a product of the centre, completed his degree in electrical engineering at the University of Ottawa, returned to Hong Kong, and chose to be baptized because of the goodness he saw in the priests at Hong Kong. Later he arrived back in Ottawa, entered the seminary at Saint Paul University, and became a Catholic priest in the Archdiocese of Ottawa. During his first few years of parochial ministry at Resurrection of Our Lord parish, he also worked with the Chinese Catholic community in Ottawa. He continued to serve the community while working on a licentiate in theology in 1987. The following year, Archbishop Joseph Plourde sent him to the Gregorian University in Rome for advanced studies, and in 1990 Father Wong completed a doctorate in theology. While serving as pastor of Assumption parish in 1991, he moved the Chinese Catholic community there. This arrangement continued for the next nine years, until 2000, when he was appointed as pastor of St. Basil's parish.

Deacon Peter Fan was baptized as a young man, pursued a Ph.D. in education at Columbia University, and married in 1973. He and his wife have three boys, who are now adults. He came from New York City to Ottawa in 1987 because Canada offered "a safer, freer life, and more opportunities." He quickly became involved in the Chinese Catholic community. He became a public school teacher and a high school principal, and experienced some discrimination. He retains the Chinese traditions of work and respect for the family, but adjusts well to Canadian mores.

In 2000, Guadalupe Missionaries, a missionary community active in Hong Kong, looked after the Chinese Catholic Community. When the missionaries left in 2005, the retired Montreal pastor Father Thomas Tou guided the community for a year. Father Wong was asked to assess the situation at the end of the year; since that time, along with Deacon Peter Fan, Father Wong has directed the Chinese Catholic Community in Ottawa. Deacon Fan also is active in the deacon formation program of the diocese.

The community currently meets for 12 p.m. Sunday mass at the Archdiocesan Centre at 1247 Kilborn Place, which offers a large chapel and ample parking. Father Wong shares the masses with three English-speaking priests: Fathers Peter Cody, William Burke, and Joseph Marattil. Father Wong says the mass in Cantonese or Mandarin, and the others say the mass in English. The community consists of students and 150 to 200 middle-aged families, of which two-thirds are very active in the affairs of the mission. The Chinese Catholic Community is currently looking for a church of its own. Conversions are made by individual contacts, and two RCIA programs are carried out in both Mandarin and Cantonese, as are the choirs. There are various groups established that facilitate active participation, such as Catholic Youth Organization and parish picnics, pilgrimages, and seniors' gatherings.

Ethnocentrism energizes the community and binds it together. The community hopes to retain the Chinese language and culture. Yet when the children become adults, they scatter to Canadian universities and are lost to the community. In a similar fashion, in the year 2000, when computer technology went into recession, many Chinese Canadians in the industry seeking new positions fanned out through North America. The newcomers to the community are young Mandarin speakers from mainland China, and include both educated and working-class people. The Chinese Catholic Community in Ottawa welcomes both as equals.

For the most part, Asian newcomers do not feel comfortable in Euro-Canadian parishes, which have different values from their own. Asians who go to a Euro-Canadian parish will often not continue attendance very long, as they do not feel part of those Catholic communities. As a visible minority, many Chinese newcomers have a hard time finding acceptance, yet they do retain their prayer life and Catholic faith. For example, some educated Chinese teachers, after coming to Canada, end up operating a take-out restaurant, because they are not accepted to teach in the school system. Even though 30 per cent of students in the system are from Asia or the Middle East, the number of teachers from visible minorities is very small. Insecurity on both sides impedes integrating Euro-Canadian and Asian parishes. [47]

Chinese Canadian Communities in Montreal

The Chinese Catholic Community

As early as 1863, Chinese residents of Montreal registered for language study at St. Laurent Catholic School. Their number remained small, with only seven Chinese Canadians in the whole province in 1881. Father Martin Callaghan PSS of St. Patrick's parish, just west of Chinatown, liked the Chinese people. After his retirement, he often spoke with them and played the violin for them at the corner of St. Urbain and de la Gauchetière streets to entertain them and to teach them English. Between 1902 and 1904, Father Callaghan baptized 58 Chinese adults. He and his brother Father Luke Callaghan paid university tuition so that a young Chinese man could study medicine.

The growing Chinese community in Montreal, led by Father Émile Girot, petitioned Archbishop Paul Bruchési in March 1904 for a Chinese speaking priest. When the Jesuit Chinese missionary William Hornsby arrived in Montreal that August for a vacation, the archbishop invited this Chinese speaking priest to preach at the Brothers of the Christian Schools for the Chinese community in October. Sunday classes for the Chinese were held in French and English, followed by catechism in Chinese. The archbishop also celebrated a thanksgiving Mass in October, at which Father Hornsby preached to a congregation of 400 Chinese.

In 1910, Father H. Montanar, a French missionary from Kwangtung, visited Montreal, where he had established a Chinese mission to organize the Corpus Christi procession for 30 Chinese Catholics. Two years later, at the request of Archbishop Bruchési, Montanar returned with a Chinese preacher, Mr. Woo, to preach at Notre Dame des Anges. By 1912, the community had grown to 1,000 members, comparable in number to the Toronto Chinese community. Father Montanar ran a Sunday school in Chinese at the Church of the Infant Jesus at the corner of St. Dominique Boulevard and St. Joseph Street, and baptized eleven young adults in 1914.[48]

Following mass for the Chinese community, Father Martin Callaghan conducted French and English classes. In June 1915, Callaghan died and Father Montanar was recalled to France for war service. The mission work was entrusted to the newly founded Society of the Missionary Sisters of the Immaculate Conception.[49] In 1916, Archbishop Bruchési arranged a new site for the Montreal Chinese Sunday School for teaching the children.[50] The catechesis was mostly in English for the 200 Chinese students. In 1917, a Chinese burial ground was purchased and set aside at Mount Royal Cemetery.[51]

The seminarian Roméo Caillé began working with the Chinese Catholic community in 1915 and, with his Chinese friends as witnesses, was ordained a priest in 1917 in the chapel of the mother house of the Missionary Sisters. With the approval of the archdiocese, he established a "personal parish," which was inaugurated on July 1, 1917, in the Académie Commerciale auditorium. Father Caillé located a permanent site for a church in 1925, at 106 rue de la Gauchetière in downtown Montreal, and the Archdiocese purchased the site for the Chinese church and school. Restaurateur Frank Lee and other benefactors generously supported the endeavour. In 1927, the parish adopted the name The Holy Spirit Chinese parish. Father Caillé, acting as pastor, baptized and registered many parishioners. The church gave assistance to new and aged immigrants. Parishioners organized a Boy Scout troop, youth club, and folk dance club. Although he admitted that he spoke Chinese inadequately, Father Caillé remained as parish priest until 1943.[52]

The Missionary Sisters of the Immaculate Conception taught the newcomers French, English, and catechism, and facilitated their integration into Montreal society. In 1916, the sisters brought a sister and a Chinese catechist from Canton to teach Chinese children. Chinese instruction continued until 1931, when many Chinese returned to China because of the Chinese

Exclusion Act, passed in 1923. In Montreal, Quebec City, and Trois-Rivières, the sisters visited Chinese families to assist them with their needs. The sisters also demonstrated their commitment to the Chinese by taking stands in favour of the new immigrants and against discriminatory legislation and racist attitudes. Their efforts did not protect the sisters from Chinese Nationalists, who suspected their Christian intentions. The Nationalists established their own Chinese language and culture programs to protect, as they explained, Chinese Canadian children from Christian missionaries. Both sides frowned upon marriage between Chinese and non-Chinese.[53]

Holy Spirit Chinese Catholic church, Chinatown, Montreal; restored in 1988

During the Spanish influenza epidemic of 1918, Father Roméo Caillé had urged the Missionary Sisters of the Immaculate Conception to rent space for a temporary shelter to care for Chinese Canadians.[54] The Chinese were well organized to raise funds to do this, utilizing both the Chinese clans and fraternal organizations. During the epidemic, the Chinese community supported the Missionary Sisters' efforts to open an emergency shelter for Chinese influenza patients.[55] The Benevolent Chinese Society paid the rent, heat, and light bills, the city paid the upkeep, the Clerics of St. Viator supplied the beds and pillows, and the Missionary Sisters offered the bedclothes, furnishings, and nursing services. "Fifty-five Chinese men were admitted and twenty died in influenza."[56] The Chinese Nationalist government awarded Father Caillé and the Founder of the Missionary Sisters, Mother Mary of the Holy Spirit, gold medals for their charitable work. The temporary shelter was closed in 1919, after the epidemic subsided.[57]

Unhappy with the shelter's closure, the Chinese community decided in January of the following year to establish a permanent hospital at 112 de la Gauchetière West, and, because of its previous experience with the Missionary Sisters, entrusted the project to them.[58] Dr. Louis E. Fortier, and later his son Dr. Henri Fortier, directed the medical progress of the hospital until 1947 and 1965, respectively.[59] Holy Spirit church also supported the nearby Chinese Hospital until the advent of government funding in 1946. The Montreal Chinese Hospital was closed in 1962, but was rebuilt three years later in the northern part of the city amidst a multicultural population. The new hospital served for 34 years, until the Chinese community decided to move it back downtown when a suitable site became available. In 1999, the new Montreal Chinese Hospital, with 128 beds, was erected in Chinatown to serve the multi-ethnic population of Montreal.[60]

The former Chinese missionary and Mandarin-speaking Father Lucien Lafond PME became pastor of the parish in 1954. Although he did not speak Cantonese, he nevertheless established the Chinese Service Association to initiate instruction in both Cantonese and Mandarin. Under the Association officers, Simon Yuen, Raymond Wong, Bill Lee, and Richard Wong, the Chinese Language School was reactivated in September 1956 at St. Laurent school. French and English were taught to adults, and Chinese languages were taught to children ages four to ten. The original 241 students increased to 278 by the following May. Government financial help was offered until the school's closing in 1971.

Fellowship of the Chinese Catholic community was both outward and inward looking. As an infant of 20 months, Gordon Wu of Toronto was diagnosed in 1991 with a fatal blood disorder. He needed a bone marrow transplant. Chinese Catholics in Montreal mobilized to seek and test suitable donors in their community. A committee was immediately struck to schedule clinic dates and prepare advertising. Parishioners arrived to assist at the clinic and to raise funds. Six hundred and fifty-five potential donors came forward to supply blood testing, and $15,000 was raised to help the Wu family with their expenses.

Since then, the Chinese Service Association has reopened the Montreal school for the education of Chinese children, and, according to *Growing with God*, "today the Chinese Catholic School has become one of the very successful Chinese language schools in all the cities of Canada." Without government assistance, 2,000 students were instructed in a custom-built building and taught at various levels of instruction by "well qualified and dedicated educators." Despite the lethargy among some Canadian-born students to learn Chinese, the teachers cultivated their goodwill and stressed the importance of learning Chinese Catholic culture for their own personal identity.

Annual scholarship awards are presented to the best Chinese students attending Montreal schools. The awards are intended to encourage Chinese students to strive for academic excellence. Seventy to 80 students receive awards annually, and many have achieved a grade average of 96 to 97. These awards motivate Chinese students to be competitive in the contemporary world and develop skills so they can contribute to the future of their family, their community, and Canada.

In the first half of the 20th century, although the United, Anglican, and Presbyterian churches had some Chinese ministers,

Chinese Catholic priests were nowhere to be found in Canada. Thus, Father Lucien Lafond petitioned Cardinal Léger in 1956 to appoint a Chinese Catholic priest to the parish. Through a connection in Rome, the Cardinal learned of Father Thomas Tou, who was completing his studies there.[61] Father Tou was invited to be the pastor of the Chinese parish in downtown Montreal. He accepted the position in 1957, and gave the next 45 years of his life to serving the Chinese community.[62] The joy of having a Chinese priest was celebrated throughout the Montreal Chinese community.

The community bought an abandoned Scottish Presbyterian church dating back to 1835, with plans to restore it. Before restoration began, the federal government seized the property for demolition, granting $900,000 in compensation. This sum was used to pay for the construction of the Chinese Catholic Community Centre. Then Quebec declared the abandoned church a historic site, and it was sold back to the Chinese parish for $1. The parish received a grant of $750,000 from the federal government for the restoration. The Chinese Catholic Community, as a result of these miraculous windfalls, found itself well established in Chinatown with a new community centre, a restored church, and a community of active parishioners in the heart of old Montreal.[63] Chinese Catholics in Canada, according to Father Thomas Tou, have a good record of supporting the Church and attending Sunday mass. The Montreal Chinese parish also served as a pillar for Catholic news and supplies to Chinese Catholics in the Maritime provinces.

The Chinese Association for the Elderly was founded in 1976 to encourage seniors to enjoy their friends and lead an active life. The restored church basement was designated as the Association's recreation centre. Games, outings, and excursions were organized. The following year, Father Thomas Tou, with the assistance of a bank loan and Canada Mortgage and Housing Corporation, was able to construct the first seniors' residence, which opened in 1982 and was immediately filled.

Three more seniors' residences were completed between 1988 and 1990. Sister Agnes Wong of the Sisters of the Precious Blood, Hong Kong, supervised the Montreal residences with the goal of providing proper health care and encouraging residents' autonomy. [64]

Chinese Culture in Canada

Language schools

Victor Lee, after his arrival in Montreal as a boy in 1958, recalled attending the Chinese school in downtown Montreal on Saturday and Sunday afternoons. He relates that "all grade levels were taught in one classroom. The lessons were given at the front of the classroom of Sister Thérèse Woo of the Missionary Sisters of Our Lady of the Angels, Sherbrooke, Quebec, who provided the lesson. She was a woman that possesses a distinctive teaching skill." As a skilled teacher, Sister Woo could maintain order in the classroom while teaching various levels of Chinese instruction. At Christmas, amidst the singing of Chinese songs and dancing, Santa Claus handed out toys to the children and their guests from the nearby Protestant church. In the summer, the Chinese school was moved to a Chinese summer camp north of Montreal. The children liked the country environment, the meals, and the camaraderie.

Canadian-born Chinese who did not speak Chinese at home, however, found themselves isolated at Sunday mass. Eugene Tam described how he "hesitantly" attended mass in Chinese. He was then introduced to liturgy sessions in English during the first part of the Chinese mass and was delighted to meet other Chinese youth who had the same difficulty. The new fellowship they experienced made their time in church a delight to which he looked forward. He also participated in Bible study sessions, annual ski trips, and numerous banquets, experiencing in the

Chinese Catholic community fellowship, sharing, and religious inspiration.

Francis Wu added that the teachers were young and full of energy and that, during the Sunday classes, they communicated the Gospel. The children were able to understand its meaning and at the same time shared fellowship with their friends. The parents sponsored biannual celebrations with the children, and the children seized the occasion to show their talents in presentations on the stage. Language loss among the Chinese born had been slight, since they generally spoke Chinese in the home, but language loss among Canadian-born Chinese was considerable. The children predominantly spoke English; only 41 per cent spoke Chinese at home.[65]

Newspapers, radio and television, art, and literature

The three major Chinese Canadian newspapers are subsidiaries of Hong Kong and Taiwan chains and are published in Vancouver and Toronto. Numerous radio stations broadcast Chinese programming, and two television stations run Chinese shows.

Chinese art has integrated into Canadian culture and is admired well beyond the borders of the Chinese community. Peter S. Li points out that "in the visual arts the work of Chinese Canadians ranges from traditional painting, printmaking, seal carving, and calligraphy to abstract images, sculpture, installations, and video." Chinese opera societies began in Victoria in the 1870s, later spreading to Vancouver, Toronto, Ottawa, and Montreal. Accompanied by original instruments, Chinese opera in Canada often relates the folk traditions and myths of the Guandong province of southern China.

In the postwar period, Chinese Canadians have contributed a new body of literature in English, including such works as *Inalienable Rice* (1979), *Many-Mouthed Birds* (1991), and *Banana Boys* (2000), which articulate the theme of the Chinese Canadian identity. In Canadian broadcasting, Adrienne Clarkson (née

Poy) and Der Hoi-Yin paved the way in giving Canada a more multicultural face. Chinese Canadians have served in public office at the municipal, provincial, and federal levels. In 1988, David See-Chai Lam of Hong Kong became lieutenant governor of British Columbia. Bob Wong served as Minister of Energy and Minister of Citizenship in the Ontario Liberal government of David Peterson in the late 1980s. Toronto lawyer Susan Eng chaired the Police Services Board in Toronto from 1991 to 1994. Raymond Chan of Hong Kong was elected a member of

Descent of the Holy Spirit upon Our Lady
and the Apostles, Holy Spirit church, Montreal

Parliament from Richmond, British Columbia, in 1993, and was appointed to the federal cabinet.[66] Clarkson was appointed Governor General of Canada in 1999; she served until 2005. Philip Lee is now the Lieutenant Governor of Manitoba.

Education

Education is a high priority for Chinese Canadians. The Chinese Consolidated Benevolent Society founded the first Chinese school in Victoria at the end of the nineteenth century. Chinese schools opened in Vancouver in 1909, in Montreal in 1913, and in Toronto in 1914.[67] Chinese and English were taught to equip a literate, bilingual population. In the 1920s, the University of Toronto offered Chinese studies and graduate work in East Asian Studies. Distinguished scholar Kiang Kang-hu presided over Chinese studies at McGill University, collecting unique library holdings. The University of Alberta, Simon Fraser University, and St. Mary's University also provided programs of Chinese studies. Chinese Canadians were twice as likely as other Canadians to finish their university degree. During the 1980s, 50 Chinese language schools opened in Canadian cities, and Chinese Catholic student groups were formed on university campuses across Canada.[68]

In Ontario, Chinese Catholic communities emerged on university campuses in London, Ottawa, Toronto, Kingston, Hamilton, and Waterloo. Students at the various campuses coordinated their activities by forming the Joint University Chinese Catholic Community to welcome newcomers on life's journey. The group provides "spiritual and intellectual interactions among all affiliated local communities" by hosting "annual retreats, prayer gatherings and bible sharing sessions in addition to the weekly meetings held at each local community."[69]

While Chinatowns remain in older sections of Canadian cities, they have shed their residential nature and have become mainly commercial districts and tourist attractions. Chinese residential neighbourhoods in Vancouver have moved from downtown to the suburbs of Richmond and Burnaby; in Toronto, to Scarborough, Markham, and Mississauga; and in Montreal, to Brossard and Pointe-Claire. The concentration of services in Chinatowns includes Chinese restaurants, foods, furniture, clothes, and services.[70]

Conclusion

Chinese Christian communities in the 20th century began to emerge in cities from Montreal to Vancouver. Finding themselves in societies rife with discriminatory practices, Chinese people sought help from Canadian religious groups that welcomed newcomers.

Throughout this period, Catholic schools in Asia had enjoyed a high reputation for preparing bright, ambitious students for an encounter with Western culture, and planted the roots of Catholicism in some. Many of these well-educated Chinese graduates of Catholic schools arrived in Canada in the 1970s, wishing to maintain contact with Chinese culture through national parishes and devotional confraternities in their own language. Chinese parishes were well established in Vancouver, Toronto, and Montreal, and more were being planned in other cities.

Chinese Canadians found themselves in a "dialogic relation," as described by Maria Castagna and George J. Sefa Dei, to search out their own personal identity through the interrelation of Chinese religion, art, music, and literature with that of their Canadian counterparts.[71] Chinese Catholics employed family values and Asian wisdom to overcome their isolation and loneliness in the Canadian social environment. They also attended English-speaking Catholic churches for communal celebration and, by the same token, put energy into Canadian parish communities.[72]

Chinese Catholics, after their arrival in Canada, found deep strength in their Chinese Catholic culture, which kept them in personal harmony during migration, transition, and integration. Chinese Canadian Catholics are the majority (Catholics, 57 per cent; Protestants, 43 per cent) among Chinese Christians.[73] Their professional competence and persistent faith helped them to overcome initial discrimination. Their well-organized parishes inspire Canadian churches to soften the dominance of Euro-Canadian influence and usher in a post-European, multicultural Canadian Catholicism.

Chinese Martyrs' church, Markham, Ontario; opened in 1994

2

Chinese Catholics:
Eleven Personal Stories

et us listen to the stories of eleven Chinese Canadian couples and one Chinese Canadian priest who chose Canada
as their home, the place where they work out their identity
as Chinese Catholics and seek their transcendent goals.[1]

Work Exploitation Leads to "Canadian Experience":
The Story of Tony Ma

Tony Ma was born in Tien Tsin City three years before the
Communist Party seized Mainland China in 1949. Members of
Tony's family were officers in the Chinese navy during the administration of Chiang Kai Chek. With the flight of the Kuomintang
to Taiwan in 1949, Tony's family moved and established a new
residence there. Tony completed his education at the National
Taiwan University and served the required time in the National
Chinese army from 1967 to 1968, a period of high tensions
between the Mainland and Taiwanese governments. His future
father-in-law, a former naval officer, then a tanker captain and
world traveller, urged his son-in-law to do graduate studies in
North America and establish a residence there.[2] After considering

the political unrest in China and Taiwan, Tony sought a better life by migrating to North America.

In 1970, Tony applied for graduate studies in business information systems at Georgia State University in Atlanta, obtaining his master's degree in 1971. That same year, he went back to Taiwan and married Lydwine Wen Liao, a graduate of World Journal College of Taipei. They moved on student visas to Georgia. Working as a teaching assistant in the information systems department, Tony continued his studies in the doctorate program of business administration, majoring in management. He finished his course work, but, having come to the end of his student visa, and now with a family, sought permanent residency in North America. He discovered that admission to Canada could be procured quickly, so he applied to Canadian immigration as a computer specialist. The family moved to Toronto in August 1974 and lived in temporary downtown housing while Tony sought his first job in Canada.

Well qualified, he interviewed for a major computer company. When it came to the crucial question, "Do you have Canadian experience?" he had to say "no." Rejected, he lowered his job expectations and chose the smallest advertisement of the smallest computer company looking for programmers. He found a company with four employees that demanded long work hours for little pay. During the job interview, his would-be employer called his university, Georgia State, to check his credentials, making him feel less than trusted. Once hired, he was paid $7,000 yearly. As he found out, his work was mainly on the night shift, although this included being called during the day for emergencies, for no additional pay. He was exploited by his employer, but accepted these unreasonable demands as the price of gaining "Canadian experience." Tony and his family remained in Canada although many Chinese student families who came from Georgia to Canada in the mid-1970s returned to the United States for the greater job opportunities.

Finding multiculturalism in Toronto refreshing, Tony forgot the Georgia social environment he left behind. He discovered that he could live in Toronto as a Chinese Canadian and did not have to fit into the American middle-class lifestyle. Yet he found that getting used to Canadian idioms was a challenge. He learned to adjust to the way of saying and doing things that Canadians do, while at the same time maintaining his Chinese culture and Catholic religious practice. Making a point not to complain about discrimination, he ignored slights and adopted a positive attitude.

Tony earned hardly enough money to live on, but his wife Lydwine helped by teaching Chinese and working for Canada Post. After seven months of low pay and long hours, and having paid the price for Canadian experience, Tony interviewed with the Ministry of Transportation and passed a brief exam with flying colours. He was hired immediately and spent the rest of his working years engaged in computer programming for the ministry. He worked there for 25 good years, retiring from senior management in the Ontario public service in 2000. One of his bosses mused that "the best contribution he made to the ministry was hiring Tony Ma!"

The three daughters of Tony and Lydwine attended Canadian schools and universities but still remain functional in Chinese. Teresa is a high school teacher with her own family. Joanna is a Canadian bank manager who is concurrently involved in a high-powered graduate school at Queen's University. Marian is a business/marketing analyst for a Canadian Internet bank. Both parents were both very involved in raising the children, and share decisions with them.[3] The parents stressed traditional Chinese values, which included the importance of education and hard work balanced by frugality and self-confidence. The daughters were given the liberty to chose their own schools and to correct their parents' English. Having grown up in a mix of Eastern and Western cultures, the daughters, given the choice, select more Canadian than Chinese values. The parents are pleased that their daughters still go to the English mass at Chinese Martyrs, respect their elders, keep in contact with Chinese culture, and live a modest lifestyle. They did not have a lot of conflict in their family, and any generational disagreements that did happen brought them "better solutions" to resolve problems.

The parents would prefer that their daughters marry Chinese Catholics in a Chinese Catholic ceremony, but would ultimately accept their choice of partners.[4] The daughters have proven themselves to be very resourceful and independent. Although the parents offered to pay their tuition or to loan them money for university, the daughters were industrious and earned the cost of their university education themselves. Having completed their years of dependency, the daughters now look after their parents, celebrate with them on festive occasions, and bring gifts to honour them. The three daughters are accomplished musicians, with one playing the organ at church services.

In 1987, Tony and Lydwine took part in the organization of Chinese Martyrs parish in Markham, and Tony was chair of the building committee for the church and community centre from 1990 to 1994. Through struggles at work and in community organization, he learned the importance of prayer in his life and the experience of transcendence. Tony does not choose specific times for prayer, but prays when he feels he is ready to pray. Sometimes he prays when he rises, sometimes when he is driving, and sometimes at bedtime. He reads the Bible, reflects, prays, and listens to God in his life. He uses no particular formula, but thanks God for his family, wife, and work, and for "loving me and giving me so much."

Tony is now a member of the oldest Chinese parish in downtown Toronto: Our Lady of Mount Carmel Chinese Catholic church, founded in 1970. He is the vice-chair of the pastoral council and a member of both the finance and building committees. He is a member of the Mandarin language group, which sponsors Bible study and picnics for seniors and looks after funerals and good works. The parish priest of Mount

Carmel, the Oblate Father Peter Ching, is noted for having an "English style," which means he knows his way around Toronto to help those who have just arrived. To recruit new members, the parishioners of Mount Carmel parish welcome newcomers and assist the Mandarin-speaking Chinese. The parish greeters are experienced in caring for newcomers who need financial aid, providing assistance to find work and English-language instruction, and helping people deal with Canadian immigration procedures. Chinese Catholics are 12 per cent of the Chinese arriving in Canada, Chinese Protestants are 9 per cent, and unaffiliated Chinese Christians are 6 per cent.[5]

Tony believes that Chinese culture can enrich the Canadian Catholic Church if the Church is open to receive it. In fact, he states that "many traditional Chinese values are similar to Catholic teachings." He points out that Chinese immigrating to Canada are diligent professionals who encourage their children to achieve academic excellence. The Chinese have high respect for learning and know that studies are of great value. Tony and Lydwine, having endured exploitation and discrimination in the workplace to gain "Canadian experience," are now retired and happy to remain in Toronto, or perhaps move to Vancouver. Yet they would also consider doing missionary work by moving temporarily to China or Taiwan to teach English or other useful skills.[6]

Cultural Seepage in the Family: The Story of Joe Chan

Joe Chan completed his training in electrical engineering at the Aberdeen Technical School in Hong Kong in 1970 and, with the hope of better employment in Canada, came to Toronto five years later. Quickly, he found work in computer engineering, but to expand his knowledge of computer software and to gain Canadian credentials, he completed programs in 1989 at George Brown and Ryerson colleges. Lucilla Lau, who graduated in nursing in 1969 in Hong Kong, arrived with her family in 1976.

Joe and Lucilla met in Toronto and married in Vancouver in 1979. They have a boy, Gabriel, and a girl, Gabriella, both of whom received their education in Canada.

Both children are university educated and understand spoken Chinese, but do not respond in Chinese. Children educated in Canada, according to Professor Wei-Chin Hwang, acculturate more quickly than their parents, and an acculturation gap results.[7] Joe and Lucilla Chan conveyed to their children the love of family values, Catholic devotion, and Chinese cuisine. However, the children, accustomed to both Canadian and Chinese food, eat both foods with equal relish. They have been brought up to respect their elders and care for family members. One of the two children continues to practise religion and attends the English masses at St. Justin Martyr. In Hong Kong, children necessarily followed the will of the parents, but in Canada the children express their views and have their own ideas about how they will conduct their lives. It is more important to Joe and Lucilla that their children marry Catholics than that they marry Chinese, but both are important values for them. Although parents and children have strong views about issues affecting them directly, they believe in open dialogue and resolving differences without open conflict. Family decisions are made jointly.

At Sunday mass, the Chans pray as a family; they also pray together at table. Joe and Lucilla say morning and evening prayers, and are involved in Bible study at St. Justin Martyr parish. Lucilla makes herself available to serve funerals at church. Although few Catholics from Hong Kong currently arrive, mainland Chinese Catholics continue to do so. They desire to have their children enrolled in Ontario Catholic schools, but fear that the Canadian schools are not as strict as the schools in China. Chinese Canadian Catholics are unlikely to involve themselves in evangelism, but do raise funds for church needs to buy clothes for the poor and show resourcefulness for communal needs. Although they are disappointed that their children are losing their Chinese heritage, Joe and Lucilla Chan are content living in Canada and remaining with their children.[8]

Chinese Culture Interacts with Canadian Catholics: The Story of Father Peter Leung

Father Peter Leung was born in Hong Kong and began his seminary education when he was sixteen. He later studied at the Urbana University in Rome and was ordained in 1972. He returned to Hong Kong for pastoral ministry. In 1981, he took a sabbatical year at Loyola University in Chicago and completed a master's degree in pastoral theology. Father Leung was invited in 2001 by the archbishop of Toronto to come to Toronto to serve the Chinese community as pastor of Chinese Martyrs parish in Markham.

Father Leung observes that the Chinese Catholic culture is changing as a result of its interface with Canadian culture. The Chinese family, moving from an Eastern to a Western culture, undergoes personal change, which can be unsettling. Discussing family decision making, Father Leung states that, in the Chinese tradition, parents make the decisions. It is presumed that the father is educated and thus the one to make family decisions. In Canada, Father Leung admits, Chinese do things differently: women also are well educated, help support the family, and play an important role in family decisions. Contributing to the family's financial stability, women in Canada have won a voice in the direction of the family. A husband or wife can play the "astronaut" role of shuttling back and forth to Hong Kong to provide adequate family income. This strategy is difficult for two reasons. Scholar David Ley contends that transnational activities are bad business and have proved unsuccessful.[9] But also, the separate lifestyle of husband and wife, even for brief periods, can place a marriage under great strain. Even when all family members have arrived in Canada at the same time, it can take considerable time to deal with the emotional trauma that fitting into a new culture can bring.

Many parents emigrate to Canada hoping that their children will receive a better education than they themselves had. The children, the second generation of newcomers to Canada, may follow one of several ways. Father Leung believes that Chinese youngsters who are older than ten when they arrive in Canada have a strong chance of retaining their language skills and fondly remember their native culture. On the other hand, second-generation Chinese Canadians who are schooled entirely in Canada lose much of their Chinese heritage. Researcher Emi Ooka points out that second-generation Chinese will remain Chinese speaking if they "are surrounded by parents and friends who can influence their cultural retention."[10] This heritage includes family events, such as celebrating Chinese New Year, gathering to eat moon cake at Chung Chau and remembering deceased members at Chiang Ming (Easter time) and Chung Yeung (All Souls). These are traditional events for Chinese Catholics, not to be forgotten. As a visible minority in Toronto, Vancouver, and Montreal, Chinese Canadians find it frustrating to lose their culture, which others presume to know. Grandparents are of great assistance for families wishing to preserve their language and culture. What works for Chinese families is to buy two houses side by side, one for the grandparents and another for the family. Father Leung says that Chinese Canadians appreciate having adequate space and find such arrangements provide living space for three generations.

In their religious affiliation, 12 per cent of Chinese Canadians are members of the Catholic Church.[11] Father Leung believes that more than 50 per cent of Chinese Canadian Catholics marry within their own religion and ethnic group, yet some marry other Christians and a smaller percentage marry those without a designated religion. The prayer of Chinese Catholics is likely to be communal when they participate in the sacraments, and private when they recite the rosary and say their own prayers.

They enjoy processions on the feast days of the saints. Chinese Martyrs church has a charismatic prayer group that meets weekly and a Focolare group that meets monthly for Bible study, sharing the Gospel and *agape* (a shared religious meal). The Rite of Christian Initiation for Adults (RCIA) commences Christian instruction for adults every three months; once the neophytes have completed the eighteen-month program, they are baptized. The new Christians are then divided into small groups for prayer and fellowship. Chinese Martyrs parish exceeds by far the other 230 Catholic parishes in the archdiocese of Toronto in the number of neophytes who are prepared for the sacrament of baptism each year. The parishioners continue to be very active in archdiocesan events, such as World Youth Days, vocation campaigns, Legion of Mary, and Catholic Women's League. Chinese Canadians embrace the universality of the Catholic Church and its Catholic organizations by their membership, their skills in doing business, and their personal commitment in faith, says Father Leung. Chinese Canadian Catholics are modestly successful in maintaining their Catholic faith over several generations in the face of a secularized Canadian nation.[12]

Gradual Assimilation for the Second Generation: The Story of Theresa Chiu and Augustine Cheung

Theresa Chiu was born in Indonesia. She was educated in Taiwan and completed her medical degree at the National Taiwan Medical University in 1962. Augustine Cheung was born in Hong Kong, began his education at the Jesuit Wah Yan College in Hong Kong, and completed it at the National Taiwan Medical University in 1962. In August of the same year, the two doctors married in Macau, the former Portuguese colony near Hong Kong, and then travelled to Canada for their medical internship at the Halifax Infirmary in Nova Scotia. Afterwards, they proceeded to Buffalo for further training in pediatrics and surgery, respectively. Attracted by the British Commonwealth connection between Hong Kong and Canada, they returned to Canada in 1965 and requested landed immigrant status in Toronto. They raised three children, who attended Catholic schools and went on to university. Their oldest child, Jerome, went to McMaster University; he works for the National Democratic Institute in Indonesia, where he is involved in the protection of human rights. While in Indonesia, he married an Indonesian Muslim woman. Theresa and Augustine's second child, Vincent, attended the University of Waterloo for mechanical engineering, and then proceeded to the University of Ottawa for medical school. A kidney specialist practising in Peterborough, Ontario, he is married to a Chinese Canadian Catholic. The third child, Michelle, went to Osgoode Law School at York University in Toronto; she is an advocate for the protection of children. Michelle is married to a Chinese Protestant, who is well disposed to the responsibilities she has undertaken as a Catholic Christian.

The children of Theresa and Augustine are partially functional in the Chinese language and appreciate Chinese culture. Their grandparents from Taiwan enjoyed year-long visits to Toronto and were helpful with the family. They spoke Chinese to their grandchildren, and the children spoke English to them. They communicated with each other in short chats but did not attempt discussions about politics or religion. In some families, there can be serious communication breakdowns when the young are no longer able to speak the language of the parents or grandparents.[13] The acculturation gap began to occur in this family. When the children were small, their mother, Theresa, made decisions for them, but in their middle teens the children became independent. The parents laid down house rules, which were stricter for their daughter than for their sons, but the enforcement was not rigid. Once the children began attending university, they were granted autonomy and were on their own to achieve their career goals.

The parents communicated the Chinese Catholic values of honesty and hard work. The children were baptized and confirmed at Blessed Trinity church. The parents encouraged their children to go beyond appearances and live a good and ethical life. Two of the three children still identify with Catholicism. Four of the five grandchildren are baptized and will attend Catholic schools. Augustine and Theresa came to Canada to study, earn their livelihood, find acceptance, and adopt Canada as their home country. Their children have assimilated the Canadian lifestyle and see Canada as their home.

The parents pray in both Chinese and English. For public prayer, they attend Sunday mass in English at Blessed Trinity or in Chinese at Chinese Martyrs. They are also members of the Mandarin language group, which fosters Bible study and group prayer. Theresa says her night prayers in Mandarin while Augustine does so in Cantonese. At Chinese Martyrs, it is conceded that Chinese Catholics are not as proactive as Protestant Chinese in the recruitment of newcomers, but nevertheless, when newcomers arrive at mass, people stand and welcome them. In fact, it was the Chinese Protestant proselytism of newly arrived Chinese Catholics that stimulated the formation of the four Chinese Catholic parishes in Toronto. Chinese national parishes in Canada have Chinese speaking pastors who say the masses in Chinese languages. But the immigration of Chinese professionals and business people from Hong Kong has eased off and, by contrast, the more recent Chinese immigrants are likely to be working people from mainland China who find housing in downtown Toronto and attend Our Lady of Mount Carmel Chinese Catholic church. The medical skills and deep faith of Chinese Catholics, such as Theresa Chiu and Augustine Cheung, is a powerful gift to the Canadian Catholic community.[14]

Chinese Catholicism Modifies Work Expectations: The Story of Patrick Yeung and Nancy Chung

Patrick Yeung was the firstborn son of Dr. George and Dr. Cissy Yeung of Hong Kong. He was named after St. Patrick of Ireland, and his siblings who followed him were named after the English, Welsh and Scottish patron saints, George, David and Andrew. The members of Patrick's maternal family have been Chinese Catholics for more than eight generations. Patrick finished his B.A. at St. Mary's College of San Francisco; he completed his M.A. in 1965 and a Ph.D. in economics in 1967 at Claremont Graduate School and University Center. Patrick's wife, Nancy Chung, completed her B.A. at the University of Hong Kong in 1964 and her M.A. in Asian history at the Claremont Graduate School in 1966. Patrick and Nancy met in Hong Kong in 1959, and were married at Claremont in August 1966.

Their four boys, Gerald, Alex, Patrick Jr. and Christopher, were born over the next few years. They were educated in the United States and Canada and, as a result, learned very little Chinese. The parents, raising their children in the United States, where Cantonese was rarely spoken, made cultural adjustments by no longer speaking Cantonese to their children once the latter started school in English. While they continued to stress the importance of Chinese culture, they taught their children prayers in Cantonese and catechism in English.[15] Their father made a point of engaging the boys in conversation about crucial issues in their lives, which he believes kept the boys close to their family. The Yeungs held functional family meetings to distribute family chores, such as cooking daily meals and leading prayers on various occasions. The family would say grace at table and share evening prayers, such as the rosary and the Consecration of the Family to the Sacred Heart of Jesus. The teenagers did not seem to mind their chores and often invited their friends for prayer and supper before they went out for the evening.

The Yeung family first moved to the University of Illinois, where Patrick was teaching, and then to Washington, DC, where he was employed by the World Bank. As for Nancy, after having raised the boys to school age in Washington, she had brushed up her typing and secretarial skills, which led her in 1976 to a career in insurance underwriting in the United States. In 1982, the family came to Toronto to join their extended family. Patrick's parents were living in Canada; they decided to retire from medical practice rather than intern anew. Nancy's parents, who had moved from Hong Kong to Canada, live in Toronto and are financially independent. After Patrick and Nancy decided to make their home in Canada, Patrick expected to return to university teaching, so he interviewed at universities in Toronto. At one interview, he was told by his interviewer that he had been "contaminated" by the American academic system. Absorbing discrimination was part of being a newcomer; Patrick lowered his expectations and settled for high school teaching. Nancy, meanwhile, was told she lacked "Canadian experience" in spite of her American professional qualifications. Discriminated against by a Canadian firm, she was hired by an American firm with offices in Toronto, which rewarded her according to her credentials.

The sons were good students, and won scholarships for university. For the most part, they did not need to rely on family funds for their education. The two elder sons lived on campus at the University of Waterloo during their undergraduate years, but the two younger sons remained mostly at home while attending the University of Toronto. The eldest, Gerald, left the Catholic Church for about ten years, but has returned, his faith strengthened by the experience. Now working in the United States, Gerald has become a successful actuary and is married to a Laotian who became Catholic. The second son, Alex, has a religious vocation to the Legionaries of Christ; he was ordained a priest at St. Peter's Basilica in Rome in December 2003. The third son, Patrick Jr., temporarily considered a religious vocation but then went into medicine and is now practising at Georgetown University Hospital in Washington, DC. The fourth son, Christopher, completed his Ph.D. in biomedical engineering at Johns Hopkins University, discerned a vocation with the archdiocese of Baltimore, and decided to become a permanent married deacon.

Since their retirement a few years ago, Nancy and Patrick attend daily mass at a nearby church and belong to a Cantonese-speaking charismatic prayer group at Chinese Martyrs parish. The group meets on the first and third Sunday of each month for meditative singing and prayer. They read the Scriptures and pray with those who ask them. They belong to a Chinese Marriage Encounter group and are involved in teaching two sections of the English-speaking Rite of Christian Initiation for Adults, which meet weekly. Both participate in the parish committee promoting vocations to the priesthood and religious life. While older Chinese Canadians were slow to encourage their sons to become clergy or their daughters to enter consecrated life in the Church, things are definitely changing. Chinese Canadian priests have been recently ordained in Ottawa, Toronto, and Rome. In other ministries, many young adults from immigrant families are fervent in Bible study groups and are now involved in preparing Chinese language programming for the Catholic television network Salt and Light. Chinese Canadian youth responded wholeheartedly to World Youth Day in Toronto in 2002. In general, Chinese Canadian Catholics seek religious freedom but are inclined to be theologically conservative, oppose same-sex "marriage," and take a strong stand in defence of traditional marriage, said Nancy and Patrick. Chinese Canadians have a strong sense of their own Canadian Catholic identity, which helps them to accept new roles in the workplace.[16]

Learning to Think in English, with Diffidence: The Story of Tony Chow and Mary Cheung

Tony Chow was born in Hong Kong. After completing his secondary education there, and then working as an office clerk, he was invited by a cousin interning in Toronto to come to Canada for university studies. When the plane landed in Vancouver, Tony felt deep in his heart that "Canada was his country." At the University of Calgary, he completed a bachelor of computer science in 1988, and met Mary Cheung. They decided to marry in Montreal, where she had moved and was working at that time, and so applied for landed immigrant status. Tony's work brought them to Toronto, where he is an application programmer; Mary found work as the parish secretary at Chinese Martyrs church in 2001. They have two children, who are in Catholic schools; Simone, sixteen, and Samuel, fifteen. Simone is functional in Cantonese; Samuel, less so. The grandparents live in Toronto but independently from the family.

Stained glass, designed by Ho-Bei Lau, in Chinese Martyrs' church

In Hong Kong, Catholic schools used English as the language of instruction. As a student there, Tony learned to read English easily, but spoke English only occasionally. As a student at the University of Calgary, he spent much of his time mastering English. When speaking English, he discovered, he had to think differently and speak differently. When he spoke English, he had to learn to think in an anglophone way. Never did he feel discriminated against, but he admits he puzzled colleagues by how he said things, and some shied away. He believes that before a person can be promoted to a leadership role, his or her communication skills must be first class. Tony also found that cultural differences cause misunderstandings. Chinese culture dictates reticence in revealing personal thoughts. Tony found that at work, while he did not discuss sensitive issues that were bothering him, his colleagues would blatantly address these issues. It took him time to learn the open straightforwardness of Canadian life.

With his family, he likes discussing current issues, but the family does not have an agenda for chats. He finds good dinners are a great help for family members to form links with one another in conversation. For instance, there was a question about which course Simone should take at school one year: parenting or history. Tony thought history would help her understand the world in which she lives, and Simone agreed, but she registered for the course in parenting. When discussing the time for returning home in the evening, Tony set the limit at midnight. Simone pressed her father to find the real limit. Tony negotiated to a point, but was forced eventually to draw the line. When Simone was at the home of a well-known family friend, Tony would compromise on the midnight curfew, but otherwise remained firm. Meanwhile, Samuel might complain that his father was tougher on him than on his sister. Despite differences, the Chow children have never openly rebelled against their parents. Familial chats kept generational conflict to a minimum, and Tony acknowledges that his children retain adequate respect for their parents.

For Tony, Catholic religious values are more important than Chinese cultural values. Within the family, he sees faith as more unifying and healing among peoples than national culture and traditions are. In Tony's view, Chinese Canadian families do their best to attend Sunday mass, say the rosary as a family, enjoy Christmas and Easter celebrations, attend parish retreats, send their children to Sunday school, and make pilgrimages to nearby shrines. The appearance of the Virgin at Medjugorje in Yugoslavia in the early 1980s, Tony believes, added new significance to the importance of the family rosary among Chinese Canadian Catholics. The members of the Chow family also pray individually. Simone does not reveal her devotional life, but is a spiritual person who has learned to trust in God. Samuel has been attracted to the Legionnaires of Christ; he attends the Legionnaires' school in Cornwall, Ontario, where prayer and study are daily exercises. Tony's wife, Mary, attends daily mass at Chinese Martyrs church, prays the rosary, and spends time in adoration before the Blessed Sacrament. Tony is active in his church, attends daily mass, says the rosary, spends time in adoration, and is a Bible study facilitator. Chinese Canadians reveal their strong faith and devotional regularity in the Toronto churches.

Tony opines that parishioners of Chinese Martyrs are not aggressive enough in recruiting new parishioners, and admits that the assertive Protestant approach for the newly arrived Mandarins is probably more successful. He believes that Protestant preaching and fellowship are attractive to newcomers and easier for them to grasp than the Catholic contemplative experience of Jesus in the Eucharistic celebration. Being a practising Catholic, he contends that Catholicism in the long run is more demanding. He believes that recent newcomers from China are attracted to Toronto's Chinatown, where they are surrounded by Chinese language and cultural symbols. Those who are Catholic go to Our Lady of Mount Carmel, near Chinatown, where Mandarin-speaking Chinese Canadians gather. Contemplating the difficulty of Canadian acculturation, Tony believes that Chinese

Catholics, as members of the 2,000-year-old Catholic Church, must be docile to this Church because their religious roots are historically not deep enough for them to give direction to such an ancient institution. In his wisdom, he demonstrates Asian reticence and the desire for transcendent prayer.[17]

Chinese Catholicism Strengthens the Canadian Church: The Story of Theresa Wang and Oakt Soun Hum

Theresa Wang was born in Taiwan and graduated in medicine from the National Taiwan University in 1964. She did an internship in Buffalo, where she met Oakt Soun Hum, a medical researcher with a doctorate in biomedical engineering. He came to Canada when he was ten years old, was educated in Ontario, and was a Canadian citizen. Theresa and Oakt married in Cornwall in August 1967; she immigrated to Canada the following November. Upon arriving in Canada, Theresa applied to do doctoral work in physiology at the University of Toronto, but was turned down as being overqualified. Undeterred, she went to work as an internist on the staffs of St. Michael's, Mount Sinai, and The Doctors hospitals. Whereas she always felt comfortable speaking English, she found she had to learn to write in English to be successfully bilingual.

The Hums had two children, who maintained a functional knowledge of Mandarin and knowledge of Chinese culture. They were encouraged to maintain the Chinese Catholic values of respecting the elderly, doing their best at all times, and not injuring others. When the two children attended Chinese Martyrs church and its Sunday school, they lived faithful to Catholic practice. The boy went to the St. Michael's Choir School of the Catholic Archdiocese of Toronto, and today is an architect in Vancouver. His sister graduated from Cardinal Carter High School and is a physical exercise trainer. She does not attend church on a regular basis anymore. Since their father was a committed agnostic and their mother a committed Catholic, the children found religious issues puzzling. The grandparents from Taiwan visited Canada a number of times for extended visits, but chose to return to Taiwan.

In family life, Oakt Soun Hum makes the major decisions. Despite the Chinese emphasis on respect for parents, the two children, in Canadian fashion, became independent at an early age. Once they began school, they were away all day with their own friends, and left their family behind. They enjoyed the youthful autonomy of Canadian students. In busy North America, says Theresa, the family as a community is forgotten, and alienation increases among family members. At times, her children could be rebellious but, as their mother, she kept dialoguing with them to be reasonable. Family discussions were irregular—about ten in 30 years. Theresa sees marriages, whether of mixed religion or mixed ethnicity, to be a difficult enterprise.[18] To accept the newly married couple, it is necessary for both families to pull together and to work out misunderstandings that naturally occur. By contrast, in her view, a couple with a common religion and culture share more human bonds, which will unite them through the years.

Theresa sees Chinese Martyrs church as displaying the strong faith of Chinese Catholics in Toronto, where parishioners attend one of the seven weekend masses. Parish teams prepare prayers for special occasions, such as prayers for vocations, discussion groups, and Bible study groups. The Legion of Mary and a charismatic prayer group meet regularly. Cursillos and holy hours are popular. The Women's Group prays together and prepares a social after Sunday masses. The Youth Group unites young people and encourages vocations. The parish has made available a Chinese prayer book, which includes morning and evening prayers, chaplet of divine mercy, rosary, daily mass and holy hour prayers.

Chinese Martyrs offers cultural enrichment to their parishioners. The Rite of Christian Initiation for Adults welcomes neophytes to the parish community. The pastor, Father Leung,

offers weekend retreats for single people, and Marriage Encounter Teams provide weekend retreats for married couples.
The pro-life group is very active in discussion and public demonstrations. To raise social consciousness, a parish group visits
Mexico periodically to live and work among the poor. Theresa is
a member of the Ontario Society for Chinese Education and sees
Chinese cultural diversity as a gift to Canada. She is involved in
organizing the Forum on Chinese Education to discuss Chinese
writings and culture. She admits that more could be done for
newcomers to help them find work. She comments that Chinese
bring with them the transcendent ideals of Confucianism and
Buddhism; they look to Christianity, which is relatively recent
for them, to enhance these ideals.[19] She sees the faithfulness of
Chinese religious devotion as a gift to Canadian Catholics.[20]

Diligence Passed Down:
The Story of Anthony Sun and Irene Ma

Anthony Sun was born in Chungking to a well-known
political family. He migrated to Taiwan in 1949.[21] He attended
the Catholic high school with his brother. They both got along
well with the teachers and chose to become Catholic. In 1958,
Anthony completed his bachelor of science at National Taiwan
University, and afterwards taught at the university. On a student
visa, he arrived in Toronto in 1963 to begin doctoral work in
medical research. He met another medical researcher, Irene Ma.
She liked Anthony, his field of research, and his transcendent
nature. Irene became Catholic, and she and Anthony married
in 1964.

Anthony had a rare gift for intense work. He could work for
days with almost no sleep, and regularly worked fifteen hours
a day, seven days a week. His father, also a medical researcher,
enjoyed a similar gift of being able to work for three days con-
tinuously before sleeping. Anthony published more than 500
scholarly papers and contributed chapters to many books. He

worked in the department of medicine with Charles H. Best who, along with Frederick G. Banting, discovered insulin. While a brilliant researcher, Anthony, as part of his accommodation to Canadian life and before starting to teach at the University of Toronto, found it necessary to take time to learn to speak English properly, so he could communicate clearly with students.

Anthony and Irene have two children: Alex, a medical doctor, and Elizabeth, a business woman. The children are Canadian educated but are still functional in the Mandarin language. Family decision making for the Suns was not methodical, and they allowed their children much freedom. Anthony conceded domestic decisions to Irene. When asked for advice by his children, he would make suggestions about their education and schooling, but let them do as they wished. Generational conflict did not seem to be a great problem between parents and children, but the children, without explicit directions from their parents, did feel "great pressure to succeed." The parents stressed family values to the children, and the whole family gathered weekly for discussion when possible. Alex and Elizabeth now go to Presbyterian churches. Elizabeth married a Korean Presbyterian, and Alex attends the Chinese Presbyterian Church for personal reasons. Irene and Anthony are now retired and remain active Catholics. When Anthony's parents died in Taiwan, he transferred their remains permanently to Toronto.

Anthony prays informally as he works. For much of his career, he has held three positions: researcher at the University of Toronto, consultant for the Hospital for Sick Children, and consultant for Connaught Laboratories. He prays formally at the weekly mass and the monthly Bible study. Irene prays privately at home and with the congregation at Chinese Martyrs. At the church, the Catholic parishioners do not formally recruit neophytes, as Protestants might. When Chinese Catholics arrive in Toronto, they seek out one of the four Chinese Catholic communities for fellowship and worship. Anthony feels that Catholics lack proper organization for proactive recruitment,

whereas, in his view, Protestants are more aggressive evangelizers. Recognizing the diversity of Chinese people, Anthony
observes that the Cantonese from the south are warm-hearted,
Mandarins from middle China are less so, whereas Mongolians
coming from the colder climate to the north are the least socia-
ble. He finds it difficult to identify specific charismatic gifts for
such a diverse people as the Chinese.[22]

Catholic Hierarchy Offers Centralized Authority: The Story of Edmond Lo and Josephine Poon

Edmond Lo was born in Hong Kong and came to Canada
as a student in 1974. While there, he decided to make Canada
his home one day. He completed his bachelor of commerce at
the University of Windsor in 1978 and returned to Hong Kong
to work in human resources and administration until 1982. That
year, he married Josephine Poon. Josephine also had a bachelor
of commerce degree and was employed at a bank. They moved
to Toronto the following year and raised their two children,
Michelle and Jason, there. Edmond completed his MBA in 1985
and is employed as a public accountant. To this degree, he added
a master of theological studies from the University of Toronto
in 2003. Michelle and Jason remain functional in Cantonese.
Edmond's parents live in New York City with his siblings.

Influenced by Western thinking during his post-secondary
education in Hong Kong, Edmond learned the importance of
shared decisions in family business. He and Josephine consciously adjust to Canadian culture, enjoy regular dialogues,
and sometimes include the children when the decisions involve
them.[23] He observes that those not exposed to Western education
will follow the Chinese custom of patriarchal decision making.
With his teenage children, Edmond advocates a balance between
the Asian respect for the wishes of elders and the Canadian belief
in freely sharing one's thoughts. He would contend that extreme
individualism can be an excuse for not listening, and fears that

Canadian education fails to teach students respect for elders and sincere listening to others. Canadian education seems to favour fun and self-expression rather than embracing the Chinese values of hard work and self-discipline.[24]

His daughter, Michelle, finds Hong Kong culture important but remote from her Canadian social life. Her father believes that "Michelle finds it hard to relate to Hong Kong culture and believes it irrelevant in the Canadian social environment." As a Canadian-born Chinese, she finds students from Hong Kong somewhat "foreign." While she is a Chinese Canadian herself, she doesn't want to resemble Hong Kong students in any way, including their culture, style, and way of thinking, for fear that her schoolmates may see her as "foreign." The same mentality causes her to resist her parents' cultural values, which in her view are essentially Hong Kong values. Edmond admits that generational conflict arises when Canadian and Chinese cultures clash—that is, when "we don't do things the same way." He concedes that Canadian Catholic schools do a good job of conveying to the young the usefulness of mass attendance, the importance of learning reconciliation in our lives, and the importance of religious issues, such as social justice.

He envisages Catholic marriages for his daughter and son, preferably Chinese Catholic marriages. This would make marriage easier for them, he believes. He finds inter-ethnic marriage less threatening than inter-religious marriage, because common religious belief can overcome the problems created by ethnic differences. "If both husband and wife are Catholic and both are serious about their faith, their common Catholic values and universal Catholic beliefs will help them to overcome any cultural or ethnic differences." Yet were Edmond's children to enter into an interfaith or inter-ethnic marriage, these unions would be respected.

Edmond and Josephine have made their life in Canada. They intend to remain in Canada and have purchased plots in Holy Cross Cemetery for their eventual burial. Since his student years in Windsor, Edmond has liked the fresh air, open spaces, and congenial environment of Canada.

Edmond begins his morning by saying the rosary. Later in the day, he sometimes jogs and prays. Before going to bed, he reflects on the Bible and papal encyclicals and prays over them. At Chinese Martyrs church, he animates the Bible study program of self-enrichment and prayer, which has sixteen study groups. Monthly attendance at Bible study averages 130 participants out of 180 enrolled in the program. Both the Bible study groups and the Rite of Christian Initiation for Adults welcome newcomers to participate.

Some parishioners are learning Mandarin to welcome new arrivals from mainland China and to assist with their adjustment to Canada. Chinese Canadians bring the professional skills of business persons, accountants, engineers, doctors, and university professors to the Canadian scene. Chinese Catholics bring a love of obedience to and reverence for the Canadian Church, which helps them fit into Canadian culture. Not entirely comfortable with democracy, Edmond feels that "Chinese Catholics are at ease with the church hierarchy and its centralized authority" in a world adrift. They like order and a clear direction for religion and society. By balancing the best of Eastern and Western cultures, Edmund and Josephine seek to deepen their Chinese Canadian Catholic identity.[25]

Chinese Canadian "Know-How": The Story of Paul Yeung and Bonny Chan

Paul Yeung was born in Hong Kong and attended a Jesuit high school. He began his university career at the University of Wisconsin. The following year, Paul moved to Canada with his family and enrolled at Queen's University in Kingston, where he completed his B.Sc. in engineering in 1995. He added an MBA from York University in 2003, and is now employed in personal financial and insurance planning. He found as a new Canadian that he needed time to adjust to North American cultural mores and idioms. In 2000, Paul married a friend from Hong Kong, Bonny Chan. Bonny graduated from a Catholic school in Hong Kong and, after coming to Canada, earned a bachelor of business administration in 1996. Paul's parents remain independent and live in Vancouver, where his brother also lives.

Vancouver multicultural Madonna

Newly married and without children, Paul and Bonny share decision making. When they do have children, they will invite them to participate in decision making. Paul points out that Chinese parents educated in Asia are less willing to share decision making with their children than parents educated in Canada. Chinese Catholic Canadians, he says, hope to pass on to their children a respect for Chinese culture, an ability to speak and write Chinese, and inspiration to retain Catholic morals and traditions. They are upset when they see "the Canadian government trying to enforce new laws that are opposed to the Catholic teaching." Paul and Bonny hope their children will celebrate cherished cultural events such as Chinese New Year, Moon Cake Festival, Ching Ming Festival (Remembrance of Ancestors Day), and the Tuen Ng (Dragon Boat) Festival.

They believe that the young are more likely to retain Catholic values when their families take time to exercise influence with them. Also, when children participate in church groups and are active in church activities, they have fewer problems in their life. When they are connected with church-minded people, they are encouraged away from the dangers and extremes of youth. Paul and Bonny point to the membership of Chinese Martyrs parish, which includes many young people. Chinese parents bring their children to Sunday mass and to parish activities to meet their peers and suitable adults. Parents are disappointed that some children do not want to go to church because their peers do not go, or are upset when one of their children adopts a pro-choice view. According to Paul, parents who were educated in Asia are stricter and more authoritarian than those educated in Canada. Parents who were educated in Canadian schools adjust more readily to Canadian values and are more likely to discuss differences with their children in an agreeable manner. With their preference for endogamous marriage, Paul and Bonny would have their children marry a fellow Catholic first; their second preference would be a Chinese.[26]

The Chinese Catholic community enjoys both Chinese and English-speaking media to receive news and information. Older Chinese would prefer Chinese television, radio, and newspapers, but the third generation of Chinese Canadians listens to CBC and reads *The Globe and Mail*. Paul and Bonny like living in Canada and intend to remain here, but would be greatly disturbed if the government were to continue on its secular course of approving same-sex marriage and abortions, which to them violate the basic structure of family life in world society.

The Yeungs say grace before meals and prayer in the evening. They are involved in a Bible study program at their church and use the Taizé prayer of repetitive singing. They pray silently with the help of icons and take time for adoration of the Blessed Sacrament. In a group, they enjoy the prayer of silence, but when all is said and done, employ different methods for personal prayer.[27]

For Paul and Bonny, the charism Chinese Canadians contribute to the world Church is organizational ability. For instance, Chinese Canadians are masterful at fundraising and are generous donors for community causes. A large number of Chinese young people have musical training, and use these talents in liturgical music, song writing, and on public occasions. At their church, they sponsor concerts for the evangelization of the Chinese community. Chinese Canadians know how to organize events and know how to raise funds for good causes.[28]

Strong Friendships Generate Strong Faith: The Story of Robin Wilson Tham and Helena Lee

Robin Wilson Tham was raised in India and graduated from the Don Bosco Technical Institute in Calcutta in mechanical engineering. In India, he had worked as a design draftsman and carried out shop supervision. He migrated to Canada in 1966 for better economic opportunities. Lowering his job expectations, he applied for a job as a grinder in a machine shop. His talent was quickly recognized and he was hired as an engineer for aerospace planning. Working in Toronto, he enhanced his credentials at Ryerson University in computers and became a lecturer in the Extension Division. Having been educated in English, he fitted easily into the Canadian workplace and did not encounter discrimination, but found it necessary to show competence. When in administration, he hired a competent female engineer and, as a result, was shunned by his fellow engineers, who resented this breach of the custom of male office control.

Robin met his wife, Helena Lee, a reflexologist, at the Chinese Centre in Toronto. They married in 1973. Before coming to Toronto, Helena had received her B.Sc. in England. Some years after their marriage, she went to the University of Alabama and completed her doctorate in holistic nutrition in 2000. Their two boys, Laurence and Anthony, are Canadian raised and are functional in Chinese. Laurence earned a doctor of chiropractic degree and practises in Australia. Anthony completed his B.Sc. and earned a teacher's certificate from the University of Buffalo. He moved to Niagara Falls, Ontario, to teach.

Robin and Helena's lives were reasonably tranquil for parents of teenage boys. They made decisions jointly and, as Robin comments, were probably "more friends with their children than parents." They sent the boys to Chinese Catholic schools in Hong Kong for four years to imbibe Chinese culture, but, Robin reports, "It didn't work!" The boys also attended Brebeuf High School in Toronto, where they enjoyed associating with their Canadian peers and playing hockey, baseball, and football. When they went out in the evening, Robin asked his sons to call home at any time, and he would come and pick them up. When they were old enough to drive, they were given equal access to the family cars. The values Robin and Helena hoped their boys would assimilate were respect for their elders, the practice of strong faith, and the sharing of their time and resources. The first son married a non-Chinese woman who took instructions to become a Catholic and was warmly received into the family. For media information, family members read both Chinese and Canadian newspapers and watch both Chinese and Canadian TV. Robin and Helena will remain in Canada after retirement, although they are tempted to join their first son in Australia.

Their prayer life is practical, in that they say prayers at bedtime and attend Sunday mass at Blessed Trinity church. When travelling, Robin and Helena enjoy visiting churches in other cities. They are members of a Thursday night prayer group that meets in homes for an hour of prayer, rosary, and hymns, and then, after an *agape*, organizes various charitable events in the community. They also participate in a Bible Study group. Robin is one of the founding members of the first Chinese council of the Knights of Columbus in eastern Canada, Our Lady of China Council. By forming the China Council, the Knights offer support to incoming Chinese Catholics to assist them in getting settled in Toronto. Currently, Chinese Catholics from the Chinese provinces arrive as religious refugees in downtown Toronto and look to Our Lady of Mount Carmel parish for assistance. The Knights are able to raise funds; they hope to unite the Chinese Catholics of the four Toronto parishes to provide food, clothing, and other items newcomers need.[29]

Catholics from mainland China come from mission churches, which are a small minority in a sea of non-Christians and are necessarily underground, defensive, and insular. The mission churches in China form one extended family, where everyone knows and helps each other. In Canada, the church is above ground and seems very businesslike to the newcomers. The Chinese Canadian Catholics in Toronto's four Chinese parishes know each other and form strong friendships with other Chinese Catholics. Throughout the city, they renew the closeness that they had enjoyed in China, which strengthens the fibre of the Canadian Church. Chinese Catholics in Toronto are a band of brothers and sisters pursuing transcendent values with a definite sense of mission for their Chinese community and the Canadian Church.[30]

Knights Encourage Volunteer Work: The Story of Brian and Clara Koo

Brian Koo, born in Hong Kong, completed his education at St. Francis Xavier's College there. Entering his family's graphic design business, he was assistant advertising manager for the

Seiko watch account. He came to Canada in 1967 to broaden his horizons and gain employment in graphic design. Discrimination was not evident to him. His future wife, Clara, finished her schooling at St. Mary's High School in Hong Kong, emigrated to Canada, and eventually became the district manager for a national retail fashion chain. Brian and Clara have two daughters, Charlotte and Camillia. Charlotte completed her master of arts and education degrees at the University of Western Ontario and now teaches art in high school. Camillia went to Ryerson University and is a stage designer. The daughters are functional in Chinese languages and work in Canada. Brian Koo's parents, who are retired, are healthy and look after themselves in Toronto.

Decisions in the family of four were jointly made. The daughters were members of the Canadian Air Cadets and developed industrious and healthy work habits. They were given a free hand to govern themselves. Camillia is a stage designer and was often out until early morning as part of her work. Brian and Clara encouraged their daughters to respect elders and Chinese culture, and to support the family trade of graphic design. The daughters maintain the love of Chinese culture, and one continues to be a practising Catholic. Charlotte married an Anglican Caucasian; he was instructed in Catholicism, and they were married in a Catholic ceremony. Brian and Clara seek media information from both the Chinese and the English language newspapers and television outlets. They intend to remain in Canada with their family, but would consider returning to China sometime in the future if it were financially possible.

Brian employs both oral and reflective prayer. He and Clara are members of a rosary group that meets each Thursday for an hour of prayer and hymns. He is one of the founding members of the Knights of Columbus, which includes prayer and charitable works. Since the Knights are unknown in China, Chinese Canadians provide information to their peers to promote the social services of the council. The Chinese Canadian Knights are interested in the media and have worked with the Salt and

Light television network to produce five programs for Chinese Catholics. A second ministry of the Knights is encouraging Chinese newcomers to volunteer. Chinese Catholic newcomers are unfamiliar with volunteering, since they would go to jail in China for doing volunteer work for their church. Once in Canada, they need to be taught that it is safe for them to help their church communities without harassment.[31]

Confirmation window at Chinese Martyrs' church, Markham, by Ho-Bei Lau

Conclusion

Newcomers, as they touch down in Canada, experience the conflict of Eastern and Western cultures and first must cope with their state of shock. When they find work, they must allow their labour to be exploited to gain the coveted trophy of "Canadian experience." Moreover, newcomers quickly learn to lower their expectations and accept the positions offered them. Professor Peter Li, not overly optimistic about automatic advancement for qualified newcomers, cautions that Chinese professionals in the 1980s continued to receive $1,300 less than members of other ethnic groups annually.[32] Ideally, competence is rewarded in time, advancement comes according to ability and qualifications, and most are pleased with the freedom of the Canadian multicultural environment and the hope of economic improvement. Nevertheless, discrimination in the workplace is a hurdle that Chinese Canadian professionals must transcend for their own benefit.

Chinese Canadian parents feel uncertain about the openness of Canadian schools and would prefer they were stricter. Yet, once Chinese Canadian young people enter university in the Western world, they are effectively out of the family home, paying their own way and making their own decisions. Children are highly programmed to be industrious, meet professional standards, and fulfill family expectations. They are given the freedom to pursue their future as they wish. They strive to meet parental expectations and retain the cherished Chinese Catholic values of family unity, academic excellence, and respect for their elders. Parents and children learn to take enough time to balance the best of the East and the West. Their new identity as Chinese Catholics is being forged in their adjustment to secular Canada.

The young people have a love of family values, Catholic devotion, and Chinese cuisine, but eat both Canadian and Chinese food with equal gusto. More than 50 per cent of the children continue to attend the Chinese mass at their parish, continue to respect their elders, keep contact with Chinese culture, and live a modest lifestyle. They are given the freedom to participate in household discussions and choose their own schools. Open conflict with parents is not intense, yet generational disagreements, once resolved, can lead to better familial friendship. Third-generation Catholics are industrious and earn their own way through university. Although well educated, the children understand spoken Chinese, but do not always respond in Chinese. They assimilate to Canadian life and enter Canadian professions such as law, medicine, the Catholic priesthood, and human rights advocacy. As their parents had cared for them in their youth, the adult children now look after the parents' well-being, celebrate with them on festive occasions, and bring gifts to honour them. More than 50 per cent of Chinese Canadian Catholics marry within their own religion and ethnic group. Two thirds of the children still identify with Catholicism, and 80 per cent of grandchildren are baptized and attend Catholic schools.

*

From the accounts of eleven Chinese Catholic married couples and one priest, it becomes evident that Chinese Catholics immigrate to Canada because Canada is a multicultural country that offers work, a well-established university system, religious freedom, and citizenship for qualified people. These newcomers see that Canada, with its size, natural resources, small population, and religious freedom, bodes well for a bright future for immigrants. Canada is a nation of democratic ideals with which to identify and a place of abundant resources in which to find a home for one's family. Chinese Canadian Catholics are hammering out their new transcendent identity from something old and something new.

Manila Metropolitan Cathedral-Basilica

3

Filipino Catholics in Asia: Postmodern Spirituality in the Making

This volume, *New Faces of Canadian Catholics: The Asians*, demands not only a study of Asian Canadian Catholics, but also a study of their spiritual roots: namely, Asian spirituality. An examination of the Asian spiritual matrix undergirding the Asian North American religious experience in the postmodern period is timely. This spiritual matrix includes Filipino business life, spiritual lifestyle, and concern for social justice. This investigation focuses on interviews with 20 Catholics in the Philippines and is based on Filipino sources. The list of names for interviewees was compiled by snowball sampling in Manila and other parts of the Philippines. Those interviewed agreed that their names could be used in this research. Filipino spirituality was selected because the number of Filipino Catholics in Asia and Canada, and their rich spirituality can be used as an analogue for Asian Catholicism. Research was complemented by some brief seminars on Asian spirituality in Hong Kong, Mumbai, Pune, and Bangkok. The study explores the extensive horizon of Asian spirituality as a foundation for understanding Asian Canadian Catholic spirituality.

Since people love to tell their stories, I divide the data collected into the religious experiences of Filipino business people, university academics, and volunteer organizations. The religious experience of Filipino Catholics is placed in the postmodern historical context. This means that Catholics and their post–Vatican II institutions—namely, local dioceses, religious orders, and lay prayer groups—are integrating and being integrated into the Asian environment while preserving core Christian values. They express themselves in language, vestments, and songs that symbolize Asia in ways they believe are suitable for them as Asian Catholics. Filipino Asians carry their religious expressions to Canada.

Business People

Francisco Colayco and Mary Anne Busuego

Born in Manila, Francisco Colayco completed a B.A. in economics at Ateneo de Manila University in 1965, and an M.A. in business management in 1969. In recent years, he has appeared on a long-running Hong Kong and Filipino radio show, in which he instructed overseas Filipino workers on "the fundamental rules of wealth generation, income, and debt management."[1] Mary Anne Busuego received her bachelor of commerce in 1968 at Assumption College, and an M.A. in business management at the Asian Institute of Management in 1970. Francisco and Mary Anne met in Manila and married in 1971. They have three daughters who have graduated from Ateneo de Manila University; two are engaged in businesses in Manila, while the youngest lives and works in Rotterdam. Francisco and Mary Anne, successful in their own enterprises, have travelled in Europe, North America, and Asia for both family visits and business.

The Colaycos have shared their values "of respect for the elderly, family ties, honesty, hard work, and love for God" with their children. Generally, they find that their children respect these values and Filipino traditions. They note that in the provinces, children are more likely to follow their parents' direction, but in urban areas such as Manila, a cosmopolitan centre of ten million people where youth are more Westernized, this is less likely to happen. Once teenagers leave home for the day, they dress as they like. They might wear short skirts, expose their midriffs, and publicly display their affection for the opposite sex. Living within the protection of the family home and attending Mass on a regular basis are less the norm in Filipino society today than 40 years ago. In urban centres, living with partners without the benefit of marriage is more acceptable. Francisco and Mary Anne share decision making in family discussions, even if ultimately the husband is credited with the decision. Francisco delights in the fact that as he is engaged in his public career and has little time for domestic concerns, while Mary Anne, in addition to her own business interests, guides the home and makes sure family functions happen.

Their three daughters attended an Opus Dei school in Manila, but were not active in the school or in Opus Dei. One daughter is unmarried. A second daughter married a Filipino Catholic; they practise their faith on a regular basis in the Philippines. The third daughter married a Dutch non-Catholic. She and her husband travel regularly on business and find it difficult to attend to religious activities. The Colaycos and two of their daughters intend to remain in the Philippines, do business, and make a difference where they can. In addition to the minimal government health-care coverage, they have private coverage, which gives them security for the future. Living in the Philippines promises a simpler, more pleasant lifestyle than in North America or Europe. Revealing their spiritual balance and maturity, the Colaycos would welcome psychiatry if necessary as it is a valuable tool by which chemical imbalances can be discovered and personality difficulties may be resolved.

Francisco is a very private person when it comes to his spirituality, preferring to pray on his own, whereas Mary Anne is more public and attends daily mass, meditates regularly, and enjoys praying novenas, saying the rosary, and seeing a spiritual advisor. Both partners find their friends from university to be their support group with whom they can talk and pray without pretensions. After many years of friendship, they all know each other well and cherish one another. These alumni groups, besides providing mutual support to members, offer education to the less fortunate, assist abused teenagers, and give medical help to those with disabilities, such as cleft palate, empowering them to take care of themselves.

The Colaycos identify the Filipino national charism as that of being caring and hospitable and doing volunteer work to help their neighbours better their lives. Filipinos show leadership by forming economic co-operatives, which lead ordinary people toward an improved standard of living. While they receive great nourishment in church services, the Colaycos regret the multiplication of the sacred liturgy in secular shopping malls on weekends, which is the Filipino custom, and the exhaustion of scarce clergy as a result.[2]

Rodrigo Naquiat

Rodrigo Naquiat completed a B.A. in philosophy at Ateneo de Manila University in 1970. He took additional courses for an M.A. in education and human resources management. Since that time, he has worked with Ayala Corporation in strategic human resources and has travelled in Asia, the United States, and Europe for business and family visits. He and Josefina Quiazon were married in 1975 and began having a family. Josefina raised the children and worked as a professional nutritionist. Later, she started her own business, which went well until she shut it down for personal reasons. Their four children were educated in the Philippines and grew up bilingual in Tagalog and English. Two children, Maria Felisa and Ramon Jose, work in the Philippines, while two, Maria Teresa and Francisco Javier, are in nursing school. After completion of her nursing program, Maria Teresa may work in North America. Rodrigo and Josefina have shared with their children the virtues they prize: personal integrity, the habit of honesty, open discussion of problems, and the role of celebration in their lives.

As members of a charismatic prayer group, Rodrigo and Josefina have learned the importance of family discussions to work out mutual problems and to bring siblings and parents closer together. They schedule suitable times for dinner, agree upon family recreations and vacations, and talk about strengthening family bounds. When their children bring home friends, the Naquiats make themselves available. They also plan family celebrations, such as when a family member comes home with a successful report card or a promotion. The children have benefited from attending an Opus Dei school, which has affirmed their faith and reinforced family dialogue. Their charismatic prayer group is not only for adults, but also prepares the youth for adulthood through its children's and young adult formation programs. In discussion groups, they discuss such topics as sports, entertainment, and group dating among the teens. In regard to interfaith or inter-ethnic marriages, Rodrigo and Josefina pray their children will choose partners who have a deep sense of faith.

The Naquiats have carefully saved for their retirement and feel that their own savings are the best insurance for health care, retirement, and a secure future. They like living in the Philippines and do not have a strong desire to migrate to another country. Both partners have siblings in the United States. Rodrigo has six siblings in California, but it is an open question whether the Naquiats will remain in the Philippines or possibly join relatives on the American west coast. Should their daughter Maria Teresa decide to emigrate to the United States, they might follow her and join their siblings there.

Beginning with traditional prayers, Rodrigo enjoys the quiet of regular prayer and moves quickly to reflection on the Scripture readings of the day. To renew his inner life, he uses the daily examination of conscience of St. Ignatius Loyola and makes a five-day retreat yearly. He delights in being a lector at some of the daily masses at Ayala Corporation. In addition to having a regular prayer life, he and Josefina attend meetings of a charismatic community. The community members support one another in Christian living and community building. They evangelize the business community by sponsoring Empowered Christian Living Seminar (ECLS) breakfasts and support the Gospel message when the opportunity arises. They sponsor seminars for youth, encouraging their relationship with Jesus Christ and their baptism in the Spirit.

ECLS has an outreach at university campuses, where seminars include talks, discussions, and prayer for the reception of the Holy Spirit. These seminars are followed with a post-initiation program to guide young people in the practice of Christian life. They evangelize single professionals to form prayer groups and develop their own career and discipleship. They teach catechism to the urban poor. People in the community tithe 10 per cent of their personal income to support these many ministries; thus, activities are free to members. Their charismatic community is associated internationally with the Sword of the Spirit, a charismatic group led by Steve Clark, who lives in the United States. The charismatic group in Manila has fostered for the Naquiats growth in the life of the Spirit through private, liturgical, and charismatic prayer, and has provided them with regular spiritual direction throughout the year.[3]

Fanny Ricafrente

Fanny Ricafrente was born in the Philippines; she received her arts degree from Santo Tomas University in Manila in 1958 and a second degree in science in 1970. In 1960, she and Mariano Quimson Jr. married in Manila. Mariano was a Certified Public Accountant in Manila; he has an MBA from Northwestern University in Chicago. He worked for the daily newspaper, the Manila *Bulletin*, for 27 years, eventually becoming its president. Moving to the *Philippine Daily Inquirer* as its president, he turned it into a major Manila newspaper. Fanny worked as a real estate broker and property manager of condominiums. The Quimsons have two daughters, Clarissa and Maria Felisa. Clarissa completed her first degree at De La Salle University in Manila and her MBA at Northwestern University in Chicago, where she now works. Maria Felisa also graduated from De La Salle University and earned an M.A. in advertising from the Newhouse School of Public Communications at Syracuse University in New York State. She is married, has a family, and works in Toronto.

The Quimsons shared with their daughters the values of personal gratitude, respect for elders, and love for extended family. As the young need time to assimilate these values, the parents maintained open lines of communication with their children. They took time to explain to their daughters "the why of every decision." As a result of their family discussions, the children were prepared to make their own decisions. For instance, the parents encouraged their daughters to marry men who have the same faith, but left their daughters free to choose. The first daughter is not married; the second married a Filipino Catholic.[4]

As a schoolgirl, Fanny began saying vocal prayers and continued praying in this fashion as a young mother. In Manila, she and Mariano became members of Bukas Loob sa Diyos Covenant Community (BLD). They learned to meditate on the Gospel and contemplate the Scriptures in the early part of the day, and to say the rosary and make an examination of conscience in the evening. The Quimsons moved to Toronto in the spring of 1990 and immediately gathered eight couples and two singles to found a Toronto prayer group. On October 17, 1990, their group constituted the first branch of BLD in North America.

Twenty-two months after arriving in Canada, Mariano was diagnosed with cancer. He died before the end of the year. During this period, BLD members and the Toronto Jesuits extended emotional and moral support to Mariano and Fanny. At Our Lady of Lourdes church in Toronto, Mariano was anointed and buried in 1992. As the grieving period was ending, Fanny accepted the advice of the rector of Regis College, Jean-Marc Laporte SJ, and enrolled in a graduate program. She completed a Master's in ministry in 1995. Now as a single person, she loosened her affiliation with BLD and worked as a part-time parish secretary at Our Lady of Lourdes church. As the trauma receded, she founded a bereavement support group at Our Lady of Lourdes. She continues to live in Toronto but returns to Manila for business and family visits.[5]

William Keyes

William Keyes was born in Brooklyn, New York, and entered the Society of Jesus in 1952. He accepted an assignment to work in the Philippines in 1956, where he still lives. He worked with the poor and needy in Manila and, after deciding to leave the Jesuits, continued to work for poor families. He completed an MBA at the University of the Philippines, then he and Nightingale Tan were married. They adopted four boys—Denis, Jerry, Charles, and Henry—who are now adults working in the Philippines.[6] William Keyes tells his own story:

> In 1976, I organized the Freedom to Build Corporation, whose purpose was to assist lower income families to achieve home ownership. The corporation's involvement in social housing dates back to more than 30 years ago when, initially, it was assisting and encouraging relocated ex-Manila squatters to improve on their initial *barong barong* (makeshift structures). It should be explained that Freedom to Build is not really a business corporation in the ordinary sense, nor is it related only to social action activities, nor is it primarily involved in programs implying direct philanthropic donations to poor communities. Its work at present is to build and develop housing projects that by price, style, and density of units are made affordable to people who could not otherwise aspire for even the lowest-cost house as developed by ordinary real estate practitioners.

It is like a business but with a social purpose: targeted at serving the poor in their housing needs. It is also targeted, as a second step, to help the new homeowners organize themselves into an ongoing community for purposes of project management, safety, athletics, social activities and basic neighbourliness. In its earlier projects, strategies included providing a construction supply store, which sold essential building materials at affordable prices and loaned tools to customers.

Freedom to Build was also engaged in conducting group dynamic seminars, setting up a network of *paluwagan* savings clubs for the relocated families, and keeping contacts open with the parish priest of the area. In 1983, Freedom to Build undertook the development of social housing projects in the Manila area, first on the southwest corner of the Ateneo de Manila University campus, and then in coordination with the Jesuit communities in four other locations, all serving some portion of Metro Manila's urban poor.[7]

The Freedom to Build program in the Manila area has built 7,000 low-cost homes for small profits. These homes, which sell for 185,000 pesos (CAN$4,405), include running water, toilets, and landscaping. A homeowners' association was created to foster the health and education of the families of new homeowners and to look after the environment of the community. Homes can be expanded by adding a room at the back, or even a second storey. Being a homeowner and having capital equity raises a formerly landless person to being lower middle class. From being squatters on government land, they become landowners—a status of great significance in Asia. This step gives the ordinary working-class family social status in their society and a stake in the community. William Keyes continues his story:

In 2001, I and my engineer/architect Eduardo Bautista launched H. De La Costa Homes V, which included, during phase one, the construction of 1,200 homes east of the city of Manila, and since then, during phase two, another 1,200 homes. They [the construction company] have found it necessary, owing to the cost of supplies and land, to increase the price of their homes to 225,000 pesos [CAN$5,357]. Sales of completed homes go rapidly, and there is a lineup waiting to buy into the community and attend community meetings. The Homeowners' Association is responsible for the collection and use of monthly dues. The dues defray basic expenditures, including garbage collection, street lights, security, and maintenance of the homes.[8]

Freedom to Build creates a community of persons committed to the economic and moral betterment of all. *The Homeowners Manual* explains that "everyone is expected to take an active part in the Homeowners Association." The owners should get to know their neighbours, get involved in community affairs, and work on gradual project improvements. Small convenience stores are permitted to open in the community, but public beer gardens and illegal drug sales are not tolerated.[9]

University Academics

Maria Elena Samson

Maria Elena Samson, born in the Philippines, was prepared by her scholarly parents for studies from an early age. Elena's grandmother, who cared for her during the week, would not let her go outside to play for fear that she would mix with children beneath her station. Nor was Elena allowed to look out the window, since that would violate the modesty expected of a young Filipina. Elena proved to be a good student, and eventually earned a master's in psychology from Indiana University and in sociology from the Asian Social Institute in Manila. She is currently involved in a doctoral program in applied cosmic anthropology at the Asian Social Institute. She has visited American, Australian, Asian, and European nations for study, business, and family reasons. Her daughter, Tara Elena, was educated at the Brent International School in Manila and earned a degree in chemical engineering from the University of Michigan. She is currently pursuing a second university degree at the University of Santo Tomas Conservatory of Music, majoring in voice and minoring in piano.

To Tara and to her students, Elena communicates the values of friendship, family solidarity, involvement in the Filipino commonweal, and love for the Catholic faith. She finds that family solidarity and love for their religion burn brightly in the hearts of young Filipinos who are sorting out their life and value systems. In her view, when generational conflict arises, it is during the adolescent period, when the young are striving to establish their own identity. Yet she admits that chaperons and group dating can still be a norm for teenage women in the Philippines. More leeway is given to 25-year-olds in serious love relationships. Marriage, she believes, is best restricted within the categories of similar religion, ethnicity, and class. Inter-racial and interfaith marriages, in her view, are frowned upon by Filipino and Asian societies and are often seen as unsuccessful.

Samson has a medical insurance plan connected with her position, and is comfortable with the equity she has in the Philippines. Although she is content to continue her work there, she would accept a call to carry the ideals of the Asian Social Institute to other communities around the world. In many ways, as with other Asians, she appreciates faith healers and herbal cures for minor health problems. But most of all, she believes that Filipinos enjoy the help of support groups—the extended family and close friends whom they feel are sympathetic. Suicides are minimal in the Philippines. Yet were psychiatric help necessary for her or her daughter, Elena would take advantage of it. She believes in using Western science and not regressing to antiquated customs. Elena has no plan to leave the Philippines at this time, but if she needed a pathfinder to North America, being culturally adept, she would send the best-educated family member. She shares decision making with her daughter, and they encourage each other in their careers.

For inspiration, Elena does meditation, reflection, and contemplation, but is also faithful to devotions, such as the rosary and novenas. She finds the Catholic Church leads her to spiritual growth, is her primary source of spiritual nourishment, and is very supportive in its care of ordinary people, in social concerns and justice. The Filipinos as a people, she believes, are concerned with the care and well-being of others. They love fiestas to celebrate with food, friends, and music.[10]

Catholics in other Asian countries may not have the same buoyant hopes as Filipinos, nor the continual need for communal celebrations, but like other Asians, Filipinos are slow to accept Western psychiatry as an assist to a healthier life. They prefer a guidance counsellor to a psychiatrist.

Paul Dumol

Paul Dumol was born in the Philippines and, after completing his first academic degree at Ateneo de Manila University, travelled to the Pontifical Institute of Medieval Studies at the University of Toronto to complete his master's and doctorate programs in medieval studies in 1994. Returning to Manila, he taught philosophy and history at the University of Asia and the Pacific and was appointed the vice-president for academic affairs in 1996. He encourages students to respect their elders, including professors and authority figures, and recommends politeness, kindness, and warmth in dealing with others. The values he criticizes at the university are excessive student docility and over-reverence for professors. Filipino students, he observes, "have difficulty finding the balance between respecting professors and critically engaging them in dialogue."[11]

Students at this Catholic university, in Paul's view, attend Sunday mass with their parents on the weekend, yet during the week do not reveal great religious sensitivity by attending an occasional mass or monthly reconciliation. While the chapel is full during weekday masses, attendees are office workers and people from the neighbourhood. College students do not have the habit of praying on a regular basis, he observes, except to pray for good results on exams or a positive result for a personal crisis. In difficulty, students may go to the chapel to speak with Jesus or look for the priest for a chat. Once the crisis is over, sincere students might make a retreat and seek further knowledge of God in their life. Prayer groups are not common on campus, but a charismatic movement is growing. Some university students can talk about their personal relationship with Jesus and Mary. Their relationship with God is intuitive through symbols and devotions rather than theological ideas. Filipino spirituality inclines to be more intuitive and practical and less rational and theological.

Lectures do not seem to change the religious life of university students, he asserts. After leaving university, a number drift from religious practices. For many, an emotional and sentimental attachment to Jesus Christ does not hold up in the educated world of postmodernism. Drifting happens as young men and women fall in love or become involved in business, which leads them beyond their limited experience. Young graduates going off to North America meet new friends, become secularized, and drop religious practice for a time. In fact, many cast off their sentimental childhood beliefs, which as educated adults they have outgrown, and find it necessary to search Catholic teaching for an adult comprehension of their lives. For Filipino students, the umbilical cord to the Catholic Church is seldom entirely severed, and, after their return to practice, they renew their commitment. Often a life crisis provokes the return to faith, but this time the sentimental attachment is replaced with adult understanding. This may demand personal guidance and serious study of the Scriptures and theology.

The control that the mother and father exercise over growing children can cause conflict between parents and children. The Filipino mother expects the children to remain in the home until marriage, and, after marriage, often wants sons to bring their wives home to live in the family compound. Other marriages are arranged for political reasons among families, with the understanding that partners are allowed to stray on occasion. In the Philippines today, interfaith marriages and inter-ethnic marriages occur.

For order in Catholic schools, girls' colleges, after enduring evangelical students preying on their students, Dumol relates, forbade non-Catholic students to evangelize Catholic students into born-again religions. The aggressive evangelization in the Philippines by a few students is looked upon as violating Filipino social and religious mores. To such Pentecostal advances, a witty Filipino Catholic responded, "Why should I believe your religion which is false, when I do not believe mine which is true!"

For Filipinos who decide to go abroad to find work or a home, Paul Dumol observes that it is the wife or mother who initiates the move—that is, she is most concerned about the financial security of the family and makes the decision. For instance, the mother might send to another country the most talented family member, who would be most likely to be accepted and do well abroad. Although Paul found intellectual stimulation in Toronto and in other cities overseas, he is strengthened by the deep sense of Asian identity he enjoys at home. He believes that the presence of Filipino professionals at home can make the Philippines a better place to live. He finds the health-care program provided by his university adequate and feels that it provides him with a secure future. Psychiatric help is not financially affordable to the average citizen, but guidance counsellors are available in the schools to help form spiritually mature graduates.[12] For his workplace and retirement, Dumol will choose to live among his lifelong friends in the Philippines. He likes living and working in the Philippines and is not interested in moving abroad.

John Schumacher SJ

John Schumacher SJ has been a professor at Ateneo de Manila University since 1965. As a Filipino citizen, he has taught Philippine history and has sage observations on Filipino spirituality. He believes that the heart of Filipino life is devotion to the family and its religion. He admits that the family is both a strength and a weakness for Filipinos. The family protects its members and makes sure they have jobs. An eldest daughter will sacrifice marriage in order to work to send their younger siblings to school or take care of their elders. On the other hand, family ties are strong factors in the graft and corruption, harming the Philippine economy and making it one of the weakest in Asia. Professor Schumacher writes that the problem is often

> fictive kinship, the so-called *compradazco* by which sponsors at baptism and marriage are bound not only by strong ties both between the sponsor and godchildren, but also by strong ties between the sponsors and the parents of the godchildren. Family ties likewise lead to family dynasties by which political offices for the provinces or regions are controlled by members of the same family over several generations.

Religion is a great inspiration for Filipinos, keeping them in harmony with themselves and others. In the past, nationalist leaders such as Jose Rizal became Freemasons while fighting for Philippine independence, but came back to the Church before they died and were buried in the same Catholic cemetery with their family and friends. As part of the postmodern period, Schumacher observes, the young reject religious and cultural traditions. Yet for some young people, Schumacher continues, devotions and pilgrimages are creeping back into vogue, and religious devotions are once again considered the right thing to do. While cursillos are dying out, charismatic groups are increasing in numbers. Spanish clergy in the nineteenth century taught a romantic spirituality of loyalty to God and the crown. Being docile students with good memories, Filipinos continued these practices of religious loyalty to the Church and secular loyalty to the government. Only recently, as foreign missionaries have left the Philippines for their own countries, have Filipinos taken full control of Filipino dioceses and religious orders. Filipino bishops, clergy, and professors lead the Church, embracing their culture in song, symbol, and language.

The young people increasingly date as they like, Schumacher comments, and many imitate the American way and dress according to American fashions. Parents have generally given up on the old Filipino ideal of arranged marriages, allowing their children to marry whom they please. Well-educated and affluent Filipinos will accept psychological help when needed, but find these services overpriced.

Young Filipino middle-class couples are currently educated to share in family decision making. Filipino families, according to Schumacher, balance the authority of the husband as the head of the family and the power of his wife as the treasurer of the family money. Among financially hard-pressed families, this situation can lead to a husband's demand for more access to family funds and, eventually, to wife beating. In the Philippines, middle-class working women depend upon the service of live-in domestic helpers to sustain the household. Yet the many Filipinos going abroad as domestics are well-educated teachers and administrators who wish to provide needed financial support to their families. The personal skills of Filipino domestics working abroad are greatly appreciated in Asia, the Middle East, Europe, and North America.

Religion is important to Asians both at home and abroad. Filipinos form prayer groups to deepen their spirituality and assuage their loneliness. In rural areas, basic ecclesial communities are successful; in urban areas, Marriage Encounter and Couples for Christ are popular. Christian Life Community and Bible study groups are important. Prayer groups among Filipinos at home and abroad are more popular and are growing in number and size. To overcome superficial religious practice, adult catechism is employed and catechists are theologically trained to undertake full-time paid positions in public schools. The NAMFREL Movement monitors elections to guarantee honesty in voting and to encourage Filipino activity in public life. Schumacher concludes that Filipino spirituality is alive in the Philippines and active wherever Filipinos live in the world.[13]

Randolf David

After graduation from the University of the Philippines, Randolf David travelled to England to begin work on his doctorate in sociology at the University of Manchester. He returned to the Philippines when martial law was declared in 1972. He had completed all requirements for the degree except the thesis. Since returning from studies in England, he has been working for the Department of Sociology at the University of the Philippines. He is married to Karina Constantino and they have four adult children—a son and three daughters. The son has a doctorate in geology from Stanford University, and the daughters have bachelor degrees from the University of the Philippines in communications, interior design, and accounting, respectively.

Exposed to various nations of the world through travel, Randolf and his family have elected to remain in the Philippines, where their ethnicity is solidly rooted. Philippine ethnicity for the Davids stresses close family ties, love of country, personal freedom, and excellence in professional performance. During their college years, Randolf and Karina were student activists, whereas their children were not. Randolf and Karina are educated and spiritual people, but do not go to church for personal reasons, whereas the children are educated and spiritual people who attend church. Dialogue and responsibility for actions have always been stressed in the family. Through discussion, the family comes to consensual decisions on schools the children should attend, which children are to travel with them on vacation, or who might live abroad for a time. The children are assertive and well educated; the son, Carlos, earned his doctorate at an American university. The eldest daughter, Kara, works in communications, had a child before marriage, but did not marry while she raised her child, because she did not feel ready for marriage. The second daughter, Nadya, designs book covers. The youngest daughter, Jovita, gave up a lucrative profession and an MBA to work as a volunteer teaching mathematics at a Jesuit school in the Palawan Islands.

A family consensus is in favour of inter-ethnic and interfaith marriages. It is the family belief that openness is preferable to bigotry. Health-care plans are modest for family members, and consist of medical benefits from the University of the Philippines and the national system. The family would welcome psychiatric treatment were it necessary, but it is expensive and, for cost reasons, avoided by most. For a secure future, the David family believes that the best health-care system is the resources of their own family.

Randolf has never needed a pathfinder in his immediate family, but in the family from which he sprang, a younger sister was the pathfinder. She went as a nurse to San Diego, where she has worked as a senior coronary nurse; she was followed by a second sister who is a medical technologist, and a third sibling who had completed law in the Philippines and migrated to the United States to manage a small printing company. His youngest brother completed a bachelor in economics at the University of the Philippines, then moved to Los Angeles, where he works for an air freight company. David's siblings are all married and active in their American parishes. One sibling in the United States is a member of the popular Filipino prayer group Couples for Christ.[14]

The Davids are a responsible family committed to personal authenticity. Randolf is a private person who needs time alone to pray in his own way. He is concerned with social justice issues in the Philippines and the world. He is a committed Filipino nationalist and wants to stay in Asia because he belongs and wants to improve by his presence the quality of life for all.

Albert Alejo SJ

Albert Alejo was born and educated in the Philippines. He entered the Society of Jesus, was ordained a Catholic priest and completed a doctorate in anthropology from the University of London. For reasons of studies and business, he travelled to Europe, the United States, India, Thailand, and Malaysia. He teaches social science and philosophy at the Ateneo de Davao University and is involved in work with labour unions and the indigenous people of Mindanao. To the students he teaches, he conveys the importance of hard work, genuine friendships with one's neighbours, and the love of country over the love of family. While students do not always follow the traditions that are handed down to them, Albert claims that they try to "adjust" as well as they can to the "different situations" in their lives. While accepting the inevitability of religious and ethnic mixed marriages, he warns that those who take this path may discover "difficult days ahead!" The conflictual nature of ethnic and religious differences can cause strife in the relationship and discord between families.

He carries a Filipino passport, has a limited national health insurance plan, and intends to remain a permanent resident of the Philippines. However, he also looks forward to participating in mission work in other countries. Understanding the benefits of modern psychiatry, he believes that Filipinos with emotional difficulties will go to a priest first and maybe later, if recommended, to a psychiatrist. In regard to family decisions, his experience in Davao is that such decisions are made by either the husband or the wife, but are seldom shared by both. When families are confronted with the prospect of immigration, he contends that it is the mother or children who are the pioneers. The father and other members of the family migrate later.[15]

Prayer for the Filipino, according to Albert, is founded on the spirituality of the body, the gathering of the community, celebration, and negotiation. For the Filipino, prayer stems from the heart, directing the posture of the body and the attitude of the mind. Prayer includes a communal act of devotion with family, friends, and community. Gathering in numbers, Filipinos celebrate in song, food, and spirit. Intercessory prayers are said in common and involve negotiation with the angels, the saints, and the three persons of the Trinity. In prayer, requests are made, promises are given, and an agreement is reached. Filipinos delight in pilgrimages where sacred places are visited and the suppliant posture is adopted. Sacred objects are caressingly touched and bargaining is carried out. A spirit of celebration surrounds the time of coming and the time of going, when songs are sung and food is shared. The gifts Filipinos carry with them to communities abroad, according to Albert, are their intense personalism and love of fun. The attention and care Filipinos show for the sick and the elderly are personal warmth and loving care. Often, in the midst of their loneliness and hardship, Filipinos seem able to generate a fiesta of music and conviviality.[16]

Catalino G. Arevalo SJ

Catalino G. Arevalo was born and educated in the Philippines, and entered the Society of Jesus in 1941. After studying theology at Weston College in Cambridge, Massachusetts, he was ordained as a Catholic priest in 1954, then taught at Woodstock College, Maryland. Doing graduate studies in theology at the Gregorian University in Rome, he completed a seminal study on the local church for a doctorate degree in 1959. He was subsequently professor of theology, dean, and president of the Loyola School of Theology, an autonomous ecclesiastical school affiliated with Ateneo de Manila University. During the Second Vatican Council, he became a consultor of the Secretariat for

Promoting Christian Unity and, in the post–Vatican II period, a *peritus* for the Federation of Asian Bishops' Conferences (FABC). He has published books and articles on the creation of the local church and the rise of Filipino theology.[17]

Interior of the Manila Metropolitan Cathedral-Basilica

He believes that the three principal values that Filipinos wish to pass on to their future generations are family cohesion, competitive education, and the Catholic religion. Filipinos turn out in force for religious events and will fill their parish churches, flood pilgrimage grounds, and turn out 200,000 strong for a Saturday evening charismatic meeting conducted by Brother Mike Velarde. Yet this overwhelming religious devotion does not always translate into the practice of honesty and social justice. Religious education, in fact, is inadequate in this Catholic nation. The private Catholic schools are very good, but the majority of Filipino children attend public schools, which do not offer religious instruction. Only 8 per cent of schoolchildren receive religious instruction; thus, most Filipinos grow up with little understanding of their faith. Despite the many Sunday masses and filled churches, only 10 to 15 per cent of Filipinos attend weekend mass. There are not enough churches and clergy to accommodate the growing Catholic population. Currently, with only one of four youths believing in eternal life, Father Arevalo contends that the erosion of the solid block of Filipino Catholicism has begun.

Family cohesion is a dominant force in the Philippines. Anything will be done or sacrificed for the family, which sometimes can include evil. Love of country pales by comparison with the dominant love of family. The rural young, and some young people in the cities, remain in submission to their parents and give the impression of not being involved in generational conflict. Sixty per cent of young women consider their mother a role model, while only 10 per cent of men consider their father a role model. Wealthy young people in the cities are likely to go through a period of teenage conflict with their parents. Among the middle and upper classes, generational tensions are often eased by prayer groups, which encourage family discussion. In traditional rural families, the father makes the major decisions and the mother holds the purse strings. Among the poor, the father, as the leader of the family, can be tyrannical in playing his role. Rural male youths moving to the urban centres, or youths going abroad, retain their traditional family attitudes toward religion but do not always practice it.

Education for Filipinos is a practical venture, says Father Arevalo. Their aspiration is seldom toward higher studies but rather the social and economic improvement of the family. Places for their children are sought in prestigious high schools and universities whose reputation will assure the success of individuals and their families.

Among Filipinos, according to Catalino, the issue on mixed marriages is not whether the future spouse will be a Filipino or Catholic, but whether he or she is kind, gentle, and compassionate. A hard-hearted or violent spouse will be rejected, as would a hard-hearted priest. Kind persons will be forgiven almost anything if they are cooperative and gracious. For emotional help in crisis, seeing a psychiatrist for lower or middle class persons is financially out of the question.

Apart from mass attendance, the rosary is the prime method of private and shared prayer. It is used in celebration and in sorrow, in need and in thanksgiving. More Filipinos are going to mass than ever before, and it has become customary to have mass at all events, rallies, celebrations, and shopping centres. Father Arevalo believes that the proliferation of sacred liturgy without suitable reason should be questioned. Among the middle and the upper class, the number of persons making retreats and the number of retreat houses increases yearly. He defines the middle class as anybody with a steady job who is earning the minimum daily wage of 300 pesos or more.

Prayer groups began among the middle and upper classes, according to Catalino, as a way of gaining salvation and avoiding damnation. Prayer groups such as Marriage Encounter and Couples for Christ emphasize deepening the marriage bond and strengthening family ties. El Shaddai, led by Brother Mike Velarde, stresses Christian fellowship and material prosperity. But since the time of the Marcos oppression, prayer groups have become socially awakened to the needs of the poor. Church people during the Marcos years were touched by the Marxist concern for needy Filipinos. At this time, many Catholics, including priests and religious sisters, joined the Communist Party in their concern for the poor. Thus, prayer groups became more egalitarian and inclusive in their membership and established outreach to the poor through affordable housing, food banks, and financial aid to impoverished students.[18] In November 2004, the national government loaned Brother Mike Velarde 370 million pesos (CAN$8,809,523) to build 22 medium-rise towers, each containing 353 units from 44.8 to 95.75 square metres in size. These 8,000 condos sell for between 1.5 million to 3.8 million pesos each (CAN$35,714 to $90,476).[19] Father Arevalo relates that Archbishop James F. Carney of Vancouver praised the vitality of the Filipino prayer groups established in Canada and believes that the newcomers bring great gifts of faith to the British Columbia churches by their regular mass attendance, renewed devotion to Mother Mary, and a sense of celebration and socializing.

Father Arevalo concluded his comments by saying that he believes the Filipino Church has not gone through the European Enlightenment. In the rural areas especially, the Church has remained clothed in seventeenth- and eighteenth-century Spanish spirituality, which has never been penetrated by the ideals of the European Enlightenment or the French Revolution.[20] In the rural areas and among the needy in the urban areas, there is simple and deep religiosity, but with little intellectual understanding. As urbanization in the Philippines is intensifying, the urban population is rapidly increasing, and the many believers cannot be catechized. Over the next 30 years, the secular media of videos, DVDs, and live programming will penetrate the people in the rural areas, and consumerism, cynicism, and violence will confront an eighteenth-century people unprepared for the 21st century. By 2035, many of the urban youth may be left with secularism and materialism but little religious faith.[21]

Volunteer Organizations

Jose Tale

Born in the Philippines, Jose Tale received his law degree from Ateneo de Manila University in 1979. Felipa Lourdes Gonzalez was born in the Philippines and earned her college degree in 1972 in business administration from Silliman University in Dumaguete City. Jose and Felipa married in 1974; since that time, they have travelled to Europe, the United States, New Zealand, and various Asian countries. They raised a family and have two adult daughters, Vida and Rica. Vida graduated from Ateneo de Manila University in management information systems; Rica finished her degrees at the University of the Philippines and is a dentist.

As a family, they gather for prayerful discussion to discern the will of God for their family and their individual careers. In matters concerning the whole family, Jose, after discussion, reserves the final decision for himself, but in regard to individual careers, family members follow their own insights. The Tale children, with the support of the Couples for Christ Youth Group, which includes discussion and retreats, have embraced their parents' values of strong faith in God, the Christian commandments, hard work, and respect for others. The parents encourage their children to marry peers who have strong faith like their own. While Jose and Felipa are content with life in the Philippines, their daughters may migrate elsewhere for the economic benefits, and the parents might then follow.

The Tales pray privately and as a family. They say the rosary together, attend Sunday mass together, and afterwards share a Sunday meal. They have been members of Couples of Christ (CFC) since 1986, and thus have matured in their prayer life since then. CFC asks members and their families to pray for fifteen minutes, read the Scriptures for fifteen minutes, and keep a prayer journal of what happens each day. The Tales have become involved in a ministry that CFC has recently embraced: building homes for the poor. Having had success with building 2,000 small homes for the needy, CFC has launched a massive project of building homes throughout the Philippines in seven years. The Tales are part of this undertaking.

Gawad Kalinga 777 (GK 777), which CFC translates as "caring," envisions "a new Philippines with no more slums" and is engaged in "building International Villages showing that poverty can be addressed if rich and poor nations learn to share resources to create a better world for all." GK 777 members desire to build "colorful, durable and secure homes for the poorest of the poor families in the Philippines." The ideal of *Gawad Kalinga* is also to provide "other physical structures such as pathwalks and drainage systems, water and toilet facilities, a school, a livelihood center, a multi-purpose hall, and a clinic. The new owners can help to finish the house by painting and landscaping the houses together with the CFC members who are helping to complete the project. Their slogan encapsulates the ideal which they try to live: less for self, more for others, enough for all."

The origin of the CFC home-building project unfolded gradually to the members through prayer and spiritual discernment. The Plenary Conference of Philippine Bishops in 1995 asked that the Catholic Church be "a church of the home" and "a church of the poor." CFC members resolved to embrace these ideals by beginning a process of discernment to decide what should be done. They followed the pattern of Tony Meloto by working with street kids—that is, youngsters in gangs who steal cars, burglarize homes, and deal in drugs. CFC opened a youth camp on weekends for these youths and saw amazing results. Chatting with the youth and building bridges with them helped; some youth even handed in their weapons and tried to find another way of life. As a follow-up to affirm this positive response of young people, a musical play about street life was produced that parodied life on the street in a way to which the young could relate. It was a great success and was performed more than 200 times in Manila and elsewhere in the Philippines!

Visiting the homes of the young people, the CFC members discovered how desperate housing was. CLC members became involved in home repair, installing running water, fixing toilets, and putting in concrete floors. The repairs made a big difference in the lives of these families, spurring them to do more for themselves. CFC members also worked with the young to help them return to school, where some of them did well. The members sought work for the unemployed parents.

At a CFC conference in November 2001, a member posed the question: "How many houses do we build next year?" Somebody offered the number "One thousand!" In February of the next year, at an International Leaders' Conference at Dumaquete, a member offered 1,000 square metres of land for home construction; the other members resolved during the weekend conference to build sixteen houses for the homeless. During the conference, the sixteen homes were completed and handed over to needy residents. The houses were 20 square meteres, including a toilet and shower, parents' bedroom, and family living space, and they were painted and landscaped. The homes cost 50,500 pesos (CAN$1,202), since most of the labour and materials were donated. President Gloria Macapagal Arroyo, present for the opening, offered government funds of 30 million pesos (CAN$714,286) to CFC to build 1,000 homes. CFC decided to match the contribution with donations from its members and benefactors. In June 2002, 60 sites were chosen and 1,000 homes were built on that weekend. The home construction event was covered on television, which brought excitement and helped raise funds. On a November weekend of the same year, a second set of 1,000 homes was built. Not only were homes built, but new communities were formed to look after the health, education, employment, and environment of the new residents.

The immediate success of building 2,000 homes generated enthusiasm and funds to expand the project. For 2003, a master plan evolved from the membership to build 700,000 homes, in 7,000 regions, in seven years. Through these experiences of home building, CFC members created a method to construct new houses and hand their ownership over to homeless people. The new owners agreed to pay a low cost for their homes by working on the construction of homes for other people. The success and enthusiasm for the project generated enough money for future inexpensive homes. The spirit of CFC and their supporters is summed up in the formula "Bleed for the cause!" Give surplus income and goods to provide homes and decent environment to others. Business corporations, such as Procter and Gamble, have jumped into low-cost home construction for their employees. McDonald's is helping to construct homes. A wealthy individual sold his BMW to travel less expensively; he donated his surplus to build homes. The homes are constructed for any homeless Filipinos, including Protestants and Catholics, Muslims and

Buddhists. The message of *Gawad Kalinga 777* is that all people can live in peace together. CFC's purpose in building homes is to strengthen families and draw youth out of drugs so that all can live a better life. The spirit of *Gawad Kalinga* has spread to Indonesia, India, and South Africa.[22]

Joventito and Jeddy Jongko

Colleagues of Jose and Felipa Tales in Couples for Christ are the Jongkos. Joventito Jongko finished his bachelor of science in chemical engineering at the University of Santo Tomas in 1965 first in his class and *summa cum laude*. He graduated with much self-confidence. He was hired by Procter and Gamble, and also taught in the evening for two years at his alma mater. Among his students was his future wife, Jeddy Joaquin. She was born in the Philippines and completed her bachelor of science in chemical engineering at the University of Santo Tomas in 1969. She also was hired by Procter and Gamble. Jeddy and Tito were married in 1970. At the prodding of his wife, Tito left the university to work full-time for Procter and Gamble. As a result of training programs and broadening assignments during his 30 years at Procter and Gamble, Tito, with Jeddy and their three children, travelled to the United States, Europe, and the Far East. Their son, Jeffrey, is completing his master's in computer science and is teaching at Ateneo de Manila University. Jennifer finished her bachelor's degree at Miriam College and is an American citizen working in Las Vegas. Janice, having earned her bachelor's degree in mass communications at Miriam College, teaches at the Ateneo Grade School while completing her master's in education. On account of their international education, the three Jongko children speak English, Tagalog, Japanese, and French.

In their early adolescent life in Europe and Japan, they attended international schools, which exposed them to Western life but with limited religious education. The children learned independence, self-sufficiency, and, as their mother described it, "selfishness." This youthful self-sufficiency contributed to generational conflict with their parents. Jeddy, meanwhile, believed that through a "look" of approval or disapproval, she could control her children and impose the Filipino tradition. The children retorted by labelling their mother "the villain."

Now as adults living in the family home, the children have accepted parental maintenance but feel no obligation to contribute to the household. In recent years, the family arrived at a consensus that the parents hoped would motivate their children to remain close to the family, continue the practice of the Catholic faith, and live a moral life. The parents desire that their children marry within the Catholic faith, since it would strengthen their children to share a common spiritual heritage with their spouse, yet the parents are prepared to accept other arrangements.

In married life, according Filipino culture, Tito made the family decisions. After Tito and Jeddy joined Couples for Christ in 1995, they replaced the male model of governance with family discussions to arrive at a shared consensus. Even after this family conversion in decision making, the remnants of hierarchical obedience hung over family decisions. Jeddy mourns her loss of dominance over her children. It is one thing for a family to share in discussion and come to an apparent meeting of minds, but it is quite another thing for all members to be internally free from the traditional expectations of Filipino family life.

When Tito retired from Procter and Gamble in 1995, his health insurance program was transferred from one company to another as he became a consultant to Johnson & Johnson, UFC/SAFI and Handyware Philippines Inc. Now that he is fully retired, the family is covered by private health-care insurers. The Jongkos have no intention of moving from the Philippines, yet if their two children who are still living there were to migrate to the United States or elsewhere, the parents might follow them. Jennifer, in Las Vegas, has initiated immigration papers for them. Their service in Couples for Christ will also influence their final decision. For the future, they put themselves in God's hands.

Both Tito and Jeddy have encountered God in prayer. In 1998, Jeddy was overwhelmed by the experience of God in her physical and psychic life. It made her "more conscious of her relationships" and more persevering in prayer, and increased her ability to meditate on the Word of God. During a Life in the Spirit Seminar, she had a "vision" of God telling her to "humble yourself, humble yourself, humble yourself!" The power of this experience freed her from the addictions of bowling, smoking, playing mahjong, and other entertainments that fascinated her.

Tito had a bleeding nose caused by the soft tissue inside the nose, for which the doctor advised minor surgery. Tito delayed the surgery, since the situation was not life threatening. This encounter with the medical profession made him look to the Lord; he received several messages "to focus on Christ," "live a simple life," and "spend more time for others rather than self." He responded positively and took leave from his public involvements, such as the Rotary Club, Christian Family Movement, Club Filipino, and Gift Association. Tito and Jeddy then gave their attention to the formation of newly recruited couples for CFC. During this time, without the benefit of surgery, Tito's bleeding nose healed, and the soft tissue inside his nose disappeared.

Tito and Jeddy are totally committed to CFC and its goals for family renewal, evangelization of society, and liberation of the poor. As chapter leaders, they recruit new members by inviting them to the twelve-week instruction for the Christian Life Program, offered twice yearly. They are active in the various family apostolates and recently became involved in the expansion of Social Ministries. CFC exists in 120 countries around the world with more than one million members.

The Jongkos feel that Filipino workers travelling overseas bring many gifts to their host country. Their ability to share their "resources and talent," their "hospitality and sincerity," their organizational skills and their religious commitment contributes to their new host country. Tito and Jeddy are very enthusiastic about the effectiveness of CFC as a method of lay evangelization. Although pastors with their own apostolic priorities can resent this autonomous and lay-run Catholic organization, the Filipino hierarchy has approved the CFC; thus, Filipino clergy are dropping their opposition to the CFC activities in their parishes. Tito and Jeddy spread CFC to Mindanao, particularly to Tito's hometown in Agusan del Notre, and built homes on his family property there.[23]

Antonio Meloto

A friend of the Tales and the Jongkos is Antonio (Tony) P. Meloto, executive director of Couples for Christ and *Gawad Kalinga* 777. Born in the southern Philippines, he received a scholarship to attend Ateneo de Manila University and complete his B.A. in economics in 1971. He has had the opportunity to travel to Europe, Asia, Australia, North America, and the Middle East for business. Tony married Amalia Dizon in Manila in 1978; they have five children. The children grew up speaking both Tagalog and English.

In December 2004, the Gloria Macapagal Arroyo government asked Tony, in addition to being the director of the *Gawad Kalinga* (GK) program, to "lead the rehabilitation effort" of the "typhoon affected areas in Quezon, Nueva Ecija, Aurora, and Mindoroa provinces." He was to harmonize the relief efforts of private resources and government agencies.[24] As a consultant to rice and the sugar cane workers, Tony strives to avoid labour discord and bring the warring sides toward a peaceful resolution of their problems. His service of peaceful reconciliation is not always appreciated, and he admits he has been called the "deodorizer." He well recognizes that the farm labourers for whom he negotiates receive barely enough pay for their family, whereas the large farm owners can afford to send their sons and daughters to urban universities, such as Ateneo de Manila and De La Salle.

With great assurance, Tony states that building houses for the poor is not about houses so much as it is about building community. It is a question of regaining the economic productivity to maintain Filipino families. Work is difficult to find in the Philippines, and many men do not have jobs to support their family. Without work, the man loses his dignity as the father of his family and his sense of being a son of God. Lacking work for their hands and money for their pockets, many Filipino men are humiliated and find themselves irrelevant to their family. They become isolated, losing the sense of family and community, and are reduced to an animal level of survival. Their animal instincts dominate them and turn them into predators of survival. Building homes is a way to lead Filipino men to productive work so that they may regain their purpose in life. They learn to transform a slum shanty into a family home, and their family becomes a warm and human resource for them.

Tony has been a member of Couples for Christ (CFC) since 1985. From 1995 to 2000, he worked in Bagong Silang, the biggest slum in the Philippines, located to the east of Quezon City. He worked with about 2,000 youths and their families, trying to understand the relationship between poverty and criminality. From his experience and observations, he learned that husbands, lacking work, are surplussed in Filipino society. They are deprived of their rightful role as provider, protector, and pastor of their home community. The restoration of Filipino manhood became a priority for CFC, which sought ways to assist them to be responsible before God and their family.

GK 777 communities organize men into neighbourhood associations to take ownership of their communities. Many men were socially alienated, violent abusers and former prisoners. Members hope to restore them to their families by using the threefold CFC ideal of productive work, family dialogue, and giving to others before oneself. By drawing these men toward this ideal, CFC believes it can restore their dignity as providers of their family and sons of God. Builders, plumbers, and carpenters work with GK clients, giving them on-the-job training. Professional workers give up their Saturday golf to help the renewal of their new brothers by preparing them to be productive workers. Men work to restore men. The affluent and the poor join together in genuine communication to build homes for the needy. The spirit of CFC is to create harmony among the needy and to assuage their anger. To do this, CFC forms partnerships with schools, corporations and the needy to regain productivity for the good of all.

According to Tony, the poor pray well because they are often in pain and need God's help to make it through the day. They pray because they believe in the afterlife and want to be part of it. They go to Mass to get help to keep their marriage together and learn to be self-sacrificing for their spouse and family. In adversity, they pray for strength to hold onto their family. CFC forms the new homeowners into household groups of five to seven families who gather periodically to talk of their faith and support their neighbours. As a matter of fact, when the poor have food, they will not eat it all; instead, they will take some to those who have less. GK 777 is designed to rehabilitate the husband's dignity and to renew the family by his real presence in that family, he says. For Tony Meloto, caring for the poor is the number one priority of any society, especially a Christian society.[25]

John Carroll SJ

John Carroll was born in Jersey City and graduated from St. Peter's College. He entered the Society of Jesus in 1943, completed his Jesuit education in New York and the Philippines, and was ordained a priest in 1955. He began a doctorate in sociology at Cornell University and finished his degree in 1962. Since then, he has been researching and teaching sociology at the Gregorian University in Rome, where he also served as Dean of the Faculty of Social Sciences, and at Ateneo de Manila University's Institute of Social Order. He was a founding director of the Institute on Church and Social Issues, together with Bishop Francisco Claver SJ, and is now a Senior Research Associate at that institute.

One of his constant interests has been the 300,000 people living at Payatas, the garbage dump in Quezon City. Many of the inhabitants came from the Philippine provinces to Manila looking for work and, unable to find it, went to the dump to become squatters and work at sorting garbage. They sort the rubbish to make money selling glass, paper, metal, and plastics for recycling. While the minimum wage in the Philippines is 300 pesos a day, they can make up to 200 pesos a day as scavengers. Others make 100 pesos daily weaving plastic doormats. Some of the people living at Payatas are construction workers, security guards, and drivers of taxis, jeepneys, and tricycles. Many are people without skills or are older than 50 and so too old to do heavy work. The young, who have no other place to go, settle at Payatas in squatters' shanties, and then marry and raise families there.

Father Carroll initiated a feeding program to supply milk for more than 500 "third-degree malnourished infants." His aim was to give the infants adequate weight to avoid mental deficiencies later in life. The Jesuit order and American friends supply the funding. "The weighing of children and distribution of the milk-powder is handled by Celing, a local volunteer and mother of four." Smart and capable, Celing proved to be "a paramedic and an all-purpose social worker in the community, assisting in the clinics, getting people into hospitals and watching by them at night, bringing in doctors from the Department of Health when there is an outbreak of cholera, being called to intervene in cases of child abuse, rape and incest in the community." Her own children, inspired by her service to others, became respectively a nutritionist, a social worker, and instructor in the Billings Method of Fertility Care. With the Don Bosco Brothers and Sisters, John initiated a scholarship program to enable 50 students from Payatas to take vocational courses; others go to a community college. Some children from Payatas have become professional workers, such as Juliet, who became chief of operations in a fast-food firm, while others got into plumbing, electro-mechanics and electronics. Transportation to city schools costs 100,000 pesos (CAN$2,381) monthly and is the major cost of this apostolate.

The religion of the people of Payatas, according to John, is folk religion, consisting mainly of baptism of infants and the family rosary. On major holidays, new babies are lined up, baptized, and celebrated. Willing parents are offered instruction on the meaning of baptism for the life of their child. The values that the children are taught as they grow up are respect and support of parents, but beyond their face-to-face family, they have "little sense" of the larger community or nation. When Filipinos go abroad, observes John, they settle, interestingly, more in regional language groups than among Filipinos in general.

The parents of Payatas find they are unable to keep their teens at home in the evenings. The young people want to go out at night and mix with their peers, and only recently have they experienced adolescent pregnancies. Sometimes there is a marriage following the pregnancy, but the couple usually waits until the following year to marry. The Billings Method of Fertility Care seems to be popular, with more than 100 couples practising fertility care and experiencing good success. The cost of the birth-control pill is prohibitive to the people of Payatas. They are not shocked by inter-racial or inter-faith marriages, but they would avoid marrying a *bumbay*—that is, an East Indian money-lender, many of whom are looked upon as being aggressive and rough. Some of the brighter young women in Payatas hope to be health workers or teachers abroad, but their language skills are limited. Some of the men hire onto vessels as seamen. Health care is fragile for most of the inhabitants. A German Doctors' Foundation sponsors a clinic at Payatas. Two Jesuit doctors visit a clinic built by the German Augustinian Sisters. Psychiatric services are not usually available, except in extreme cases, when a resident is taken to the National Mental Hospital.

As mentioned above, Father Carroll notes that religious practices at Payatas are mainly folk religion. For some, the Church is "a place where one can cry, ask for help in trouble, tell God our sins, ask forgiveness, and come away feeling better." Churchgoers believe that "Jesus is my friend who understands me and keeps me from committing suicide." Only a small percentage of the inhabitants of Payatas attend Sunday mass or know the responses and songs at mass. The prayer groups that John's associates guide include born-again Christians and members of indigenous sects. They appreciate the Bible study and mutual support they receive in the group. The Catholics know the basic prayers, such as the Our Father and the Hail Mary. Religious appreciation can be demonstrated in the novena of pre-dawn masses before Christmas, which draw more people than any other religious occasion. These Christmas masses are celebrated with candles and bells, a sung Gloria, white vestments, Christmas carols, and often a *noche buena* of ginger tea and hot pastries afterwards. As a long-term chaplain at Payatas, John Carroll feels that the charism of Filipinos is offering the world, even in their economic distress, the joy of celebration.[26]

Denis and Alicia Murphy

Denis Murphy was born in New York, entered the Jesuits, and completed his early studies at Cebu in the Philippines. Later, he completed a master's degree in social work at Fordham University in New York. As part of his university education, he travelled in Europe, North America, and Asia. As a Jesuit, he worked with the urban poor. When he decided to leave religious life, he continued his work among the urban poor and, in 1976, married a fellow worker, Alicia Gentolia, who had graduated from Far Eastern University in the Philippines. They currently work in non-governmental organizations and have one daughter, Marifel, who was educated both in the Philippines and at Fordham, where she now works.

Denis and Alicia work together in a small office for the Urban Poor Associates. Denis writes newspaper articles and fiction. The decisions Denis and Alicia make at home and at work are shared decisions that they discuss until they arrive at a consensus. They shared with their daughter their active concern for the poor, an interest in world affairs, and the importance of respect for other people, including an elderly housemaid. As a teenager, Marifel had to be encouraged to turn off the radio, do homework, go to bed, and get up on time. For a while, she preferred fashionable fast food to Filipino home cooking, but on her own, Marifel learned to look after troubled children. Denis and Alicia would welcome mixed marriages, whether they be interfaith or inter-ethnic marriages.

Given the fact that the American dollar equals approximately 42 pesos, Murphy says that they could not afford to move to the United States. Rather, they have a network of health plans, both American and Filipino, which work for them. They enjoy a happy personal and work relationship and intend to remain in the Philippines working with the urban poor. Spiritually balanced and mature, they found psychiatric guidance helpful for their family.

Murphy believes that most Filipinos enjoy personal and communal prayer. He believes that Filipinos rely mostly on the oral prayers of novenas and rosary. Yet he also explains that oral prayer leads a person to deeper reflection as one thinks through problems in God's presence. Like Abraham, by trading off their promises of faithfulness, regular observance, and heroic sacrifice, Filipinos bargain with God to get answers to their petitions.

The Urban Poor Association, which Denis and Alicia Murphy direct, is funded by the international cooperation of the Dutch, German, and Canadian churches. Denis and Alicia inspire and mobilize the urban poor living in shantytowns to put political pressure on the government to recognize their needs.

They strive to come to agreeable solutions to problems such as potable water, proper sanitation, surface drainage, and adequate electricity. Security is a major problem for squatters who live on public or private land from which they can be evicted at any time. The Urban Poor Association uses legal procedures to gain squatters time for relocation and provide them with adequate security. The association also acts to keep drugs away from the communities and to show concern for the deterioration of education in public schools. Classrooms are filled to overflowing, with 40 to 80 children sharing textbooks, which they cannot take home at night to study. As a result, much time is spent writing things out, and the quality of education is poor. Good teachers give up teaching because of the low salaries and arduous workload, going abroad as domestic workers to earn adequate income to feed their family. Filipino overseas workers, giving personal care to others, have a splendid reputation as nurses and domestics.

In general, Denis observes that the public health-care system does not work well. At government health clinics, there are few nurses, fewer doctors, and no medicines. In the Philippines, the minimum daily wage is 300 pesos (CAN$7.14), which is effectively below the poverty line of 8,000–9,000 pesos (CAN$191–$214) monthly. For someone who works a six-day week, the average daily income of 300 pesos adds up to 7,200 pesos (CAN$171) monthly. The average family income in squatter areas is 6,000 pesos (CAN$143) a month. Three thousand pesos go for rice, and the rest for transportation and rent. This means that the average person has a lean diet, and no money for vitamins, medicines, or health care.[27]

By becoming personally inspired during retreats, single and married volunteers become religiously committed to live a modest life and serve the needy. Volunteers have proven to be effective among the abandoned and the hurting of the Philippines. These volunteers work with street kids and their families, feed the hungry, build homes, construct communities, educate the poor, and look after their welfare. They work with the home-less throughout the cities to protect squatters from losing their homes and possessions. Volunteers also work at the city dump, providing both material and spiritual services to the forsaken. Committed women and men can have a strong influence on the families, community, and Church of the Philippines.

Conclusion

Since the People Power Revolution (the EDSA Revolution) of 1986, which toppled the administration of Ferdinand Marcos following allegations of widespread cheating in the presidential elections, business people, academics, and volunteers have gone through personal conversions to devote themselves with new seriousness to the care of the poor and to attack poverty itself. These are healthy signs indicating that Filipino spirituality is be-ing transformed and a postmodern spirituality is in the making. Filipinos take responsibility for their own lives and take owner-ship of their own spirituality. For instance, the Colaycos pursue their careers, raise their family and, at the same time, seek out Filipino overseas workers to provide these workers with financial guidance. They also lend support for the education of challenged youth. The Quimsons came to Toronto to extend a worldwide prayer group and to foster Marriage Encounter weekends to strengthen newcomers' marriages for cultural accommodation. The Keyes in Manila build low-cost housing for a small profit to provide affordable housing for workers receiving minimum wage. Segments of the Filipino business community show themselves able to slough off the pitfalls of societal corruption, to do honest business, and to show compassion for the poor begging at their gates. In regular communication between the Philippines and Canada, Filipino spirituality is carried by Filipino Canadians and influences Canadian spirituality.

Among Filipino academics, women such as Elena Samson become autonomous by seeking out a university career to educate the youth. Paul Dumol points both to the secularization of university life and to the quality of Catholic piety, but he also is surprised by the student drift away from traditional devotion when conflict enters their lives. John Schumacher reveals the loyalties deeply ingrained in Filipino history, and the generational tremors that result from the young seeking independence when parents continue to dominate. Filipino shrines offer numerous religious models of female strength and resourcefulness, but little is offered to boost the male ego. A unique style of postmodern spirituality is fashioned by intellectuals such as Randolf David and Francisco Colayco, and they find it nourishing. Albert Alejo sums up the intuitive nature of Filipino religiosity as being based on the bodily expression of communal celebration and reaching its apex in spiritual negotiations with God, the angels, and the saints. Catalino Arevalo sees the breakup of the classical Spanish/Filipino piety in the absence of public religious education, the youth no longer believing in the afterlife and the modern media confronting an eighteenth-century rural piety in the far reaches of the Philippines. By contrast, in the urban areas, university academics strive for personal authenticity in themselves; they are postmodern Catholics who recognize the change occurring in Filipino spirituality.

Couples for Christ, such as the Tales, Jongkos and Melotos, direct their own ministries in building homes and communities in the Philippines. Among the volunteers, women often dominate religion in the home and perhaps the nave of the church building, but the entrenched clergy dominate the structured Church of the sanctuary and the sacraments. Other volunteers, such as Father John Carroll, visit the inhabitants of Payatas to provide food, education, homes, prayer groups, and Sunday mass. The Murphys guide the Urban Poor Association to motivate squatters to look after their own needs and mobilize public pressure to protect them from capricious land developers.

Volunteers in the Philippines put much energy into their numerous endeavours to forge a better world for all. These self-directed lay people and involved clergy are learning to discern the will of God for their communities, revealing an incipient, dynamic, and involved postmodern spirituality. Filipino spirituality flows in the hearts of Filipino migrants to Canada, who bring with them a spirit of caring and renewal to Canadian Catholics.

A Filipiniana event in Toronto: organizers Eusebio Aquintey,
Luis Ignacio Jr., Paula Ignacio, and Constante Ignacio

4

Filipino Canadians: Easy Integration

Filipino Catholics, as newcomers to Canada within the last 40 years, have been the subject of little historical research. Since the late 1960s, they have migrated to Canada indirectly from Europe, the Middle East, and the United States, and, more recently, directly from the Philippines itself. Filipinos speak English and are familiar with Western thought patterns and lifestyle. Eleanor Laquian tells us that Filipinos in Canada in 1972 numbered 25,000 and were likely to be young female professionals living in Ontario.[1] Some came to study at Canadian universities and others to pursue work opportunities. As teachers, engineers, medical professionals, skilled technicians, and commercial graduates, they gained work in health care and other assorted fields and then applied for landed immigrant status. During the last quarter of the 20th century, Anita Beltran asserts, Filipinos supplied 4 to 6 per cent of immigrants, placing themselves among "the top ten sources of newcomers to Canada."[2]

According to the latest available Canadian census figures, Filipinos in Canada increased numerically to 327,550, of which 82 per cent (or 268,591) are Catholic.[3] Filipino Catholics in Canada assimilate easily into Catholic parishes, and their numbers in Canadian cities continue to rise. In Toronto, for instance,

30 Filipino priests minister in parishes; in Winnipeg, twelve; and in Vancouver, five. In 2001, Filipino Catholics in Toronto numbered 115,132; in Vancouver, 50,471; in Winnipeg, 25,592; in Montreal, 15,568; in Calgary, 14,313; and in Edmonton, 12,343. Urban Filipino Canadians have mass available to them in Tagalog if they wish.[4]

During this period, Filipinos in the United States, along with other Asians, have gravitated to the metropolitan areas of Los Angeles, San Diego, and San Francisco. It is said that Filipino immigrants seek out Los Angeles to settle, while Chinese gravitate to New York. According to William Fry, migrants in these cities are quickly entrenched "in well-defined occupational niches—[and] for some groups—extremely low levels of political clout will make their road to full economic and political incorporation challenging."[5] Others end up at the high end of the economic spectrum. The third generation, speaking American English and identifying themselves as "hyphenated Americans," suggests "a potential for later assimilation, linked to both upward and outward movement." Other American cities attracting Asians by their high-tech industries are Las Vegas, Atlanta, Phoenix, Dallas, Houston, Minneapolis, Portland, Boston, Seattle, Detroit, Denver, and Miami.[6] The United States Census of 2000 counts the number of Filipinos to be 2.4 million.[7]

In this chapter we will first discuss the ability of Filipino Canadians to acclimatize to the Canadian social and cultural environment. Then, we will treat the personal and cultural clashes that grandparents, parents, and children experience as part of the rite of passage to a new home. Lastly, we will investigate the positive contributions made by Filipino Canadians in the process of their integration into Canadian life. It must be added that these three themes of acclimatization, cultural clash, and contributions to Canada are intermingled through the three sections, but it will be helpful for readers to recognize each theme in a particular sequence. Statistics Canada 2001 helped to focus the study on the three principal centres of Filipino Canadian demographics:

Vancouver, Winnipeg, and Toronto. The research sampling was determined by snowball or convenient sample.

St. Patrick's Parish in Vancouver

Filipinos in Vancouver may be found at Holy Rosary Cathedral, Good Shepherd, and St. Patrick's parishes; in Richmond at St. Monica's, St. Paul's (15 to 20 per cent) and St. Joseph the Worker (40 per cent); and in Burnaby at St. Helen's.

St. Patrick's serves 3,000 families, 75 per cent of which are Filipino. The pastor, Father Donald Larson, remarks that Filipinos enjoy coming to church on Sunday and staying for a good part of the day. For spiritual strength during the week, they also come to daily mass and make church visits. Filipino children fill St. Patrick's school, and there is little need for special language classes since Filipinos speak English. In Vancouver, Filipinos network with one another, and information is passed along by word of mouth.[8] In an unpretentious manner, Filipinos reveal their flexibility to new situations and acclimatize quickly to the Canadian workplace, schools, churches, and culture. Geraldine Sherman points out that information for Filipinos does not need to be in print, such as in a tabloid or newspaper. As a matter of fact, when two Filipinas meet on public transport, their conversation goes like this: "We smile. We start talking. 'You're Filipino?' 'Yeah, I look after kids, how about you?' 'I do too.' We exchange phone numbers."[9] A friendship is easily made and will not be forgotten.

At St. Patrick's, the Rite of Christian Initiation for Adults (RCIA) serves mainly the members of the Chinese minority, not the Filipinos. The Filipinos, being baptized at birth, feel they are charter members and have little need for the RCIA. Father Larson says that baptisms at St. Patrick's number 100 yearly, but the baptized are Chinese adults and Filipino babies. The Legion of Mary has formed several prayer groups, which meet in members' homes. Members visit parish shut-ins and engage in other ministries. Filipinos are highly active in this ministry, but allow themselves only brief periods for reflective prayer. Father Don concludes that in their busy schedules, which often include two or three jobs, Filipinos leave themselves little opportunity for a deeper understanding of the faith and do not get beyond the appearances of Catholic devotional life. They shy away, he feels, from the theological distinctions of Western culture and its confrontational style.[10] Filipino theologians Dindo Tesoro and Joselito Jose write, "The Filipino tends to focus more on the unity of human existence's multiple dimensions (mental, volitional, psychic, physical) rather than on their separation and distinction (in a sense this view appears closer to the Biblical vision of human reality, and farther from Platonism, with its strongly dualistic and spiritualistic tones.)"[11] As a colonized people for 500 years, Filipinos exude gentleness and kindness and avoid being *hambog*—that is, being boastful and lording it over others, preferring to fit into a community peacefully.[12]

When Filipinos first arrive in Canada, they follow the Filipino system of church support in which lower- and middle-income families are expected to contribute only small change.[13] Historically, the Spanish crown gave the land, transported clergy to the Philippines, and supplied them with small stipends. Filipinos built the churches by *corvee*, or labour. Thus, in the Filipino church, a weekly collection was not part of the Sunday Observance, but parishioners were accustomed to paying stole fees for what they asked of the church, such as baptisms, marriages and burials. "As a Spanish heritage, active Catholics will contribute generously to building of a new church, with the wealthy expected to give substantial amounts," observes Philippine historian John Schumacher. "Among more educated people, this is gradually changing, depending on the quality of service of the priest."[14] Upon arriving in Canada, the challenges of finding employment, coupled with the need to send money home to their family, add to the challenges facing newly arrived Filipinos. Yet after a Filipino family becomes established in Canada, buys a car, owns a house, and adjusts to the higher cost of living, the family learns the Canadian volunteer church system of contributions and donates generously. For instance, St. Patrick's, which is predominantly Filipino, completed a $6.5-million church and is constructing a $3.5-million recreation centre—all paid for by voluntary contributions.

The lay members of St. Patrick's church formed Couples for Christ (CFC) as a covenanted charismatic community. CFC began among the middle class in the Philippines in 1981 and, from the zeal of three couples, spread quickly to 140 countries around the world. CFC was founded to strengthen the marriage bond between husband and wife and to incorporate the children into family dialogue. The group is strongly devotional and well organized, forming "households" of extended families. They have a strong commitment to Christ and the Church but, as Father Don Larson suggests, are not well catechized in understanding the Christian faith.[15] Father Don contends that they have a definite Western orientation, and many of their priests, sisters, and laity travel to the West for higher degrees because Western academic degrees are looked upon as being widely recognized and more marketable. While in Western nations, they put down roots and remain. The Catholic Women's League at St. Patrick's is divided into three groups: one for young mothers, another for adult women, and a third for senior women.[16] Filipino Canadian men are beginning to show interest in the Knights of Columbus. Membership for many years has remained under Irish Canadian control, so Filipino men were reluctant to join an organization where they felt uncomfortable.[17] In the Philippines, parishes are large and overflowing communities compared with the smaller North American and European parish communities. Similar to Italians, Filipinos presume charter membership in the Catholic faith, and feel that they intuit its beliefs without further investigation.

Filipino women are traditionally heroic in their self-sacrifice for their family. A self-effacing and long-suffering commitment (*mahinhin*) is expected of the Filipina, writes therapist Emilio Santa Rita.[18] It is a Filipino phenomenon that a family will send the eldest daughter or young wife ahead, asserts sociologist Anita Beltran Chen, to immigrate to a North American country.[19] These women are usually admitted as domestics with the expectation that they will earn permanent resident status to bring their families to the new country. Father Don relates the story of a Filipino mother to illustrate this point. Her family of three children in the Philippines included a disabled son who needed expensive medical treatment. She sought work in France and then in Germany in order to send money to the Philippines for her son's medical treatment. To care for a friend in Canada, she next migrated to Vancouver. Eventually, she was hired by St. Patrick's church and was able to sponsor her husband and two children. During the lengthy separation, the couple focused on their eventual reunion and remained faithful to each other.[20]

The strength of the Filipino mother is graphically demonstrated in this story. With the family reunited in Vancouver and the number of wage earners increased, they soon moved from an apartment to a house and sponsored a third daughter and her husband to come to Canada.[21] The Filipino commitment to the family and the Church is deep seated. Families morally support absentee mothers by taking care of their children, and these heroic sacrifices gain the mothers prestige and power. Myriam Bals comments on this personal heroism, writing that "Filipina women are supported by their religious faith, believing that God has sent them on the difficult mission in order to strengthen them"; she goes on to comment in her study of foreign domestics that, in contrast, Moroccan women can be "completely destroyed" by similar experiences.[22] Heroism and family loyalties become a stabilizing consolation to lonely Filipinos in a foreign land.

Couples for Christ in Richmond

St. Paul's parish in Richmond is the centre for 7,700 Catholics in a multicultural context. One of most active groups in the parish is Couples for Christ. Arturo and Rafaella Macapinlac were active in CFC in the Philippines. While helping a friend file landed immigrant papers at the Canadian embassy, Rafaella spontaneously decided to file papers for her family. When Arturo learned of this, it caught him by surprise, but both partners felt migration to Canada might give their son educational opportunities. In the Philippines, Arturo was a production manager for a food company. Coming to Canada in 1991, he found employment with an Internet company in Vancouver. Arturo and Rafaella established themselves in Richmond and became Canadian citizens. They did not encounter racism or other difficulties finding work, indicating they were being readily assimilated into a multicultural society. During the first year, they did encounter cultural difficulties, such as when they discovered that Canadians talked too fast for them easily to understand.[23]

In March 1993, Arturo and Rafaella came together with Marilen and Jojie Catibog and Luis and Angie Untalan in Richmond. This meeting, they believe, was the result of the Holy Spirit bringing them together in a foreign land to found the first Canadian branch of Couples for Christ. Soon, three more couples from the Philippines, Bert and Ely Barte, Butching and Carrie Locsin, and Clem and Anning Mabasa, were added to their numbers. They initiated a ten-week Christian Life Program to train future members and "the first seeds were sown."[24] Nine volunteer couples arrived from the Philippines at their own expense to help train the new members, bringing with them the episcopal approval of their home archdiocese in the Philippines.[25] After establishing themselves in Richmond, which is part of the Vancouver archdiocese, the leaders of Couples for Christ, Luis Untalan and Arturo Macapinlac, established a working relationship with the archdiocesan director of Marriage and

Family Formation, Father Joseph Hattie.[26] In the spring of 1994, Luis and Arturo asked for archdiocesan approval of Couples for Christ and their Christian Life Program. Nine months later, a letter arrived stating that CFC "did not fit into the pastoral orientation of the archdiocese at that time."[27] The letter indicated that enough married couples' organizations already existed in the diocese, so the duplication of services already offered was not desirable at present. As a result, episcopal approval would not be given.

Meanwhile, there was a growing line-up of couples clamouring to take the Christian Life Program and join the CFC. As this was happening, the administrator of St. Monica's parish, Father Bede, complained of a dead parish and asked the leaders of Couples for Christ to help. The parish administrator reasoned that as the archbishop had said "no" to a diocesan organization, he would not object to a parish group. During the ninth week of their ten-week program at St. Monica's, the archbishop called Luis and Arturo and told them to stop the program and come to his office. After the interruption of the program, Father John Malloy of Our Lady of Good Counsel parish in Surrey asked CFC to hold the tenth and final session of the program in his church hall.

When the archbishop heard about this, he summoned Luis and Arturo to his office. He welcomed them, peered at them, and asked with a firm voice, "What in my letter did you not understand?" Luis explained that the acting pastor of St. Monica's had, for pastoral reasons, asked them to help revive parish spirituality. Leaning forward and sitting on the edge of his chair, the archbishop repeated his opening question: "What in my letter did you not understand?" Luis replied that Vancouver Filipinos were looking for prayer groups, and Father Bede of Good Counsel invited Couples for Christ to come and help. How could they refuse? After this explanation, the bishop softened and assured them, "What you are doing is good," and promised to look at it again.[28]

CFC scheduled a Christian Life Program for February 24, 1995, but needed the archbishop's approval. They knew that Archbishop Exner was flying to the Philippines in January 1995 for World Youth Day. At that time, CFC was the only volunteer group in the Philippines with the resources to organize World Youth Day. Arturo immediately contacted CFC in the Philippines, asking them to talk with Archbishop Exner and show him that the prayer group was the most resourceful of Catholic organizations in Manila. CFC searched the hotels but could not locate the archbishop. They discovered that, as an Oblate religious, Archbishop Exner was staying with his confreres in the Oblate house and not in a hotel. Contact with Couples for Christ in Manila and the Philippine bishops transformed the archbishop. When he returned to Vancouver, he found a beautifully crafted but "impatient" letter from Luis Untalan urgently petitioning for approval.[29] Having exercised his prerogative of allowing time to pass for observation of CFC in the archdiocese, the archbishop approved its ministry in early February 1995, in the nick of time for the scheduled Christian Life Program. Archbishop Exner also appointed the Chinese born Father Peter Chiang as the spiritual director for CFC.

The archbishop's letter arrived in Luis Untalan's mailbox on February 14 and proved to be a wonderful St. Valentine's Day greeting for CFC.[30] Thus, in the shadow of Vancouver, 25 couples gathered to launch Couples for Christ. The Christian Life Program was immediately initiated in St. Monica's, St. Matthew's, and St. Francis of Assisi parishes. In a short time, the membership increased to 400 couples, along with the related groups of 200 youths, 100 singles, and 50 widows and widowers. In the next few years, CFC spread to Edmonton and Calgary. At the second anniversary mass in 1997, the Vancouver cathedral was filled, and Archbishop Exner presided over the ceremony of joyous CFC members.[31] Father Peter Chiang, pastor of St. Paul's, relates that the Couples for Christ are divided into spiritual households that are Christ-driven and very evangelical. They attach themselves to local parishes and are solidly committed to the Church. They have yearly conventions for couples, youths, men, and women. Father Chiang points to other groups active in St. Paul's parish—the Legion of Mary, El Shadai, Bukas Loob Sa Diyos (BLD), which means "Opening up to God," Knights of Columbus, Catholic Women's League, two large Bible study groups, the very active Alpha group, three youth groups, and five choirs for the six weekend masses.[32]

Filipinos have a natural empathy for the broad-based Asian culture of British Columbia and acclimatize easily to this environment. They come to improve their economic prospects. Under the stress of long workdays, their faith remains firm but can become spiritually static if there is no time for them to deepen religious insight. Filipino religious faith is intuitive, in the Eastern tradition, and not analytical, as in the Western tradition. When family members go abroad, there is much stress on the family remaining in the Philippines. Filipino families send abroad their most prized family members. Yet much humility is demanded from these workers to adjust to the host country, and much patience is demanded of the family left behind in the Philippines. A sustaining element among lonely Filipinos is the warm-hearted sharing of Catholic devotional life. Prayer groups like Couples for Christ travelled across the Pacific Ocean and are welcomed in Canadian churches. By intense activity and constant agility, the Canadian Filipinos in Vancouver endure the hardships of the Canadian workplace to gain landed immigrant status and establish their hearth and home in this country of their choosing.

Integrating in Winnipeg

Recruited from the Philippines and the Netherlands, the first Filipinos to arrive in Winnipeg during the 1970s came to work in the garment trade. Initially, most of the newcomers were women, but this study also focuses on the arrival of Filipino professionals who followed and deliberately chose to come to Canada. Five Winnipeggers were chosen from St. Edward's parish for the focus of this study: a single woman, a married couple, and two parish priests. We will examine their integration into the Winnipeg community and the resulting cultural clashes between parents and children, young and old.

Cultural Continuity Maintained: The Story of Manuelita Mejos

Manuelita Mejos came to Winnipeg in 1972 as a single woman to join her sister. In the Philippines, she had earned a bachelor of education degree in 1967 and had taught for four years. Arriving in Winnipeg, she found her degree and teaching experience were not recognized by Manitoba. Making the best of a bad deal, Manuelita found a job as a nurse's aide before discovering that she could requalify as a teacher in Canada by enrolling for a second education degree at the University of Manitoba. Completing her studies in 1983, she taught for thirteen years in northern Manitoba in Frontier School Division No. 48. When choosing a teaching position, Manuelita selected Pelican Rapids School, located near a parish church. She adjusted to the northern Canadian climate and culture, but found teaching in English very challenging. Different pronunciations abounded, so she began pronouncing words exactly as she heard others say them. When she retired from the northern school division, she continued to work in Winnipeg at a daycare centre and taught English as a Second Language classes.

Retaining her traditional values, Manuelita preserved close family ties and remained single. The young Filipino Canadians she knows struggle to retain their heritage, but at the same time quickly adapt to Canadian life. The Filipino Canadian parents she observed found themselves all but unable to impose Filipino family discipline and Filipino customs on their Canadian teenagers. Families in the Philippines would express similar reluctance to impose traditional discipline on their children who are adjusting to Westernization.[33] But even more than the reluctance to impose their values on the youth is the lack of time parents in Canada have to relate with their children and to see that they are cared for. In Canada, both parents have jobs and household tasks that demand their attention, which is not the way it is in the Philippines. Back home, working parents of middle-class families would have several domestics to prepare meals, answer the telephone, drive the car, clean the house, and do the laundry. Filipinos in Canada are middle-class; they miss the domestic support they would presume in the Philippines. Manuelita has relinquished her Filipino passport and will remain in Canada. For her health, she prefers readily available herbal remedies to becoming dependent on pharmaceutical drugs. Manuelita teaches catechism to students who do not attend Catholic schools. As a member of the Catholic Women's League, she welcomes new arrivals and recruits some for future membership. She maintains family cohesion, remains close to her Church, and is an active participant in Canadian life.[34]

Lowered Job Expectations:
The Story of Sonia Salazar and Alberto Sangalang

Married couples also discover anxieties and cultural conflicts in moving to Canada. Sonia Salazar completed her bachelor of science in chemical engineering at the University of the Philippines in 1972, then worked for a government corporation doing research in metallurgy. That same year, Alberto Sangalang completed his degree in architecture at St. Louis University in the Philippines and gained experience by working for a number of government corporations, such as Human Settlements, Farm Systems Development Corporation, and the Satellite Housing Contractors Corporation. Sonia and Alberto married in 1980 and looked forward to establishing their own family. When they made the decision to immigrate, Canada was the logical choice to raise and educate their family: since Alberto had family in Winnipeg, they decided to follow family links to join relatives there.

Arriving in 1991, Alberto was anxious to get work in his profession, but resolved to take the first job he found. He accepted work on the night shift at a sewing machine factory, and six years later got a better job on an assembly line elsewhere. Alberto's experience is not uncommon for newcomers to Canada. Susan Brigham comments that "many migrants experience down grading of their credentials by Canadian professional institutions. This is a move of Canadian institutions to protect the interests of their current membership more than by the need to ensure parity."[35] Alberto did not allow the downgrading from his profession to inhibit his ability to support his family and to get on with life. In a similar job shift, Sonia welcomed the opportunity to leave chemical research behind when she came to Canada and decided to try her skills in accounting. She has taken a variety of positions in Winnipeg, including administrator of cooperative housing, accountant for a nursing home, and parish secretary. Her positive attitude to life allowed her to accept the adjustments demanded of her in the Winnipeg workplace.

The Sangalangs found it took time to adjust to the Canadian climate, culture, and language. For instance, Alberto discovered that a large number of Canadians were uninformed about Asian geography and hardly knew where he and his family had come from. Also, the Sangalangs quickly learned how much Filipino culture differed from Canadian culture. Educated in American English, Filipinos must adjust to Canadian pronunciations and idioms. Alberto and Sonia were trained in a formal school tradition that assigned much homework to students and demanded high academic performance. Filipinos in the lower schools have been meticulously drilled in proper grammar and correct spelling—mechanical skills the Canadian system does not stress. Alberto found that Canadians use contractions in speech that are difficult for newcomers to hear and understand. Newcomers are surprised that they look different from other Canadians and that their credentials when they report to the workplace look different from Canadian credentials. They do not receive acceptance until they become embedded by a home in a neighbourhood and have proved their skills in the workplace.

Sonia and Alberto have communicated to their adult son, Pierre Jordache, the Filipino values of honesty, celebration, family honour, and the importance of education. In Canada, children can report their parents to the authorities for being abusive; thus, Filipino parents find it difficult to know how to discipline their children. Some parents find the young are less respectful to their elders than the parents would like. In Asia, young Filipinos were expected to listen politely to elders as part of the discipline. Thus, when young people in Canada openly express their opinions, Filipino elders see the young as being disrespectful. A language barrier inevitably develops between the traditionalism of the old and the spontaneity of the young. The grandparents have Asian expectations of their grandchildren, which can cause generational conflict; parents feel caught in the middle. In Canada, school-age Filipinos blend Canadian values along with their Filipino values and are eclectic in what they retain from the two cultures.

Filipino Canadians, who began their education in the Philippines and are completing it in Canada, are good students for the first few years, but as they become more Canadian, they ease off. They find that Canadian schools encourage the young to become better persons, caution them against the dangers of competition, and animate them in the direction of the cooperative model. The personal feelings and social welfare of students in the Canadian schools are more important to educators than trophies and ribbons. In Asia, there is more concern for academic achievement and less concern for the students' personal adjustment and "fitting in." In the Philippines, good schools impart to their students the professional skills that will give them a competitive edge to do well in business and support their family. Since a minimal social network exists in the Philippines, Filipinos do not look to their government for benefits, retirement funding, or medical assistance.

Sonia and Alberto came to Canada as a family and now carry Canadian passports. They appreciate the Canadian medical system but, when returning from the Philippines, they bring back to Canada Filipino home remedies for colds and flu. They are also familiar with home healers in the Philippines who use natural methods of healing. As a team couple for both Marriage Encounter and Engaged Encounter, they make family decisions by means of dialogue and shared responsibility. They are also involved in a number of prayer groups, such as the Lord of Pardon Association, which was founded in the Philippines and brought to Canada in 1979, and the Worldwide Marriage Encounter, which arrived in Canada in the early 1970s. To keep their spirits high in leisure time, Sonia and Alberto enjoy singing "I'll Never Find Another You" or humming "The Impossible Dream" from *Don Quixote*. Prayer groups and singing are at the heart of a charismatic Filipino spirituality. These spiritual movements promote solid friendship among married couples, dedicated service among clergy, and bible studies, block rosary (where families from the same neighbourhood gather to pray the rosary), and family prayer among the laity.

In Winnipeg, Sonia and Alberto participate in welcoming new Canadians in fellowship by a potluck supper and invite them to a Marriage Encounter weekend. The weekend retreat is followed by introducing the new parishioners to parish life and encouraging them to become active members. During their presentations for the weekends, Sonia and Alberto share their life experiences with the couples taking the weekend. The Sangalangs brought to Manitoba their religious values, hard work, and regular church attendance. They adjusted to Canadian culture, managed their family life, and helped mould a close-knit Winnipeg Catholic community. They encourage other couples to see how, by dealing with the cultural differences that arose in their lives, they have acclimatized to Winnipeg culture, language, and even weather. [36]

Horizontal Transfers: The Story of Fathers Vicente Tungolh and Francisco Francis

Filipino Canadian laity are struggling not only to adjust to Winnipeg, but also to Canadian clergy. Thus, the archbishop of Winnipeg invited Father Vicente Tungolh to come to St. Edward's in 1995 to serve Winnipeg's growing population of Filipinos. Father Vicente had completed his seminary education at Divine Word College and San Carlos Seminary in the Philippines. Afterward, he served parishes in the Philippines for five years, and then was assigned as military chaplain for the next 23 years, until his retirement from that work. He arrived fluent in English but found Canadian speech fast, often spoken in a low voice, and laced with strange idioms and different vocabulary. He learned to like the Canadian medical system and, upon retirement, intends to remain in Canada, with occasional visits to relatives in the Philippines. When in difficulty, Asian Catholics, according to Father Vicente, look to the priest for support. When Filipinos have "mental, behavioural, financial, or spiritual problems," they first seek out their pastor, and, perhaps later, accept referral for financial, medical, or psychiatric help. This approach reflects the Filipino lack of confidence in officials and their agencies, and their confidence in the priest as the most credible person to consult.

Father Tungolh makes an effort to retain Filipino customs and to attract newcomers. He finds Filipino Catholics in Manitoba are regular churchgoers who look for devotions they recognize from home. For instance, in preparing for Christmas, the Misa de Gallo brings out Filipinos at the early hours of the morning for a novena of masses. On Holy Thursday and Good Friday, the seven last words of Jesus are sung in Tagalog during the Pabasa. The parish dramatizes the Encuentro, the meeting between Jesus and his blessed mother following the resurrection. Prayer groups are also active at St. Edward's, including Couples for Christ, two charismatic groups, the Miraculous Medal, and Santo Niño. Father Vicente believes that older parishioners born in the Philippines embrace these devotions eagerly, but that younger, Canadian-born Filipinos have difficulty with such religious piety. Canadian distances and winter snow militate against easy church attendance for devotions at Christmas and Easter. Children and seniors have to be driven to church, and in cold weather, outside processions are impossible. Fellow priests in the archdiocese are grateful that Father Vicente and his associate, Father Francisco Francis, are serving the needs of Winnipeg Filipinos in the way they deserve.[37] On the other hand, some Anglo-Canadian Catholics raised in a Protestant environment are dazzled by the elaborate Filipino devotional style and the free display of sentimental emotion.

Young Filipino Canadians do not always attend family meals and prayer. They force their parents to be open to the demands of Canadian secular life. Separated from the Asian way of raising children, parents are not always sure how they are permitted to discipline their children, Father Vicente explains.[38] After being educated in Canadian schools, young people can lose their taste for family events and church devotions. Among Filipino Canadians, inter-racial and interfaith marriage is common, as it is among Euro-Canadians. On the positive side, clinical psychologist and university professor Maria Root believes that "mixed" marriages will expand the Filipino community and make it more diverse and flexible.[39] This view is shocking to senior Filipinos, who recall that weddings in the Philippines, where choices were adequate, were exclusively Filipino Catholic. It could be pointed out, however, that the memories of the older generation are not always indicative of what is happening in the Philippines today, and that Westernization has meant for the Philippines more inter-ethnic and interfaith marriages. After Canadian Filipinos are married, they retain the tradition that husbands are the leaders of the family who pay bills and resolve family problems. Wives seldom contest this custom and are willing to give their husband due respect, while quietly holding the purse strings and developing their own lifestyle and interdependence.

Filipino Canadian organizations to assist newcomers in their adjustment are not proactive, as Canadian organizations would be. Father Vicente explains that Filipino Canadians wait for the need to arise before taking action. Filipino assistance to others, whether in the Philippines or Canada, is spontaneous and heartfelt but decidedly short-term. Once the crisis is over, the help ceases, and both the helper and the helped get back to normal. From their culture of generosity, Filipino Canadians down on their luck know that they can ask for help and it will be forthcoming. Filipino families will not turn away the needy.[40]

Father Francisco Francis completed his seminary training at San Carlos Seminary in the Philippines, working as an associate pastor for seven years and pastor for 25. He arrived in Winnipeg in 1996 at the invitation of the archbishop of that city, and began work as associate pastor at St. Edward's parish. Father Francisco likes to promote traditional Filipino Catholic devotions, such as novenas and the recitation of the rosary, and encourages family ties, home visits, gift giving, and assistance to those in need. At St. Edward's, he is the spiritual director of the Catholic Women's League and the Legion of Mary. Their members carry out the visitation of parish homes and help a nearby parish with a yearly lunch for the needy. Filipino women's groups are integrated into Manitoban and Canadian Church structures through diocesan, national, and international organizations. Avoiding an ethnic ghetto, Filipinos become part of Canadian Catholic national organizations, and Filipino devotional life reinforces Canadian devotions and enriches Canadian piety with its regularity and faithfulness.

Father Francisco finds that Canadians use slang in speaking English; thus, it is difficult for a person from another culture to know exactly what is being said. He believes that children who are well nurtured by their parents at home are more likely to attend Filipino devotional and social events. When parental guidance is accepted, Father Francis insists that generational conflict is avoided. Yet he admits that in Canada, young people preparing for marriage often live together before the wedding. He observes that what Canadians do, Filipino Canadians will do. In the Philippines, he postulates, such conduct is frowned upon.[41] However, others would add that when adult children outside the Philippines live with partners without the benefit of marriage, parents learn to tolerate the new reality.[42]

While Father Francisco consoles the lonely Filipinos living in Winnipeg, he maintains dual Philippine and Canadian citizenship. He personally likes the Canadian medical system but intends to return to the Philippines after retirement. In his senior years, he would prefer the warmth of a family home in the Philippines to a private nursing home in Canada. His diocese will offer him a health-care plan when he returns.[43] The research of professors H. Billones and S. Wilson show that "elders want to return to the Philippines when they are incapacitated and they want to be cared for by their other children and family members in their home country."[44]

It becomes apparent that Winnipeg Filipinos endure cultural conflict and adjust to the new workplace, accents, and discipline for the sake of their children. Lacking "Canadian experience" when they arrive, they must lower their job expectations but acknowledge that the work they do offers better salaries than in the Philippines.[45] They must adjust to Canadian verbal sounds and dialectical idioms. Their children are educated in Canadian schools, which teach them how to deal with the Canadian culture. Through these cultural challenges, families keep their courage high by close ties with the Filipino Catholic community. Filipino clergy coming to Winnipeg in the 1990s strengthened the resolve of the Canadian Church to reinforce a struggling ethnic community. For Filipinos, it is important to preserve their identity. E. San Juan Jr. affirms this process when he writes that "the construction of a Filipino ethnic identity as a dynamic, complex phenomenon" defies the American assimilationist model.[46] Yet in the multicultural Canadian society,

Filipinos, like Irish, German, Ukrainian and Polish immigrants before them, are asked to describe their origin and identity. It is important for Filipino Canadians to resolve the clash of cultures they experience and to work out a clear idea of who they are and from where they came.[47]

Pursuing Employment in Toronto

In Toronto, Filipinos cluster principally in eight core parishes, but are also found in substantial numbers in other parishes throughout the urban area. Of these eight principal parishes, masses in Filipino are celebrated monthly at Blessed John XXIII, St. Anthony, St. Catherine of Siena, and St. Paschal Baylon in Toronto, and at St. Joseph in Mississauga. Filipinos also make up 50 to 70 per cent of the attendees at Our Lady of the Assumption, Our Lady of Lourdes, and St. Thomas More. Filipinos are 10 to 35 per cent of attendees at Christ the King, Prince of Peace, St. Aidan, St. Bartholomew, St. Boniface's Scarborough, St. Edward's North York, St. Joseph's Highland Creek, and St. Martin de Porres. In these Catholic parishes, sizable Filipino communities are active and make positive contributions to parochial life.

Father Rodolfo Imperial was the pastor of Blessed John XXIII and the chaplain for the Filipino community in the Archdiocese of Toronto. The Filipino community sponsors yearly Marriage Encounters, Life in the Spirit Seminars, a Filipino choir, and a community service committee. According to Father Imperial, parishes attended by Filipinos are energetic in family activities, such as the baptism of children, community services, and choral singing. The 3,000 parishioners of Blessed John XXIII are composed of 40 to 50 per cent Filipino, with 27 other ethnic groups being represented, including Chinese, Vietnamese, Korean, and East Indian Canadians. The Rite of Christian Initiation for Adults is mostly run for Chinese and East Indian Canadians. The Filipino parish was moved in August 2008 to Our Lady of the

Assumption parish in Forest Hill. Filipino Canadians represent 70 per cent of the 9,000 parishioners, Euro-Canadians 25 per cent, and the remainder Caribbean Canadians. Father Ben Ebcas is the new chaplain, and a mass in Tagalog is celebrated weekly on Sunday evening at 5:00.

While welcoming substantial numbers of Filipinos, these Toronto parishes are also open to other ethnic groups, integrating Italian, Portuguese, Chinese, Korean, Vietnamese, and East Indian Canadians into one worshipping community.[48] At Our Lady of Lourdes, just north of St. Michael's Cathedral in downtown Toronto, Filipino Canadians represent about 65 per cent of the 13,640 parishioners, which include 15 per cent Tamils and a sprinkling of Hispanic, Vietnamese, Korean, Caribbean, English, and French Canadians. In 2001, the average number of parish baptisms in the archdiocese was 84. In this same year, parishes with a heavy overlay of Filipinos baptized more than the average number: Our Lady of Lourdes baptized 195; St. Paschal Baylon and St. Joseph of Mississauga, 184; Blessed John XXIII, 127; and St. Anthony, 130.[49] Filipino Catholics in Toronto number more than 115,132, and are positively changing the Catholic demography and customs in the archdiocese.

Among Canadian prayer groups that help Filipinos manage the transition to life in Canada are Bukas Loob Sa Diyos (BLD) and Couples for Christ. BLD members in Toronto and St. Catharines gained diocesan approval in 1990 and have met regularly since then. As we learned in Chapter 3, Philippine BLD members Mariano and Fanny Quimson came to Canada in 1990; along with eight Filipino couples and two singles, they resolved to found a Toronto-based BLD.[50] In a short time, 500 to 700 BLD members were gathered to provide Marriage Encounter Weekends, Life in the Spirit Seminars, and Basic Bible Study.[51] Members meet monthly at healing masses at Assumption Church and gather weekly to share common faith and worship. They group themselves into ministry teams to pray together, reflect on the Scriptures, and serve the community.

Organizing a First Friday Charismatic celebration at Assumption church in Forest Hill, BLD attracts 500 to 700 Filipino Canadians each month. Having lived in Toronto for fifteen or 20 years, BLD members have found regular employment, purchased homes, educated their children in Canadian schools, and become established Catholics. They have found BLD a source of personal inspiration and a good forum for dealing with adjustment and generational tensions. Yet some Filipinas who are doing domestic work in the neighbourhood will not attend the Friday evening celebration because of their own sense of Filipino class consciousness and the established appearance of BLD members.[52] The newly arrived, especially young women, can bring with them from the Philippines their memories of a class-conscious society.[53] Similar cultural conflict can arise when three generations of a family live in the same house. The first generation grew up with the phantasms of the tropical environment, indigenous religious culture, and speaking both Tagalog and English. By contrast, the second and third generations are growing up with the phantasms of urban apartment dwellers, hockey playing, secular Canadian culture, and the English and French languages. The three generations of Filipinos do not share the same worlds, which are as dissimilar as the Philippine tropical climate is from the Canadian winter.

Concerned with the plight of new Filipino Canadians, BLD offers a program of service. BLD members, involved in their local parishes, offer spiritual and physical support to the newly arrived. When individuals and families in difficulty seek help through the parishes, Filipino volunteers are ready. They are willing to do menial tasks in parish organizations, which sensitize them to the needs of the local community to learn who needs help and what has to be done. While Filipino Canadians in the 1970s did not find immediate acceptance in Canada, the passage of time has seen Filipino Canadians find more genuine acceptance. Thirty years later, Euro-Canadians are impressed with hard-working Filipino Canadians and welcome them fully into their workplace and neighbourhoods.[54] The staunch devotion of the Filipinos in Canadian churches gives genuine encouragement to Euro-Canadian Catholics.

BLD members Roberto and Paciencia Santos, a professional couple, described their unusual route to Canada in the 1980s . Bert and Cita knew each other growing up in the Philippines. Cita arrived in New York to study medicine; soon after, Bert, an engineer, established himself as a Canadian citizen in Toronto. When Cita completed her training, she and Bert returned to the Philippines to celebrate their wedding among family and friends. After the wedding, they returned to Toronto to initiate their professional careers. Initially, they experienced discrimination. For example, they bought a house with the help of colleagues in a pleasant mid-Toronto neighbourhood. A nosy neighbour, seeing Bert at work on his lawn, inquired how they could afford a house in such an upscale neighbourhood. Becoming more insistent, the neighbour demanded, "Where are you getting your money from? What work do you do? Where are you from?" Bert recalled that "when I told him that we were from the Philippines, and my wife is a medical doctor, and I am an engineer, he seemed surprised. What about the money? We worked hard and saved money to buy what we want and, in this case, our house. He asked me further about the geographical location of the Philippines." Reflecting on this experience, Bert now views these probes as stemming more from ignorance than from discrimination.[55]

Employed by a multinational company for eighteen years, he encountered discrimination in the workplace. As assistant manager of his division, he was known to be "the firefighter for the company, crisscrossing the country to solve problems." Despite his position, competence, and seniority, he was passed over three times for the manager's position. Bert realized that he had "reached my glass ceiling and it was time to go." In 1984, the Canadian government published the document *Equality Now*, which perfectly described Bert's situation: "Barriers ...

exist for the advancement and promotion through relegation of the minority persons to low status and low-income positions, through seniority policies, and through limited exposure to new job openings."[56] Discrimination in the workplace is a constant factor used by those who are protecting jobs for themselves and their associates.

In contrast, Cita Santos, with a North American degree, did not experience professional discrimination. Canada was in need of her skills as an anaesthesiologist, and with her American degree and four years of additional training in Canadian hospitals, she was "welcomed" into her profession. She became an associate professor at the University of Toronto and Chief of the Anaesthesia Department at the Orthopaedic and Arthritic Hospital in downtown Toronto.[57] Arriving in Canada 40 years ago, Bert and Cita Santos were Filipino pioneers in Toronto. They experienced Canadians becoming more appreciative of the positive value of Filipinos.

After their son, Neil, and daughter, Maria Theresa, were born in Toronto, Bert and Cita focused on the importance of family bonding by speaking Tagalog at home and celebrating Christian holidays. Following the Filipino custom, Neil and Maria Theresa were not allowed to go to other family homes for sleepovers. Such a breach of family etiquette was considered unacceptable to Filipinos. The parents' desire for the children to speak Tagalog, however, never materialized, as Neil and Maria Theresa preferred responding in English. Again, rather than choosing the Filipino sport of basketball, Neil preferred playing hockey. Nor did Neil pick a Filipina as his bride, as his parents might have expected, but chose for his life partner Jennifer Aycan, an Armenian Canadian, who has since become dear to the parents and the entire Santos family. Bert and Cita, as second-generation Filipinos, attend church weekly, and are lectors and ministers of bread and cup in their parish. They are involved in BLD as a team couple for Marriage Encounter Weekends. Neil and Jennifer, as members of the third generation, go to Sunday mass when they are free but are not involved in their church community. The strategy of Bert and Cita proved to be effective, since their children continue to enjoy their friendship and, in Filipino custom, visit their parents on Sundays.

Filipino Canadian children celebrate their First Communion at Our Lady of Lourdes church, Toronto.

Filipino Canadians retain many of their Asian customs and instill them in their children. They try to maintain Asian discipline, retain religious devotions, and will sponsor a debutant party if possible when their daughters turn eighteen. Bert and Cita admit that Filipino Canadian parents are puzzled when they are cautioned against using physical punishment, which is acceptable in Asia but not under Canadian law. Parents wish to have a voice in the marriage of their children, resist interfaith and inter-ethnic marriages, and expect married children to visit on Sunday. They have great hope for the first male child that, when he becomes adult, he will do well and provide younger siblings with school tuition and assure the parents of a respectable retirement.

Susan Brigham believes that in the 1980s and 1990s, this phenomenon was responsible for the first child of Filipino families coming to Canada to set up a household and to sponsor other family members. If the first child was a woman, she might have been admitted as a nanny on a temporary work visa for two years. The next step was to begin a permanent residency period of three years, to establish a home and bring out the family.[58] Filipinos follow practical wisdom, which says, "Wherever there is a loophole, fill it." The North American Filipino family is an extended family rather than a nuclear family; it may include an uncle, aunt, in-law, or friend of the family who has just arrived. Parents try to guide their growing children and find it difficult when the children attend Canadian schools. The parents dress modestly and encourage their children to follow the Christian Gospel and the Golden Rule. Yet the children demand from their parents more freedom to mix and choose to hang out with their friends rather than the family. Parents are shocked to find their daughters calling boys on the telephone and receiving calls after 9 p.m.[59] Children are under peer pressure to conform to Canadian youth mores, while parents feel pushed to make concessions.

Similar in many ways to the Santos family, the Marquezes had to make profound adjustments to Canadian culture. Armin Marquez and Florinda Mapa were married after finishing their university degrees in the Philippines. At first, Armin worked as a contract personnel officer in Saudi Arabia, while Linda remained in the Philippines working as a teacher. Their desire to live together as a married couple brought Linda to move to Saudi Arabia to work as a private tutor. They discovered the economic advantages of working overseas, especially when they began raising their children, Aurora and Armand. Soon Armin moved up the ladder of company management, and Linda opened a play school for their children and the children of their associates. Through their enterprise, they became more financially stable. When their children reached school age, they attended an American international school. A chance visit to Toronto impressed the Marquezes that it was a city in which they could live and work comfortably, especially in the light of the increased educational opportunities it offered to their children. They landed in Toronto as immigrants in 1996. Armin found a position as a student counsellor at the University of Toronto, while Linda was hired as a claims specialist by a Toronto insurance company. A host of transitions faced the couple, as Armin adjusted from guiding workers to counselling students, and Linda switched from teaching children in the Philippines and Saudi Arabia to working in the business world. Putting aside the dawn-to-dusk hours of a Filipino teacher, Linda entered into the nine-to-five world of Canadian business; she enjoyed the shorter hours and better pay.

By this time, Aurora and Armand were teenagers attending Canadian high schools. It was important to Armin and Linda that the family retain its religious identity, prayer life, and sense of respect for the elderly. While the family held onto its Filipino values, the pressure to conform to Canadian ways soon proved daunting. When Aurora reached age eighteen, she wanted to date, which would be considered comparatively late for Canadian teenagers. This seemed to her parents much too soon for a Filipino girl. Linda's time frame was age 25, and then only in the company of a chaperon. Linda was aghast at her daughter's Canadian ideas, but Armin was more receptive. Upon meeting his daughter's date, he requested that a 10 p.m. curfew be respected. Linda and Armin also learned to accept the possibility of interracial marriage as part of Canadian society. Armin adds that such marriage unions must involve strong persons who are deeply in love in order to cope with the misunderstandings that will occur among family and friends. Armin and Linda and their adult children find that Toronto offers excellent opportunities for the future and want to be rooted in Canada. In their view,

Canada offers a better quality of life, and a Canadian passport provides entrance to most nations of the world without visas or additional payments.

Linda has discovered racism in herself and has encountered North American racism in Canadians. On the street in Toronto, she and her young daughter Aurora were frightened by an African Canadian, and she remarked to her daughter that one has to avoid black people. Her Canadian-educated daughter admonished her mother, "Mom, you're a racist. We don't say that in Canada!" Linda admitted that her daughter was right, and Linda began to change her attitude. Yen le Espiritu, in *Home Bound*, comments that "Filipinos live within and in tension with a racist system that defines white middle-class culture as the norm."[60] On a cruise in the Caribbean, one of Linda's fellow passengers asked her where she was from. Linda replied that she was from Canada. The person responded, "But you don't look like a Canadian!" In Toronto she encountered this bigoted comment: "Why did you come to Canada? Go home to your own country!" According to researcher Susan Brigham, this comment is typical of Canadian-born bigots to strangers they meet.[61]

Linda and Armin were warmly welcomed by Couples for Christ when they arrived in Toronto, and CFC members were helpful to them for their first years in Canada. Linda and Armin became involved in numerous parish activities at Our Lady of Lourdes. They made the Spiritual Exercises of St. Ignatius Loyola, which helped them decide to commit themselves in service (*bayanihan*) at the downtown Toronto parish. They are team members in marriage preparation and deeply involved with the parish social ministry. Through volunteers like Linda and Armin, Lourdes parish helps new Canadians adjust to Canadian ways and assists them with the demands of the Canadian immigration department.

As members of the Engaged Encounter Movement at Our Lady of Lourdes, preparing young couples for marriage, Linda and Armin openly share their marriage experiences with the young couples. Their artistic and dramatic talents are employed to motivate parishioners to understand the neighbourhood needs and alleviate them. They believe that Filipinos, because they are English speaking and bicultural, blend well into Canadian parishes and the Toronto workplace. In fact, Filipinos bring to those they meet in Canada the gifts of song and celebration. Armin surmises that "Filipinos by virtue of their centuries of colonial background are raised to serve, help, and provide service. Their eagerness to serve is carried out as welcomers, choir members, and volunteer workers in the Canadian church."[62] What this means, according to Susan Brigham, is that the "Filipino's nature [is] not to respond in a confrontational manner" but to handle conflict quietly and at a suitable time.[63] Family therapist Emilio Santa Rita confirms this Filipino style of "*delicadeza*, or nonconfrontational communication."[64] Theologians Dindo Tesoro and Joselito Jose contend that "the Filipino instinct" seeks "harmonious human relations," a "conciliatory rather than confrontational bent."[65] Professor Felipe M. de Leon Jr. argues that "Filipinos are essentially unitive, harmonious, [and] non-confrontational."[66] To the many parts of the world where they work, Filipino overseas contract workers are missionaries who bring the tranquility of the Christian Gospel to the Euro-Canadians from whom they originally received it. In doing so, migrant Filipinos complement the culture and religious customs of their host countries.

Employment Problems

Manuel and Elizabeth Gorospe were from middle-class families in the Philippines. Blessed with five children, they both held executive-level positions and were able to take care of their family needs. "Almost everything we earned," Bessie wrote, "went to the children's education ... and our medical/health needs." After the fifth child, Manny decided to resign from his position and set up his own business. The business failed, but he was offered a position as a branch manager in his family firm in

Manila. Unhappy with their slow financial progress and praying for God's guidance, Manuel and Elizabeth decided to leave the Philippines for Canada in 1990, mainly for "economic reasons." As they soon discovered, it turned out to be the wrong time to arrive, as the Canadian economy had slowed down.

Jobs in Toronto were hard to find, and Manny, desperate to get going, took a job as a low-paying mail clerk. Elizabeth, a bank officer in the Philippines, found employment working as a benefits administrator for an insurance pension plan of a Canadian bank. Working as a team, Bessie and Manny initially sought financial help from BLD, but soon gained their own financial stability. Manny was overqualified and overworked in his job. Through his company's educational program, he studied and acquired his licence as an insurance broker. Wishing to help others, he tried to assist a female co-worker who was having difficulty, and, owing to verbal and cultural misunderstanding, was accused of sexual harassment. Convinced of his innocence, he refused to follow his supervisor's suggestion that he resign voluntarily. The axe fell, and Manny lost his first Canadian job. As a religious leader in his community, he was humiliated and hurt by the incident. His community became his source of encouragement and strength as members prayed with him and shared generously with his family. His dismissal turned out to be a lucky break in disguise. After a year of unemployment, he found full-time work on the assembly line at the Ford plant. Even though this was his first experience of physical labour, he found the pay and benefits beyond his expectations and worth the hard work. Together, he and Elizabeth were able to buy a Canadian home in the suburbs. They remain loyal and grateful to their fellow members in BLD.

Adjusting to Canadian culture for Manny and Bessie was not easy or automatic. They were schooled in the Asian culture, which proved entirely different from Canadian culture. In the Filipino way, they taught their children not to talk back to adults and always to respect their elders. When their children arrived in Canadian schools, however, the teachers taught them to speak out and say what was on their minds. This shift in approach caused conflict between parents and children about who had greater wisdom and what was right. Their family in the Philippines was accustomed to having servants who cleaned the house, prepared the meals, and cleared the dishes when dinner was over. The Gorospes had to learn in Canada that house servants were a luxury and financially impossible for them. This meant that the five children, along with their parents, had to pitch in and do their share of household chores. These tasks demanded family adjustments, which included cooperation. The spiritual encouragement and guidance of BLD was especially helpful in keeping the family together through this period of adjustment and assisted them to overcome divergent attitudes. The sacrifices the Gorospes made proved to be the price of passage for integration into Canadian life. Through these labours, they became very appreciative of the benefits of living in Canada.[67]

Isabelle and Fernando Escaño, who lived in Hong Kong, came to Canada in December 1989, when the Canadian economy was in recession. In Hong Kong, Andy was the managing director of an international bank, and Belle was marketing manager for sales at a travel agency. Because of his high position, Andy enjoyed expatriate benefits—free luxury housing, car and driver, paid vacations, and other privileges. The Escaños were enjoying a comfortable lifestyle and were at the peak of their careers. But things were about to change. The impending Communist takeover of Hong Kong was like a menacing cloud hanging over their political and economic future. They seriously considered moving to Canada.

Feeling pressure at the bank, which was in a bullish and expansionary mode, Andy thought he was having heart problems. In fact, the bank was demanding from him total commitment and loyalty. Belle and Andy were invited to a Marriage Encounter Weekend sponsored by the BLD community in Manila.

The experience spoke to both Belle and Andy, and they ended the weekend "hungry for more." They joined Life in the Spirit Seminar and encountered God through profound spiritual experiences. The retreat weekend was a turbulent time for Belle. Vivid flashbacks of her youth, long forgotten, passed before her. This spiritual experience released her from past anger from which she had suffered as the result of having an alcoholic father. Psalm 147 assured her in an inner way that the Lord "heals the brokenhearted, and binds up their wounds." A powerful bright light came into her life, and she trembled in front of the Holy One. Belle was overwhelmed by the weekend singing and praising of God. Andy's experience was a peaceful one, not quite as dramatic as Belle's. Having encountered the love of God deeply in Manila, Andy and Belle joined BLD when they returned to Hong Kong.

They joined for emotional and social support, preferring it to similar organizations since it was more substantial in its liturgical and educational programs. Its communal prayer and liturgical programs anticipated the Word of God to be read at Sunday mass. Although carefully prepared, the BLD community worship could also be spontaneous, but within a structure.

Without telling their family, Andy and Belle applied for landed immigrant status in Canada as a backup if life under the Communist government in Hong Kong started to go bad. To their surprise, the Canadian embassy notified them within a short time that they had been accepted for immigration to Canada. They were given six months to make their initial landing. As this decision was not an emergency for them, they did not think to share it with anyone else. In the meantime, their last three years in Hong Kong had been exciting, since they were involved in their community. They assisted the parish community as catechists and choir members, and became active members in BLD.

As the deadline for departure to Canada approached, Belle and Andy asked the Lord's guidance on whether to go. They

sought the counsel of some of their elders, and together discerned the will of God for their life. Reflecting over the Scriptures
and using devotions, they prayed constantly for enlightenment.
One morning during Belle's prayer, she asked the Lord if it was
his will that they move to Canada and, if it was, to reveal it to
her in a clear way so that she would know without doubt that it
was the Lord speaking. The Lord, knowing "the number of the
stars" and whose "wisdom there is no limit" (Psalm 147), answered
her that he understood what was best for them, and they should
not fear. As she read from *Our Daily Bread*, the words "Never fear
an unknown future to an all-knowing God" jumped off the page.
The words assured her that the Lord was speaking to her heart
and revealing his plan for them.

At a prayer meeting at their church, when Belle was feeding
song sheets to the overhead projector, one of her friends, looking
at her, heard the words again and again singing in her heart, "Belle
is going to Canada!" This friend did not know of Andy and Belle's
application to the Canadian embassy and could not explain the
source of her knowledge. At another prayer meeting, this same
friend saw a vision of Belle and Andy standing in front of packed
suitcases with labels stating the destination: "Canada."

They consulted their BLD elder about going to Canada. He
asked them bluntly why were they leaving Hong Kong when
they had no friends and no jobs in Canada. With the Canadian
economy in recession, he cautioned them that in Toronto, Filipino
men often end up as househusbands while women become the
breadwinners, since it is easier for women to find work. Could
Andy, he queried, live with that possibility? Andy argued within
himself that they did not have to go and that they could serve
God just as well in Hong Kong. Yet, Belle and Andy were deeply
stirred by the Scriptures telling them the Lord was building the
new Jerusalem and called them to help and "give freely what
you have freely received." Believing that they should "consider
unclean your silver-plated idols and your gold-covered images"
(Isaiah 30:22), they decided to give up the privileges of Andy's

position in Hong Kong, go to Canada, put themselves in the hands of the Lord, and form a BLD group there.

In mid-December 1989, they arrived in Toronto. They stayed with a BLD couple they had met in Hong Kong. The couple welcomed them with open arms, and their visit was a great social and spiritual success. Every evening, they reflected on the Scriptures and prayed with their newfound brothers and sisters living in "the House of Israel."

Job hunting, however, was bleak. They were told that economically, they were in the wrong place at the wrong time. Putting aside the temptation to seek employment in a New York City bank, Andy remained in Toronto and put himself in God's hands. Increasingly discouraged, Andy and Belle returned to Hong Kong for a number of months. Andy went back to his position at the bank. He didn't know what to do. Should he resign permanently or not? The words of the Scripture came back to their minds: "The Lord will give you the bread you need and the water for which you thirst .... And you shall consider unclean your silver-plated idols and your gold-covered images" (Isaiah 30:20-22).

The bank in Hong Kong was in the process of expansion; Andy was a key player in this operation. He was caught in a dilemma of whether to obey God or mammon. He telephoned his boss in London, explained his situation, and tendered his resignation. His boss, who was saddened at the thought of losing Andy, countered that he did not want Andy to leave the bank. He offered to speak to the shareholders and see if they would agree to reopen the dormant office in Toronto. Andy and Belle rejoiced.

A few weeks later, Andy received a telephone call from his boss in London advising him that the shareholders had decided to reopen the Toronto office and that he was to be its general manager. Belle and Andy exclaimed to each other, "God's generosity can never be outdone!" By June 1990, they had returned to Toronto, and Andy had assumed his new position. Belle and

Andy began the work to which the Lord called them. Weekly, they met with their BLD brothers and sisters to pray and seek the Lord's will. In August 1991, the couples officially founded BLD in Toronto. Since then, BLD has renewed marriages, strengthened families, and formed disciples of the Lord.[68]

Pursuit of Identity

A well-educated Filipina, Rosemary Abigania, feeling oppressed by her overprotective middle-class Filipino family, came to Canada in search of her own identity. In the Philippines, she had worked as a training coordinator for the Agricultural Credit Administration. Her position provided her with the opportunity to represent the Philippine government in a program sponsored by the United States Agency for International Development. She was driven here and there to welcome dignitaries and ensure they were given proper orientation of the Land Reform Program in the Philippines.

She spoke English in the Philippines in her business and social contacts. When she arrived in Toronto, she found work as a medical secretary but had difficulty understanding Canadian English and pharmaceutical terms, and was let go from her position. She hoped to achieve a position in management training, for which she had been educated in the Philippines, but was never given the opportunity in Canada to apply for a parallel position. As a result, she was cut off from the skills she brought to Canada to contribute to the business world.

Nevertheless, being intelligent and determined, Rosemary eventually obtained a position with the Labour Tribunal of the Ontario government. The intricacies of processing cases at the Labour Board challenged her legal propensities, and her intensity gave her mastery of the procedures. In the meantime, she was a single parent of a child who is now an adult. Her son, Enrique John (EJ), who has autism and Tourette's Syndrome, has developmental disabilities and lives at Kerry's Place, a residential home for people with autism. Rosemary is a watchful advocate for his welfare. She spoke Tagalog and Ilocano to EJ so he can mix easily when visiting family members in the Philippines. She also taught EJ her strong commitment to the Catholic religion and Filipino culture. She has conveyed to him the Filipino values of humility, honesty, and respect for the elderly. Although generational conflict is not prominent between mother and son, there is some personal conflict. In fact, the relationship is dominated by EJ's need for personal acceptance and his fear of rejection.

Rosemary has found her identity in Canada by stepping away from her need for self-esteem and learning to rejoice in the intelligence God gave her. She feels as a member of a minority group in Canada that she no longer relies for her identity on the superficialities of clothes, social position, and family status. A cultured, self-possessed Filipina, she has a strong sense of her role in life as a mother. She has purchased a townhouse in Toronto and intends to remain in Canada.

Both in the Philippines and in Canada, she has maintained strong relationships with members of religious orders and Catholic clergy. They sustained her through the troubling times of pregnancy and during her son's childhood. After taking a weekend spiritual encounter in September 2001, and its follow-up Life in the Spirit Seminar, Rosemary joined BLD in the Single Parents Ministry. When she moved into her home, her "shepherd" and other members rallied around her and held a potluck supper for the house warming. The members looked after her when she was undergoing medical care and saw that she was not alone. For Rosemary, BLD goes beyond physical and moral support and includes helping its members to encounter the Lord in the joys and sorrows of their lives. In difficult times, she has learned to sing in her heart, "Lord, teach us to pray; I will trust in you."[69]

Domestic Employment

Five thousand Filipina domestics have arrived in Canada each year since the 1990s, so that now 80 per cent of Canadian domestics are Filipinas. In Ontario, where over two thirds of these Filipinas work, they are paid the minimum wage of $10.45 per hour for a five-day week, have Saturdays, Sundays, and holidays off, and are given summer vacation time.[70] After 24 months of live-in service with one employer, they can apply for permanent residency in Canada.[71] Canadian families seek Filipina domestic workers who "have created a genuine bond of mutual respect" with the families they serve. These women have interesting stories to tell.[72] Jean La Torre and Audie Olano speak of their quest for work, first in Hong Kong and then in Canada. For seven and nine years respectively in Hong Kong, their lives were very busy, with long hours of work, but socially they shared activities at the Filipino Catholic Centre. Filipino religious sisters were stationed by the archdiocese of Hong Kong at the Filipino Centre in 1989 to welcome Filipinas in their off hours. The two attended weekly mass and socialized with their compatriots.

Leaving Hong Kong, Audie came to Canada in April 2003 and found domestic work in Toronto; Jean arrived in June 2003, and was also employed as a domestic. Jean immigrated to Canada since doing so would give her access to relatives and friends in Seattle. For financial reasons, Audie decided to migrate to Toronto to establish a home in a city to which she could bring her brothers and sisters. Compared to the long hours of work in Hong Kong, Jean and Audie found the hours shorter and working conditions more agreeable in Toronto. Ontario winters were initially to be feared, and they stocked up on vitamin pills.

From her fond memories of the Philippines, Jean misses the affectionate titles given to family members and elders, such as "po" or "opo." She also finds the public display of affection by young couples in Canada inappropriate. They also find that the excessive use of makeup by Filipino Canadian young people upsets their parents and causes family tension. Although not married, Audie believes in the Filipino custom of married faithfulness until death, and both she and Jean admire North

Americans for keeping romance alive in marriages. They like the custom of visiting the Philippines and returning with an abundance of *pasalubông* (gifts). Both Filipinas have little difficulty with inter-racial marriages as long as couples have strong love for each other. Both have experienced discrimination in Hong Kong, but not in Canada, except in situations where they found their English inadequate. Both completed bachelor's degrees in the Philippines along with a one-year caring course. In Canada, Jean, after completing her initial two-year work period, would like to study chiropractic or reflexology; Audie would like to prepare for teaching.

In Hong Kong, Jean and Audie attended Mary Queen of Love Prayer Group, founded by Filipinas who were looking for social and religious groups, at the Filipino Centre, which offered Bible study, social outreach, and sharing prayer, but in Toronto they have yet to find a similar prayer or social group.[73]

Telling a similar story of loneliness is the widow Virgincita Cepeda. Leaving the Philippines as a domestic for the third time, she sighed, "I would have loved to work here [the Philippines], where I can be close to my children, but my earnings as an elementary school teacher can never sustain my five kids." When she returned home after two years in Canada, she grieved that her four-year-old "didn't recognize me anymore. The older kids seemed cold and distant." When in Canada, she worried about her children growing up in the Philippines undisciplined and disrespectful to their parents. Homesick in Canada, she "couldn't sleep" and worried "about my kids and their condition; if they were eating well; if they are doing their schoolwork." But, sending home $400 monthly compared with $180 earned by teachers in the Philippines, she confessed the benefits: "When it's a matter of family survival, do we really have a choice?"[74]

Some commentators from her homeland would dispute Virgincita's choice and argue that it was unfortunate for her family that she was away so much. It is contended that in the long run, money sent home from foreign nations is not beneficial to the Philippine economy and leaves wounded families. The money sent is used often for school and survival but also for luxuries. Opponents might say it would have been better for Virgincita to be present in her home "to rear her children in good moral values and live within their means." They would argue that it is more useful for the Philippines and for her family that she use her teaching skills in Filipino education, which, in the long run, would improve the national standard of education.[75]

A study of the Asian Development Bank states that in 2004, Filipinos sent home to the Philippines more than CAN$9.1 billion; informally, it was perhaps twice this amount. The report continues that "the money that workers and emigrants send home each year is spent putting sons, daughters, nieces and nephews through school, while the rest is blown on food and village fiestas as well as ill-advised small-business ventures that usually fail." These remittances represent 11 per cent of the gross domestic product and are thought to be financially important to the Philippines. The study goes on to comment that "considerable spending" was used "for non-essentials and luxuries" and could be employed "for more productive use and as a tool for poverty reduction."[76]

Conclusion

Employing caregiving, medical, and managerial skills, Filipinos fit into Canadian life quickly and make a positive contribution. The immigration department and the Canadian populace recognize these services. Filipinos nurse in most Canadian hospitals, and Filipino doctors and dentists are busy in many cities. During the SARS crisis in Toronto in 2003, the three medical workers who gave their lives for the health of their neighbours were Filipino Canadians: two nurses and one doctor.

Since the 1990s, Filipinos have dominated the field of domestic employment in Canada. They are treasured as domestics because they have a good sense of homemaking and are loving toward children. To the business community, Filipinos bring excellent organizational skills and strong company loyalty. They are positive and cheerful and have a vigorous commitment to the Canadian Catholic Church. They are generally from middle-class families, personally attracted to the medical, teaching, and caring professions, and less intrigued with the world of business, economics, and politics.

The question arises whether Filipinos in Canada prefer to be sojourners, earning income and then taking it home, or to establish themselves permanently in Canada. Many Italians, for example, came as sojourners and returned home with earnings in hand after a few years.[77] By contrast, Irish immigrants in the nineteenth century came to Canada as permanent settlers.[78] Do the Filipinos fall into the category of temporary workers, like the Italians, or of permanent residents, like the Irish? In Hong Kong, Singapore, and Arab countries, Filipinos are necessarily temporary workers, not allowed to remain once their employment contract expires.[79] In Canada, Filipinos, like the Irish, become permanent residents because immigration policy encourages this decision. Many Filipinos have integrated permanently into Canadian society, giving their adult skills to the nation and sponsoring their family to join them.

Filipino parents see their brand of Catholicism as offering a healthier lifestyle than Canadian secularism. They believe Canadian schools to be less competitive than Filipino schools, but know that Canadian university degrees carry prestige around the world. Parents adjust their family lifestyle to accommodate the Canadian climate and cultural imperatives, but remain committed to Filipino Catholic cultural values. Generational conflict is muted when families, through regular discussion, soften their desire to maintain Filipino traditions and make adjustments to Canadian culture. Yet it must be admitted that Canadian-educated third-generation Filipinos are less committed to Filipino traditions and Catholic religion than their parents and grandparents are.

Filipinos encounter discrimination in Canada until they adjust to the new culture by getting work, finding a home, and sending their children to Canadian schools. They appreciate the Canadian medical system, with all its surgery and wonder drugs, yet Filipinos, like other Asians, find natural remedies suitable for minor illnesses. Empirical research reveals that Filipinos are "less likely to use mental health services through both primary care and psychiatry" than Canadian-born citizens.[80] Jonathan Okamura writes that the common perception of any nation is an "imagined" reality of a people scattered in far distant lands perceiving themselves to be united as a people. Filipino communities in Canada have this imagined sense of unity with Filipinos around the world, but this same ethnic community is also reinforced by the international religious bonds that weld it into world solidarity.[81] Using the techniques of narrative analysis and historical research, it becomes more obvious that Filipinos, as a people, share the double bond of faith and ethnicity. Despite external pressures, we see in this study that the ethnic identity of Filipino Canadian Catholics, which includes a deep commitment to the preservation of religious and cultural values, remains intact in the first generation, as Anita Beltran Chen also pointed out, but is considerably weaker in the second and third generations. The Canadian-born generation of Filipinos assists older Filipino Canadians in casting off the colonial mentality by retaining the core traditions of Filipino culture. Immigration trends tell us that Filipinos in Canada are a strong, cohesive, inculturated Catholic community, but, as Professor Chen points out, the future remains to be written.[82] Filipino Canadians over the past 40 years have shown the flexibility to integrate and the ability to resolve cultural clashes between the first and following generations. In the process of integration, Filipinos have contributed energy to the Canadian Church, offered health care to the Canadian nation, and have deepened their own identity as Filipino Canadian Catholics.

St. Andrew Kim, the first Korean martyr saint, 1845

5

Korean Canadians:
Cohesion and Acceptance

K orean culture goes back through the corridors of time more than 5,000 years.[1] Korean Christianity can be traced to the seventeenth and eighteenth centuries, when Korean scholars made annual visits to China.[2] On one of these visits to Beijing, Lee Seung-hoon sought out Christians at the South Church; he studied the Christian books Matteo Ricci wrote in Mandarin in the seventeenth century and dialogued with his Jesuit successors. Lee Seung-hoon asked the Chinese Christians for baptism and received his wish in early 1784. Returning to Seoul with Christian books, crucifixes, and images, he instructed and baptized his friends Lee Pyök and Francis and Ambrose Kwon. This date of 1784 since then is celebrated as the beginning of Christianity in Korea.[3] Three brothers were also converted—Jung Yak Chon, Yak Chong, and Yak Yong, the latter of whom was a favourite advisor to the king and was later martyred for the faith along with his whole family.[4] A lay community of Christians emerged from these early beginnings. Working from the description of Catholic practices in the Chinese books, they confected the sacraments of the Church as they understood them. "It is significant to note," as G. Thompson

Brown points out, "that the founding of the Catholic Church in Korea came about by the spontaneous efforts of the Koreans themselves."[5]

It was over 60 years later, in 1846, that Andrew Kim Tae-goon was officially ordained as the first Korean Catholic priest. Some of the courtiers, jealous of Christian influence at court, plotted to persecute Christians. The emperor feared Christians as agents of Western imperialism and ordered more than 10,000 of them put to death. Andrew Kim and more than 100 Koreans martyred in 1846 were canonized by the Catholic Church in 1984.[6] At the beginning of the 21st century in South Korea, Christians are 41 per cent of the population of 49 million, and Buddhists are 23 per cent. Protestant congregants number 16,550,000, or 31 per cent, whereas Catholics represent 4,900,000 or 9 per cent. Catholic evangelization since the Second World War greatly increased the Catholic presence in Korea.[7] According to Thomas Fox, the Catholic population doubled to over four million, and "today the Catholic Church in Korea is experiencing the highest annual adult baptism rate in the world, a trend also true among Koreans living in America."[8]

In Canada, according to the 2001 Census, there are 100,660 Korean Canadians, of whom approximately 16,106 are Catholic, 66,436 are Protestant and 4,026 are Buddhist.[9] In Surrey, British Columbia, the pastor of the Korean community of 6,500 persons is Father Joseph Tae Woo Lee at St. Andrew Kim Church. In Edmonton, Father John Baptist Joo-Ho Lee is the pastor of 650 persons at St. Jung Ha Sang Korean Catholic church. In Calgary, Father Yong Sik Hwang is the pastor of the Korean community of 1,500 persons at St. Anne's Korean church. In Saint-Boniface, Father Philippe Tae Koo leads the Manitoban Korean Catholic Mission of 50 families at Holy Cross parish.[10]

A Montreal community was formed soon after Korean immigrants began arriving in Canada in December 1976. The Archdiocese of Montreal, under the Fabrique Act, formed the Assumption of the Blessed Virgin Mary Korean Mission in 1979.

Father John Pellissier was appointed acting pastor, and six members were named as wardens. In 1982, Father Joseph Yong-Ho Kim arrived from Daegu, Korea, as the new pastor for Koreans in Montreal. Monseigneur Willard was appointed temporary pastor in 1984 when Father Kim transferred to the Boston archdiocese. The following year, Father Bernard K-Hong Kim from Busan, Korea, arrived as acting pastor. Benedictine Sisters from Busan joined the Korean Mission in 1990. Father Matthew Jong-Ok Ko became the acting pastor in 1991. Numbering more than 200 families, the Catholic Mission was renamed the Korean Martyrs' Catholic Mission in 1995. Father Pierre Ki-Tek Sung in 1998 was appointed pastor to replace Father Ko, who retired, and the following year the Korean Mission celebrated its 20th anniversary. Two Sisters of the Immaculate Heart of Mary of Mirinae arrived at the mission to share in the ministry. The community in Montreal grew to 250 families.[11]

Seven hundred Koreans now gather at the old Saint-Cunegonde, which has been renamed Saints-Martyrs-Corées, on rue Saint-Jacques. Of the 3,760 Koreans in Montreal, 700 are Catholic, and on average 250 attend the Eucharistic celebration on Sunday in the great baroque church.[12] Most parishioners live in West Montreal and drive into the city for Sunday mass. Others attend churches in their neighbourhoods. Korean Martyrs is the only Korean Catholic church in Quebec. By contrast, there are eleven smaller Protestant Korean communities in the province.

Korean Martyrs church in Montreal has about 15 adults in the RCIA program preparing to receive baptism. Six children will also be baptized during the year. Parishioners are divided into ten prayer groups. Meetings include prayers, Bible readings, personal sharing, and a meal of Korean food. Youth gather weekly in two groups, according to age. A seniors' group meets one afternoon a month for prayer, a time that includes a social and occasional pilgrimages. They pray as a group for their deceased ancestors. Other prayer groups at Korean Martyrs include the Legion of

Mary, which has five presidia (groups), Marriage Encounter, and the Cursillo movement. Our Lady of Peace prayer group meets weekly, as does a charismatic group. Parishioners especially appreciate the time for contemplative prayer during exposition of the Blessed Sacrament and the holy hour on Thursday. The Korean Martyrs' mission in Montreal has no parish hall for community gatherings and celebrations. [13]

In Toronto, the Korean Catholic community first gathered at the Catholic Information Centre in 1968. By the beginning of the 21st century, two Toronto Korean Catholic communities gathered in two locations: St. Andrew Kim parish in Toronto, guided by Father Gregory Choi, and Sacred Heart of Jesus parish in Etobicoke, guided by Father Antigonus Min-Kyu Park. St. Andrew Kim lists 7,000 parishioners, while Sacred Heart has 2,700. For the purpose of this study, 21 members of St. Andrew Kim parish were interviewed, along with the Father Gregory Choi, Father Antigonus Park of Sacred Heart of Jesus, and Father Pierre Ki Tek Sung of Korean Martyrs in Montreal.

Economic Acculturation

Slow Recognition: The Story of John and Elizabeth Park

John Chong Kook Park graduated with a B.A. from Dan Kook University in Korea in 1964. He entered the South Korean Air Force and achieved the rank of major, managing aircraft maintenance. Elizabeth Hyung Za graduated with her B.A. from Myung-Ji University in 1969 and taught junior high and high school. John and Elizabeth married at Seoul in 1970 and had two children, Julie and Peter. Elizabeth's sister, Theresa Oh, already in Canada, agreed to sponsor them as newcomers. Desiring an improved economic standard for their family, they arrived in Canada in 1974.

John hoped to work as an aircraft engineer, but upon coming to Canada had to lower his job expectations. Changing his language of work from Korean to English was difficult for him, as it is for most Koreans.[14] When applying for his first job, he was asked whether he had "Canadian experience." The demand for Canadian experience means that the applicant understands English well enough to negotiate the job, understand Canadian workers, and meet customers' needs. To get Canadian experience, John had to load chickens on a truck for a day and a half and clean rooms in a warehouse for a day. Then he landed a job as a motion mechanic on an aircraft assembly line at De Havilland. His technology skills were recognized and, in due time, he was made an aircraft mechanic, yet his management skills remained unrecognized. After fifteen years on the job, he was appointed an upgrader inspector, which continued until his retirement. He had to pass intermittent tests in English on new aircraft technology, which demanded careful study and preparation. In a published article, Chai-Shin Yu sums up the difficulty, writing that "most Korean immigrants are not able to continue their professions in Canada .... They lack knowledge of English, have no Canadian educational background, or Canadian work experience. They would be unable to get well-paid jobs, and in low-paying jobs, they would experience discrimination and isolation."[15]

In Korea, most women stay at home, but in Canada 74 per cent of Korean women go to work.[16] Elizabeth also had to lower her job expectations and develop English language skills. While an elderly Korean woman looked after her two children, Elizabeth worked on the assembly line. She took classes at Seneca and Centennial colleges and the University of Toronto to upgrade her English comprehension. She eventually got a job as a secretary at the Toronto District School Board, which employed her for 24 years. On weekends, she taught at the Korean school, which grew to five classes, and eventually she became its principal. She had five volunteers working with her.

John is a cradle Catholic. Elizabeth was a Buddhist who, after coming to Canada, investigated Christianity, first as a Presbyterian, but eventually chose to be baptized a Catholic in 1981. They say morning and evening prayers, the daily rosary, the stations of the cross and novenas to the Sacred Heart of Jesus and Our Lady of Mercy. Elizabeth likes to meditate on the Bible and contemplate before the Blessed Sacrament. At St. Andrew Kim, John and Elizabeth have leadership positions on numerous committees, being directors for the Korean Canadian School, Seniors' Bowling Club, and Korean Air Force Veterans Association. The prayer groups at St. Andrew Kim offer assistance to new Canadians getting settled in a house, finding work, and enrolling their children in school. Scholar Young-Sik Yoo points out that the churches function as information centres "where traditional Korean values and those of the new Canadian society can coexist under one roof."[17] St. Andrew Kim prayer groups also reach out to visit nursing homes. The Korean Canadian community is socially active in civil and religious affairs.

Family decisions for the Parks were made by ongoing arrangements. To buy a house or car or some major object of mutual concern, the family discussed the decision before it was final. The parents encouraged their children to attend Korean language school, honour their ancestors, celebrate holidays, and enjoy Korean foods on national days such as Independence (August 15) and Korean New Year. In regard to schools for their children, John and Elizabeth sent Peter to Brebeuf High School and Julie to University of Toronto Schools. During high school, the children stopped attending Sunday mass, and their decisions were respected. By the time the question of university came along, the children were old enough to make their decisions. Both chose the University of Toronto: Julie for archeology and Peter for chemistry. The parents encouraged their children to speak Korean, but the children preferred speaking English. The parents admitted that the children politically and socially follow their own insights, and when the question of marriage comes up, will make their own decisions. John and Elizabeth arrived at a modus vivendi with their Canadian children; although some conflict took place, it was manageable. The parents use both the Korean and English news media, and for entertainment, choose bowling, golf. and gym workouts. Their adult children live mostly in English and use the English media. As educated professionals, John and Elizabeth Park never regained in Canada the full status of their Korean employment, but they were able to adapt to make a reasonable transition. Although their credentials were slow to be recognized, they gained sufficient earning power in Canada to enjoy life and be middle-class Canadians.[18]

Changed Expectations: The Story of Peter Yang Hwan Oh and Othilia Young Sook Oh

Peter Yang Hwan Oh was born in Korea, completed his B.A. at Yonsei University in 1979, and began working for Samsung Electronics Company. Othilia Young Sook Oh was born in Korea and baptized a Catholic at Hong-Ik University in 1980. She completed her Master of Fine Arts in 1986, taught fine arts and began to paint. Peter and Othilia married in 1986 in Seoul; they have two boys, Michael and Anthony. In Korea, Peter had a long workweek, which included the consumption of alcoholic beverages, which was destructive. Against the wishes of his Protestant mother, he became a Catholic in 1990; Catholicism gave him the moral support to stop drinking and begin immigration proceedings. Peter took his family for a visit to New Zealand in 1994. But after checking the United Nations' report on the living conditions of various countries, they decided in 1998 to immigrate to Canada to improve their environment and the education of their children. With 30 per cent of Korean newcomers possessing university degrees, Korean Canadians are the most highly educated national group to arrive in Canada.[19] Their new country offers them the hope of a shorter workweek to improve the quality of their lives, prayer, and spirituality. Peter, having spent some years working in Saudi Arabia, was accustomed to speaking English; he adjusted to Canadian English and began selling real estate. Othilia, who found English difficult, returned to school to polish her schoolgirl knowledge of the language so she could function more professionally.

Their children—Michael, 18, and Anthony, 17—began their education in Korea, where they received Catholic instruction on Sunday. When in Toronto, they attended public schools but, owing to a conflict in the schoolyard, moved to a Catholic school where they felt better accepted. St. Theresa's High School required school uniforms and instructed them in religious knowledge. This move improved the quality of their lives. The boys understand and speak Korean and enjoy Korean food. Their parents believe Korean food is healthier than Canadian food because Korean food is cooked with a variety of vegetable oils and includes tofu, beans, and kim-chi (the spicy Korean national dish of pickled cabbage, onions, and seasonings). The boys attend mass in Korean on Sunday with their family. Peter and Othilia, learning from the Cursillo movement and Marriage Encounter the importance of joint prayer and family dialogue, share their religious faith with their children. They realize that young people must be led to God, which takes time, gentleness, and patience. After the tension of migrating and becoming established in Canada, the family was drawn together by prayer and dialogue. The boys love working on their computers and play computer games by the hour. The parents encourage them to be faithful to God and to study diligently. The boys do not smoke, drink, or date. Michael has enrolled in life sciences at the University of Toronto, and Anthony will pursue dental technology at George Brown College. The parents expect them to marry Korean Catholic women when they arrive at that point in their lives.

Peter and Othilia connect with Canadian life primarily through their colleagues and via the English media, news outlets, and videos, although they do like reading Korean newspapers.[20] They are involved in Canadian life and intend to live out the rest of their days in Canada. In a study on acculturation, Uichol Kim and John W. Berry concluded that the "preferred" path for Korean Canadians is to adopt a "dual identity," Korean and Canadian, and integrate into the host society by avoiding assimilation to or separation from the host culture.[21]

Peter made a Cursillo in 2003, which changed his life. He realized that for him "prayer is the beginning, the process and the end of life." Othilia made a Cursillo soon after Peter, and the following year, they both made a Marriage Encounter Weekend. At home, they have a prayer room, say morning and evening prayers, invoke the help of God the Father, the Son and the Holy Spirit, and pray for the intercession of Mother Mary. Peter and Othilia read the Bible and contemplate the Scriptures to receive the gift of the Holy Spirit. They discovered that prayer helps them to adjust to the demands of Canadian life and is a miraculous gift for positive thinking. Professor Tan points out that a careful reading of the Bible reveals that "the primary concern of the Bible is our identity formation, that is *who we are* in the grace of God rather than moralistic exhortation for what we must do."[22] As part of his prayer life, Peter likes to sing and share his religious life freely with others. He prays throughout the day and, as he sells real estate, tries to imitate the life of Jesus. Othilia, through her faith, encounters the love of God in her prayer. She and Peter attend daily mass when possible, but feel especially nourished by being present at Sunday mass. They read spiritual works such as Thomas H. Green's *Opening to God*, Tom Keating's *Open Mind and Open Heart*, and the fourteenth-century mystical work *The Cloud of Unknowing*. They are members of Cursillo, Marriage Encounter and a Bible study group. They believe that Korean Canadians bring to the Canadian Catholic Church the gift of the Cursillo movement, which results in a strong faith in God's love and an unbreakable marriage bond.[23]

Deception Turned to Opportunity: The Story of Joseph Lee and Kathy Kyounghee

Joseph Lee completed his bachelor of science in Korea in 1982, then served in the South Korean Army. Kathy Kyounghee completed her first science degree the same year. Kathy and

Joseph married the following year. Both desired further studies. Kathy returned to Sungkyunkwan University, completed her master's degree in 1984, and began working as a pharmacist. Joseph wanted to study abroad and begin work on a doctorate degree. They found an advertisement in a Korean newspaper from a Toronto pharmacy offering pharmacists a work visa for $5,000 to help solve the shortage of pharmacists in Canada. Joseph and Kathy agreed that they would move with their small children to Toronto to find work, and Joseph could pursue his doctorate degree, after which they could return to Korea. Joseph and Kathy and their two children, John and Elizabeth, arrived in Toronto in 1989. The Canadian pharmacy owner who had offered the job said that owing to a economic recession, he was not interested in hiring at that time, and Kathy should look for work elsewhere. Later, Joseph and Kathy found out that he was running a racket of handing out employment letters for large sums of money without ever hiring anybody. They wrote off the $5,000 they had paid for the so-called work visa as the price of learning Canadian ways. They see the letter that offered them work as facilitating their passage to Canada.

Despite the downturn in the economy, Kathy and Joseph found positions in pharmacies, and Joseph enrolled part-time at the University of Toronto in toxicology. He earned his Canadian pharmacist licence in 1990. Kathy earned her licence in 1991. Joseph was working as a licensed pharmacist and going to university, but his colleagues questioned why he wanted to take time from a professional salary to pursue a graduate program at his own expense. Their reasoning impressed him; after ten months, he terminated the graduate program and settled into the Canadian daily work routine. Meanwhile, Kathy worked for a local pharmacist who hired her specifically because she spoke Korean to his Korean clients. After a time, the store owner invited Kathy to take over management of the store; Joseph soon joined her at the pharmacy, and they became partners with the owner. The deception that brought them to Canada turned out in the long run to their benefit as they became owners of their own pharmacy.

Family decisions for the Lees are made through casual chats between parents and children without necessarily waiting for a family discussion. The parents have taken the Parent Education and Training program to improve dialogue skills with the children. Kathy and Joseph have tried to instill in their son and daughter respect for their elders, the celebration of Korean festivities with Korean food and traditional dress, and the practice of the Catholic faith. The children, their parents admit, reveal thus far little sense of religious faith in their lives, but do join the family at church as a shared activity. On the lunar New Year, the children come to their parents and ask for their blessing, and then receive a small purse of money. John and Elizabeth understand Korean and can speak the language. John graduated from high school at University of Toronto Schools in 2003 and chose to enroll in architectural studies at the University of Waterloo. Elizabeth completed high school at Havergal College and is pursuing pharmaceutical studies at Albany College of Pharmacy. When their children were in school, Kathy and Joseph would have welcomed more contact with the teachers, but found that linguistic difficulties and cultural differences prevented more direct conversations.

Koreans in general do not approve of inter-ethnic marriages. Kathy and Joseph hope that their children will marry Korean Catholics, but are prepared to accept the Canadian system of the young making their own choices. If a choice were necessary, their religious choice would be more important than their ethnic choice. Kathy and Joseph would prefer a Catholic in-law who is not Korean to a Korean in-law who is not Catholic.

Joseph's mother lives in Korea and is supported by his siblings there. Kathy's mother is an independent, self-supporting retired fashion designer who likes to spend the winter in Korea and the summer in Toronto. She speaks Korean with her grandchildren and makes them aware of their Korean roots and culture.

The dissimilarity of the Korean language to English is a major problem for Korean newcomers. When Joseph was first working at the pharmacy, he feared the ringing telephone for the problems it would bring him when he picked up the receiver. He tried to understand the English speakers but his worst nightmare was understanding the slurring words of sick or intoxicated patrons demanding service. When Kathy and Joseph discovered they were able to anticipate telephone requests, they felt more comfortable and were at ease on the job. As they integrated into Canadian culture through the years, their primary concerns changed. In their home, they rely on the English media for news and information, but still enjoy Korean films and videos. They no longer plan to return to Korea, since it makes more economic and personal sense to remain in Canada as their chosen country.

Both Joseph and Kathy have made Annotation 19 retreats in the Korean language to learn Ignatian meditation and contemplation. Their parish is divided geographically into small prayer groups that meet monthly to reflect on Bible readings for the following Sunday. Their group reads a scriptural passage three times, reflects on it, and discusses it. Joseph likes to pray by picking up his guitar and singing gospel hymns. Kathy and Joseph are members of Marriage Encounter, meeting monthly to share with married couples their faith experiences. They also are members of the Cursillo movement and the Christian Life Community. Other prayer groups in the parish are the Legion of Mary, with 400 members and 30 presidia (sections) who pray for the church and work actively among the Korean community.

Korean Catholics have websites in Korean with some English, which offer information on the Korean churches in Toronto and in Mississauga. The Korean Catholics have two large churches, whereas Korean Protestants have 250 small worshipping groups. Koreans Catholics have two pastors assisted by other clergy, whereas the Protestants have a multitude of pastors competing for the loyalty of Korean Christians. A Korean Catholic committee provides help to newcomers to find apartments, schools, and church services. According to Joseph and Kathy, Korean Catholics in their care for others bring to the Canadian Catholic Church strong faith, fervent prayer, and cohesive marriages and families.[24]

Forgiveness and Dialogue: The Story of Jerome and Margaret Hong Kim

Jerome Hong Kim was born in Korea, completed his architectural degree at Hanyang University in 1966, and worked nine years as an architect for the Korean Air Force and the Korean Ministry of Education. Margaret Ran was born in Korea, completed her degree in graphic arts at the University of Hong-ik in 1970, and worked as the art director for large corporations. Both Buddhists, they were married in 1975. Living in a geographically small country with high population density, Jerome decided it was time to go to Canada, which offered open space and economic opportunity. For Margaret, Canada, with its thriving economy, was an economic dream, and with its extensive geography was a spacial vision, so she agreed with Jerome's decision. A Korean doctoral student at the University of Toronto echoed their thoughts in a chapter of his dissertation where he developed the image of Canada as "God's Country."[25]

Jerome and Margaret arrived in Toronto in November 1975. In the new year, Jerome started searching for work, while Margaret, who was pregnant, remained at home. After five months and about 200 interviews, Jerome found his first job in Canada. Although his Korean credentials were not recognized, he found a position as an architect. In fact, he was paid according to the work he did, which turned out to be in line with the salary to which his credentials entitled him.

Jerome and Margaret, who had learned English at school in Korea, sometimes spoke English at work there. In Canada, a central problem for Jerome was not the language but the shift from the Korean to the Canadian context. Awkward situations arose. Trying to decipher the body language and cultural meaning in the words of Canadians caused both of them considerable anxiety.

They invited Jerome's mother to Canada. She cared for their daughter so Margaret could look for work. With a freshly prepared portfolio of her work, Margaret found a position as an art director in an advertising agency. Shortly afterward, her firm merged with another firm, and the work became highly competitive. Staff members were laid off. She kept her position, but found that at a certain point her professional integrity demanded that she leave the office because of its shoddy printing work. After an impasse with her boss, she was fired, but was soon hired by another firm. Anger from this bad experience lingered in her heart.

Jerome and Margaret had participated for ten years in the small Buddhist groups in Canada. In 1987, Margaret started testing Christian churches, for she was missing something in her life and longed for more meaning. She began attending Protestant churches, but her search led her to the Catholic Church. "For the first time when she walked into a Catholic church, she felt at home right away and was at peace. Her spiritual journey had begun, and she never forgot the feeling she got the first day she walked in the church. When she was baptized in 1988 with their children, Jerome was somewhat surprised at the speed of Margaret's move, but he was fully supportive." After many debates, Jerome started attending baptism preparation class the following spring. Margaret's wish to see Jerome become a Catholic was "so strong" that it in fact turned him off. He would not promise to be baptized, but "hoped to get a certain calling by attending the preparation class."

In September 1989, at Margaret's insistence, Jerome and Margaret went on a Marriage Encounter Weekend. Although Jerome felt forced to attend the weekend, it was at this weekend "where he encountered his inner self." He realized that he did not have to be perfect and that he could forgive himself and others their faults. "After this inner experience, Jerome became easy with himself and his surrounding and he decided to become a Catholic." Jerome was impressed with the Marriage Encounter Weekend because it encouraged a dialogue of mutual sharing, opening couples to each other in mutual acceptance. Jerome and Margaret became a team couple, which meant sharing their married experience openly with those taking the weekend.

Margaret, involved in a charismatic prayer group, learned to forgive her former boss for the hurt he had caused her. The long, simmering anger in her heart disappeared "like snow melting under the warm spring sun." This forgiveness healed her upset stomach, renewed her energy, and made her appearance more youthful. Her family, arriving in Canada after this event, remarked on her bright appearance and positive mental attitude. Learning to forgive her former boss was an important forward step for Margaret. "It was similar to the Israelites being led by Moses from the slavery of Egypt through the Red Sea to the freedom of the Promised Land." She and her husband came to Canada for material prosperity, but instead found happy spiritual lives, which they had not sought. She now wants to know more and more about Christianity. Through the process of becoming Canadian Catholics, the Kims discovered what it means to experience the risen Christ in their lives. Margaret brought herself to seek reconciliation with her former boss by mailing him a beautiful, handcrafted Christmas card. Margaret eventually began freelance work, which gave her time for her work and her children.

Their children, Eunice and Brian, were born in 1976 and 1980, and Margaret took time out from her career to be with them. The children were educated in Canadian schools and embraced Canadian culture. Jerome's mother acquainted them in their early years with Korean language and culture. The children understood Korean but responded in English. Margaret loved her mother very much and was happy with Korean nurture for the children. She believed in raising the children according to the Korean customs in which she was raised. The Korean scholar Young-Sik Yoo explains that "modern Korean cultural values and social structures are still based on the vertical, hierarchical model derived from Confucianism." The children are "taught to obey their parents, honour their elders, and protect the family name."[26] From Jerome's point of view, this meant that the children were trained to say "yes" to their parents and "yes" to their teachers without the benefit of developing their own identity and views. Jerome read current literature about parenting and chose the liberal approach of discussion and giving the children leeway to enjoy their own successes and regret their failures. He believes that in Canada, where there is more space and opportunity, young people need to be educated to utilize the creativity of their own skills and develop their own identity. The diverse approaches of their parents left Eunice and Brian in some confusion, but they recognized that each one has to work out his or her own Korean Canadian Christian identity.

Margaret, even more than Jerome's mother, tried to imbue their children with Korean culture. This meant teaching the children the importance of family reverence and visiting the cemetery to remember the deceased. Margaret admits that she is much less interested in teaching their children Korean ways than in teaching them Christian ways. She sees little conflict between Buddhist/Confucian and Christian religious practices. On Memorial Day, the Kims honour deceased family members by visiting the cemetery, and on Christmas and New Year's, they attend Mass and home celebrations. They find that Eunice and Brian have to be enticed to embrace Korean Christian culture, but are currently going through an awakening in this regard. When they were younger, they were not enthusiastic to kneel before their parents and ask for a blessing on New Year's Day, but now, after Eunice's visit to Rome, she and her brother have become better friends with their parents, giving them reverence and affection, and going with them to religious and national celebrations.

Margaret and Jerome pray their children will marry Catholics, or people who might become Catholics in the future. They hope their children will choose a Korean spouse, but would not insist. The Kims rely mainly on the Canadian news media for information and are committed to spending the rest of their lives in Canada.

Margaret spends time in front of the Blessed Sacrament contemplating the life of the Lord. She reads the lives of the saints, attends a Bible class, has attended the New Catechism class at St. Andrew Kim, and has talked to the class about the Lord's Prayer. For twelve years, she has been a member of the World Apostolate of Our Lady of Fatima. Two years ago, Margaret joined the Legion of Mary, which inspires her greatly by its good works. The Marian Movement is especially precious to Margaret. Many of its principal teachings are found in *The Marian Movement of Priests* by Father Stefano Gobbi. This volume has given her spiritual direction and had a powerful influence on her life. The Blessed Virgin Mary has taught her to transcend her own problems and to reach out to others. Margaret has moved from the more enthusiastic prayer of the Charismatic Movement to the quiet prayer of the Marian Movement. The Catholic sacrament of reconciliation has taught Margaret the Marian way of contemplation and graciousness.

Jerome, when praying in the evening, likes to sit down and reflect. He likes to pray while listening to music, playing golf, doing Tai Chi, and reading good books, such as the life of the Dalai Lama. He feels God's presence through these activities and finds a link to prayer. A prayer group he and Margaret like is the neighbourhood Korean prayer group. Newcomers who do not yet have work and are anxious to meet others also attend this group. Jerome and Margaret recruit couples for Marriage Encounter Weekends, which enrich the lives of married couples. They attend daily mass together, say the rosary before they retire for the night, and know they are together on the spiritual journey of life.

What do Korean Canadian Catholics contribute to the Canadian Church? Korean Catholics, according to Margaret and Jerome, are very faithful Catholics who attend mass and cultivate their spiritual life. They add that Koreans avoid individualism, are group oriented, and desire to belong to something bigger than themselves. Korean culture demands obedience from its adherents and the ability to give of oneself fully. When Koreans transcend the language and cultural differences of becoming Canadian, they become involved in Canadian society and give themselves generously. Korean Canadians admit that Euro-Canadians are more outgoing, and that Korean Canadians must learn this outgoing style in Canada. They learn much from their prayer groups, but how they ultimately integrate into the Euro-Canadian Church is yet to be determined. Jerome and Margaret Kim believe it is important for Koreans to accept limitations, be open, and contribute to the Canadian Church through their inherited gift of ethnic cohesion and strong faith.[27]

St. Andrew Kim church, Surrey, BC

Cultural Accommodation

Cultural Retention: The Story of Peter Choi

Peter Choi came with his family from Korea to Canada in 1988. His family, which included his mother Stella, his father Simon and his bother Paul, travelled first to Argentina and then to Canada. His father believed the family would be economically better off in Toronto than in Korea or Argentina. Back in Korea, his father was an engineer, but in Canada his father necessarily changed his employment expectations and opened a dry cleaning shop, which he and his wife Stella operate. Peter, after four years of high school and one year of English as a Second Language, attended the University of Toronto engineering program, studied philosophy at the Dominican College in Ottawa, and entered St. Augustine's Seminary in Toronto. He completed a Master of Divinity degree and was ordained a Catholic priest in May 2004.

Growing up, the two boys were not rebellious, and completed the tasks their parents set for them. While Peter was completing his divinity degree, Paul did a degree in business at York University. Both are fluent in English and Korean. Father Peter has a peer group of Korean Canadians from St. Andrew Kim parish, which helps him maintain his Korean culture. They read Korean newspapers on the Internet and subscribe to Korean magazines. They maintain their familiarity in the Korean language and culture to retain their personal identity as Korean Canadian Catholics. They respect their elders and savour the taste of Korean food. Both Father Peter and his brother are Canadian citizens and are permanently employed in Canada. When they gather in Toronto as a family, they speak Korean, and at home Paul and his wife, Elizabeth, speak Korean with their young daughter. They consciously work to retain the Korean Catholic culture among Korean Canadians. For Father Peter's young niece, when she grows to a marriageable age, he will suggest she marry a Korean Catholic husband, but for the young couples he prepares for marriage at St. Anne's parish in Brampton, he readily accepts their choice of interfaith and inter-ethnic marriages.[28] Korean scholars tell us that for Koreans, "the church is both an acculturation agent and a resource for preserving culture and ethnic identity."[29]

To cultivate his own spiritual life, Father Peter likes to read the Bible, catechetical books, and commentaries on the Bible. He meditates on the Scriptures, prays the rosary daily, and says mass for parishioners each day. He makes the yearly diocesan retreat and enjoys meeting with his priestly support group. He sees the strong faith of the Korean community as a contribution to the Canadian Catholic church. This Korean gift to Canadians results in numerous vocations to the priestly and religious life. Korean Canadian Catholics, like other Asian Catholics, are not aggressive evangelizers among their own ethnic community. They are reluctant to seek out Korean Catholic newcomers, but wait patiently for newcomers to come to Catholic churches in Canada. Charity to others is spontaneous rather than proactive. Their Catholic faith gives them inner peace and helps them to intensify their ethnic solidarity.[30]

Diverse Paths of Integration: The Story of Stephan John Wone Choi and Cesillia Soon Ae Choi and their Children

Stephan John Wone Choi was born in Korea and earned his degree at Sung Sil University as a computer programmer.[31] In 1979, he married Cesillia Soon Ae Choi, and they soon became parents to two daughters, Suki and Ju Yeon. Stephan worked for a major Korean electronics firm, while Cesillia raised the children at home. Cesillia was from a Catholic family and graduated from a Catholic High School in Korea, while Stephan was from a Buddhist family. Stephan's Buddhist mother was a formidable force, casting a shadow on her son's marriage. For domestic peace and better education for their children, Cesillia made plans for the family to immigrate to Canada. They arrived in Canada in 1996; Stephan looked for a job in computer programming and sales, but was not successful due to his English. In Korea, he had had ten years of instruction of English grammar and syntax, but little practice speaking the language. Cesillia studied textbook English for six years in Korea, but also had no conversational experience. Thus, they decided to open a convenience store and work together as owners and operators of the store.

Their daughter, Suki, was fifteen when the family arrived in Canada. She finished her secondary education at Cardinal Newman High School in Toronto and graduated from York University in psychology in 2005. Her younger sister, Ju Yeon, went to Notre Dame Catholic School in Toronto and will go to university. While Suki is more Korean and traditional in her attitudes, Ju Yeon is quicker to embrace Canadian ideas and lifestyle. For instance, she does not always speak Korean at home. As a family integrating the Korean and Canadian cultures, they have seen the importance of family discussions and shared decisions in regard to purchasing a home, buying a car, courting the opposite sex, or choosing a university. The parents try to imbue their children with knowledge of the Korean language and culture, respect for elders, and regular practice of Catholic spirituality. The children are encouraged to volunteer to read at mass or serve at the altar. Cesillia regrets the fact that her family no longer attends daily mass as often as they did in Korea.

When parents return home from work, it is customary in a Korean home for the children to greet them at the door. Preoccupied with homework and the Internet, Canadian children are reluctant to leave what they are doing and wait at the door for their parents' return. The possibility of an interfaith or inter-ethnic marriage is not something the family wants to think about or discuss.[32] Suki's friends are mainly Korean Canadians, but Ju Yeon casts a wider net for friends. Korean Canadian professor Bo Kyung Kim discovered in his research that, whereas Korean youth showed the highest scores of identification with their parents and Canadian youth showed the least identification, Korean Canadians appeared "in the middle" between over-identification and under-identification.[33] In Suki and Jue Yeon, we see two siblings taking diverse paths of identifying with their parents and Korean tradition, with one child identifying more closely and the other less closely. The parents rely on Korean newspapers and videotapes for community information, whereas their children monitor both Korean and English media. The Choi family members are accommodating to Canadian life and intend to live out their lives in Canada.

For spirituality, Stephan and Cesillia attend daily mass and say the rosary. They attend Korean Bible Study, Legion of Mary, and charismatic prayer meetings. They also enjoy the monthly meeting of the Korean neighbourhood prayer group. Since 1988, they have been members of the Marriage Encounter movement. Suki attends Choice, which is a Marriage Encounter–sponsored group for the children of Korean members. Cesillia, as a group leader of the Legion of Mary, welcomes new Korean Catholics to Toronto and invites them to attend religious activities and social events at St. Andrew Kim. A number of Christians of other faiths joined St. Andrew Kim parish to be part of the many activities that dot the liturgical and social calendar. Korean Canadians also visit the various neighbourhood seniors' homes to assist with mealtime feeding.

The particular hallmark of Korean Canadian Catholics is their strong faith and regular devotional life. This is seen in the number of vocations they contribute to the priesthood and religious life. Small families generously contribute a son or a daughter to the service of the church. A busy community, St. Andrew Kim church conducts more than 100 baptisms yearly. Korean Canadians, and also Catholics from Korea, visit Madonna House at Combermere, Ontario, for retreats and longer periods. Madonna House has opened more than 20 Friendship Houses in Canada and around the world to care for the needy. Four young Korean Canadians of St. Andrew Kim parish have joined the religious community at Madonna House.[34]

Linking East and West: The Story of John Jai Don Lee

John Jai Don Lee was born in Korea, ordained to the Catholic priesthood, and completed his master of theology studies in 1985 at the Catholic University in Seoul. Upon the recommendation of environmental theologian Father Thomas Berry, the archbishop of Seoul asked Father Lee to enroll for doctoral studies in the Faculty of Theology at the University of St. Michael's College at the University of Toronto. He arrived at Toronto in 1997 to study ecotheology and completed his doctorate in 2004. The following year, he returned to Seoul to serve in the diocese. Offered the opportunity to teach graduate courses on Asian Theology, Ecotheology, World Religions, and Interreligious Dialogue in the Faculty of Theology at St. Michael's College, Father Lee returned to Toronto in 2006 to teach and do research in ecotheology. After two years at the Faculty of Theology, Father Lee returned to Korea to lecture at the theological centre at the Catholic University in Seoul.

Koreans, according to Father Lee, are traditional people, and Korean Canadians favour keeping Korean customs. Koreans born in a heavily populated, narrow peninsula are open to change, but in Korea they have little contact with outside influences to offer them alternative models. Korean Catholics hold very firmly to their religious life, church attendance, language and culture. They delight in Korean music, dance, and food. According to Father Lee, the young are receptive to retention of these values, and the Canadian Heritage Program supports them to maintain their language and culture.

In regard to the Korean family, Father Lee states that the father of the family is expected to make the principal decisions, but it is acknowledged that mothers in the quiet of the home have influence. Arranged marriages in Korea, and even more so in Canada, are disappearing. However, inter-ethnic marriages are not readily accepted by Korean families, nor would interfaith marriages easily be embraced. For instance, an ecumenical marriage between a Catholic Korean and a Presbyterian Korean would be problematic because of the puritanical rigidity of Presbyterian Koreans, says Father Lee.

A professional student of Asian theology, Father Lee sees the backbone of Korean spirituality to be the daily rosary, mass and the Legion of Mary. These devotions also include morning and evening prayers, and occasional weekends of Cursillo or Marriage Encounter. The devotional life among Korean Catholics is strong and well accepted into Catholic Church life in Canada. Korean Catholics make an effort to link Eastern and Western traditions in their Canadian devotional practices. Korean Canadian Catholics are a homogenous and cohesive group and offer the Canadian Church the solidarity of their strong Christian community. Although language is currently a barrier to easy integration into the Canadian Church, the Canadian Catholic Church allows visible minorities using their own language to thrive despite the dominance of[35] the English language group in the Archdiocese of Toronto.

Faith Community: The Story of Lisa Hye Young Min and Alexander Young Dai Kim

Lisa Hye Young Min graduated from Seoul National University in 1987 and began a career in music as a flute teacher and orchestra member. Alexander Young Dai Kim completed his bachelor's degree at Chun Ang University in 1987. Lisa and Alexander met when they were teachers in Sunday school. They married in 1989 in Seoul and had three children: Grace, Angelo, and Bona. The Kims moved to Canada in 1998. Before they came to Canada, they dreamed of opening a musical instruments store. They came to Canada hoping to make this happen. However, they found it difficult fitting in, so they started a convenience store and operated it for four years. As they worked, they learned more about Canadian culture and its people. As the years rolled by, they felt confident and thought that it was possible to achieve their dream. So they opened a baroque music store, which Lisa operates, and a convenience store, which Alexander operates. The English language was a central problem for them in acclimatizing to Canadian life. Lisa found, despite her textbook knowledge of English from grades 7 to 12 in Korea, that her spoken English was inadequate. For example, she went to a Canadian postal station to speak to a clerk. Not expressing herself clearly in English, she was simply ignored by the clerk. In confusion and frustration, she burst into tears. On another occasion, when she went to a bagel store that advertised a dozen bagels for a special price, she selected her twelve bagels and went to pay. The clerk, looking at her as an enemy alien, humiliated her by counting the bagels, as if she could not count them herself. Her son Angelo, after having the assistance of a tutor for three months, made the transition from being a Korean speaker to becoming a bilingual speaker. But when Angelo first attended a Canadian school, he remembers how the other kids in the class "made fun of my differences."

Family decisions are made together, but the parents chose the Catholic schools that the children attend. The parents want their children to retain the Korean Catholic customs of acknowledging adults by bowing, by additional bows on New Year's Day, and on their birthday to eat the birthday soup commemorating their gift of life. Angelo says that he and his sisters maintain these Korean Catholic traditions. The parents want their children one day to marry Korean Catholics, but Angelo would like to choose his own marriage partner when the time comes. The family relies on both the English and Korean media for news, information and for carrying advertisements of the music store.

The Kim family prays the rosary together in the evening, but each member also prays individually. Besides working full-time, Lisa and Alexander are members of Marriage Encounter, Cursillo and the neighbourhood prayer group. Korean Catholics assist new Korean Canadians to find housing, a car, schools, and church events, and help with other needs they may have. Angelo, a teenager, is a member of the Altar Servers, Readers and Youth Group, which helps teens to know each other, meet Korean Catholics, and help new arrivals to adjust. The deep faith in the Korean community helps it draw closer to God so they feel more comfortable in their new Canadian faith environment. Korean Canadians express their faith through regular prayer, the desire to go on pilgrimages, such as to Medjugorje and Fatima, devotion to Mother Mary, and supplying clergy for the archdiocese of Toronto.[36]

Religious Accommodation

Animating the People: The Story of Gregory Choi

Gregory Choi moved from Korea to St. Louis, Missouri, in 1970 to enroll as a graduate student of economics at St. Louis University. Completing his degree at Chicago in 1972, he taught English to Korean nurses, saw their need for priestly help, and sought to enter a Catholic seminary. After his acceptance in 1974 at St. Augustine's Seminary in Toronto, Gregory applied for immigration to Canada. He wished to become a priest and to work with the Korean community in Toronto. His competency in English was excellent, so he did not experience difficulty or discrimination.

The Korean community in Toronto first gathered in 1968 for Mass in Korean at the Catholic Information Centre on Bathurst Street. Over the next few years, the community grew from a few families to more than 7,000 parishioners today. The Korean Catholic community went through a series of chaplains, including Fathers Sung-Woo Lee and Byung-Do Pak, and a number of locations, including the churches of St. Helen, Our Lady of Mount Carmel, St. John the Baptist, and St. Paul. Father Matthew Ko was appointed the chaplain of the Korean Catholic community in 1969, opened the Korean Catholic Community Centre at St. Helen's, and became the first pastor of St. Paul's in 1981. Gregory Choi was appointed administrator of the Korean parish in 1976 and its second pastor in 1982. After the canonization of the Korean martyr Andrew Kim in 1984, and the completion of the $5.5 million church in North York in 1997, the Korean Catholic community adopted St. Andrew Kim. A rectory was purchased in the neighbourhood for the clergy, and a convent for the sisters.

In 1976, Father Choi and parishioners established the Korean Catholic Church Credit Union, which has generated $8.6 million in assets. Two years later, the Korean Language School was founded to educate third-generation Koreans. In 1982, it was renamed the Korean Heritage School. This school is one of 62 across Canada.[38] The school meets on Sunday afternoon from 3:00 p.m. to 6:30 p.m. and includes 300 students, twelve teachers and 31 volunteers. Korean parents are involved in the school "to help in the spiritual and cultural formation of their children," and the Korean Consulate has high praise for this work. Koreans are very musical; the parish also mounts an orchestra and numerous choirs for weekly liturgical celebrations.[39]

Father Choi believes that his principal ministry is to educate Korean Canadian Catholics in the Christian Scriptures, Catholic thought, and sound spirituality, and to facilitate their integration into Canadian life. He has the assistance of Father Justin Kim, a Korean graduate student at Regis College, and Canadian Fathers Terry McKenna and David Norris SJ. Their combined labours are rewarded by high attendance at the five Sunday liturgies, and the many confessions they hear.

Korean Canadians, according to Father Choi, are changing the way they care for the sick and the elderly. Seniors are traditionally cared for in the homes of their children. But two thirds of Korean Catholics have accepted Canadian ways to allow their parents to be professionally cared for in seniors', retirement, and nursing homes. Seniors are living longer, and many suffer from deterioration of their health; thus, their working children and their families find it difficult to provide the necessary care. Professor Chai-Shin Yu concurs with the changes in the Korean Canadian community as the second generation of

Korean Canadians, with both husband and wife working, "find it impossible to look after disabled parents."[40] Also, conflicts can arise between the mother and the mother-in-law living in the same house, which can make family life difficult. Seniors often initiate the move to their own accommodations in a retirement home, and encourage their peers to lower the tensions of home life by moving into a seniors' residence. The St. Andrew Kim community hall becomes a meeting place for seniors. The parish makes seniors a priority by facilitating semi-monthly meetings, including morning mass, lectures, prayers, and entertainment.

Family decision making, Father Choi believes, is changing among Korean Canadian Catholics. For instance, women are in the workforce helping to support the family, and, Father Choi estimates, are making 60 to 70 per cent of the family decisions. Many religious groups, such as Marriage Encounter and Couples for Christ, are encouraging husband and wife to share decisions and to consult with their family. But in Canada, Korean prayer groups promote the retention of Korean customs when possible, including the language, lunar New Year, respect for elders, and ancestral devotion.

Conflict arises between Korean parents and their Canadian-raised children. Parents may think that the children do not listen to or obey them. They are confused by their children's aggressive behaviour. The children, for their part, according to Father Choi, are highly motivated and study hard, but will call the police if the parents strike them. Wives suffering spousal abuse will do the same.

Koreans want to marry Koreans, but occasionally Korean Canadians will marry Chinese women, but not Euro- or Afro-Canadians. The resistance stems from ethnic or personal reasons and not from Church regulations. The Catholic Church will accept inter-ethnic or interfaith marriages, but asks that couples properly prepare. Father Choi observes that Korean men who have married a non-Korean wife can, as they age, again crave Korean food and regret that they have not married a wife who can cook Korean food for them. Not being in the habit of cooking, in their later years these men miss the aroma and taste of kim-chi cooking. In some cases, Father Choi asserts, this nostalgia can cause marriage breakup.

Ecumenical relations between Korean Catholics and Korean Protestants are not very warm. More than 200 Protestant ministers with limited education and strong denominational views are highly competitive with one another. They are responsible for about 250 small congregations in Toronto, their congregants are small in number, and their congregations are not affiliated with any of the mainstream Canadian Christian religions.[41] For them, anti-Catholicism is natural and has been passed down from decade to decade, from father to son. The ministers are zealous to maintain their position and, thus, are eager to recruit neophytes among the newly arrived Korean Protestants and Catholics.[42] By contrast, says Father Choi, the two Korean Catholic pastors guide two large parishes in North York and Etobicoke and limit their evangelizing propensities to their own parishioners.

The social welfare committee of the parish assists newly arrived Korean Catholics to find housing and schools and provides a translation service. In 1962, the first immigrants began to leave Korea to travel to the outside world in pursuit of work as miners and nurses in Germany. Immigration to Canada reached its peak between 1968 and 1980. After 1990, groups of Korean professionals, technicians, and investors arrived in Canada. For Koreans unfamiliar with English, learning the language is difficult.[43] When they were able to get work, it was hard to keep their jobs. With few language skills in English, many ended up operating convenience and fruit stores, dry cleaning shops and restaurants. They were taught how to operate the stores from early Korean arrivals and how to improvise when working in the Canadian business community. For Koreans living in an English or French milieu, language is the perennial problem. Father Choi says that in future at St. Andrew Kim, he will make English as a Second Language (ESL) classes a first priority of the parish.

Public schools are not very helpful to the Korean community because, desperate for funding, they tend to use ESL funds for other purposes.

Information is available through the local Korean newspaper and radio station and on the Internet. TV channels in Korean are beamed from Los Angeles and Seoul to Toronto. Some Koreans are able to live in Toronto without speaking English, relying on their family and the community for essential information. In contrast, their children are bilingual and take advantage of the media in both languages. Father Choi believes that 90 per cent of Korean Catholics remain in Canada as their country of choice, whereas the remaining 10 per cent have not yet made a decision about whether to stay.

The prayer groups at St. Andrew Kim are numerous and active, according to Father Choi. The Legion of Mary is a highly regarded Korean devotional group, of which the parish has 34 presidia (sections). They evangelize Korean Catholics and give hours of community service. The members say the daily rosary and carry out their *lectio divina*—pious reading—in front of the Blessed Sacrament. They make yearly Ignatian retreats. Parishioners, in general, are well instructed in prayer, and some are members of the Franciscan third order. The Charismatic Movement came to St. Andrew Kim in 1982 and meets every Thursday evening from 7:30 p.m. to 9:30 p.m. More than 1,000 parishioners have participated in the Charismatic Seminar. The Cursillo movement has welcomed more than 700 parishioners to weekend retreats, and another 700 parishioners have participated in weekend Marriage Encounters. The various prayer groups provide multiple spiritualities for the needs of parishioners.

Yet it is the weekend Eucharistic celebrations, which 35 to 40 per cent of parishioners attend, that unify and bind the parish together. According to Father Choi, Basic Christian community has 70 cells of ten to fifteen families each, which meet monthly for *lectio divina*, scripture study, and social life. The Basic Christian communities and the Legion of Mary are the evangelical arms of the Korean parish; members seek out Korean Catholics who might like to attend church services but who have not yet made connections with the community. As a refresher course, the parishioners study *The Catechism of the Catholic Church;* the program offers two sessions in the fall and two in the spring, according to Father Choi.[44] The director of lay ministry of the archdiocese of Toronto, Father Robert O'Brien, believes that St. Andrew Kim parish has proven to be "a highly effective model of organization and animation of lay people."[45]

Korean Canadian youth at St. Andrew Kim church, Surrey, British Columbia

Commitment to Prayer: The Story of Andrew Moon Young Ahn and Lucya Joe Eun Song

From a prominent Buddhist family, Andrew Moon Young Ahn completed his university degree at Korea University in 1971 and began a teaching career. From a Catholic family, Lucya Joe Eun Song finished her college degree in Seoul in 1974 and left for Canada to seek her fortune. She took English courses in Toronto and returned to Korea the following year. Lucya and Andrew were married at a Catholic church in Seoul in 1976. Although not a Catholic, Andrew promised to be baptized the next year. Andrew and Lucya had two sons, Louis and Lawrence, and a daughter, Christine. An uncle encouraged them to move their family to Canada, and, in 1977, they arrived in Toronto hoping for better life. Andrew wanted to enroll in graduate studies at the university, but gave up that ambition in order to meet immediate needs and adjust to Canadian life. He fulfilled his promise to Lucya and was baptized a Catholic in 1977.

Their first problem on arrival in Toronto was to generate cash flow to provide their livelihood. Andrew began work on the assembly line for a window and door company, while Lucya began on the assembly line for a glass company. For both, this was not only exhausting but dangerous work. Because of limited language skills, Andrew and Lucya decided to open a convenience store as the best way to get into the Canadian economy. From 1979 to 1988, they operated the store, working long shifts to keep the store open from 7:00 a.m. to 11:00 p.m. The long work hours prevented them from attending language school and upgrading their English. Their English deficiency showed up in various ways. For instance, a customer arrived at the store and asked Andrew for ketchup. Ketchup was not part of the Korean diet or vocabulary. Andrew shook his head, saying he did not have any ketchup. In disbelief, customer made a quick survey of the store and came back with the ketchup bottle in her hand, saying, "Here it is!" Embarrassed, Andrew rang it up, knowing he had learned a new word. One time when Lucya was tending the store, a customer asked her for *The Sun*. Lucya replied that "her son was at home in bed asleep. Why do you ask about my son?" The customer looked befuddled and insisted the store must have her favourite newspaper, *The Toronto Sun*. The tabloid was located, and the customer went away happy. Andrew and Lucya now laugh about these early encounters with Canadian culture.

To ease off on the long and punishing hours of labour at the convenience store, they closed the store and opened a sandwich shop at Yonge and Queen Streets from 1988 to 1994. They opened early in the morning to serve breakfast and lunch and continued until five in the afternoon, Monday through Friday. They accumulated a $0.5 million debt but, as a matter of conscience, refused bankruptcy and continued to pay off creditors. Lucya fell sick during these years from the long hours and continual worries. Scholar Young-Sik Yoo has commented that small Korean businesses "face a bleak future because of their owners' unhappiness in the face of the social and economic challenges confronting them."[46] Yet, the upside of the sandwich shop for Andrew and Lucya was that the shorter hours afforded them time to attend daily mass on a regular basis, which buoyed their spirits.

Between 1994 and 2003, they managed stores and restaurants for others, calling these years "their golden time." In 2003, they opened a fish and chips store, which serves lunch and supper six days a week. They admit that through the struggle to establish business in Canada, they learned to pray better and to bring their spiritual values into line with their life goals. Despite their hard work and financial setbacks, they give thanks to God that he has enriched their lives with a spiritual life of honesty and integrity.

At the Ahn home, family dialogues happen on an irregular basis. Being raised in Canada, their boys, Louis and Lawrence, did not learn to read and write Korean but do speak the language. Daughter Christine, having attended Korean classes, reads, writes, and speaks Korean. The parents sent the children to Catholic high schools: Louis and Lawrence went to Brebeuf and Christine to St. Joseph Academy at Morrow Park. When the time came to enter university, Louis chose Seneca College because he wanted to be a teacher. He likes sports and plays soccer, baseball, and hockey. When playing Triple A hockey, he was captain of his team. He dropped out after three years at Seneca

College to become a poker dealer for a charity game. Lawrence chose York University and is a sales manager for Procter and Gamble. Christine is an order person for Nestlé and may in future enroll at university. The children live at home with their parents. They like to watch Korean videos, sing, and celebrate Korean holidays. For the Ahn family, Canada is their country, and they watch English media for information and entertainment.

Lucya's father was a committed Catholic who gave her strong faith. She loved her father and wanted to pass on her faith intact to her children. Christine says, "Mommy's too Catholic!" but attends church on a regular basis. The boys attend occasionally. Bo Kyung Kim's study shows that "Korean Canadian female adolescents may create more intensive value conflicts with their parents" than their brothers, since the girls tend to be more independent.[47] Christine was dating a man who was neither sympathetic to Christianity nor a believer in God. Lucya spoke with her daughter about the long-term prospects of dating someone whose ideology is incompatible with her Christian beliefs. Christine appreciated her mother's wisdom and stopped seeing the young man. (It might also be pointed out that the Canadian style of heterosexual dating is not the Korean way.) Lucya and Andrew would like their children to marry Korean Catholics.

For prayer, Lucya loves to read the Bible and reflect on the Word of the Lord Jesus. For entertainment, she writes out the Bible, chapter by chapter, book by book. When she was sick, she relished the opportunity to contemplate scenes from Bible stories. As a family, she and Andrew say morning and evening prayers, pray the daily rosary, and attend daily mass at a nearby parish. They are members of the Legion of Mary, Cursillo, and the neighbourhood prayer group, of which Andrew has been a leader. On Thursday evening, they attend the Holy Spirit group, which prays over the mass readings for the next Sunday. While they prepare food at their restaurant, they listen to tapes and CDs of spiritual talks by well-known spiritual writers and theologians. The Legion of Mary is especially skilled in helping Korean newcomers in Toronto to locate housing, schools, health care, stores and transportation. Lucya and Andrew believe that Korean Catholics bring to the Canadian Church their intense prayer life. For the Ahns, the deep commitment of Korean Canadians to prayer strengthens familial cohesion, is productive of priestly vocations, and facilitates the newcomers' integration into Canadian life. [48]

Prayerful People: The Story of Theresa Eun Joo Lee and Paul Sun Young Lee

Theresa Eun Joo Lee completed her teacher training at Seoul Teachers' College in 1978 and began a teaching career. Paul Sun Young Lee finished his bachelor degree at Hanyang University and found a position in an office. Theresa and Paul were married at a Catholic church in Seoul in 1981 and began raising two children, Helena and Daniel. Paul's brother recommended that the family go to Canada; Paul agreed that this move would improve their quality of life and their children's education. They arrived in Canada in 1996 and opened a dry cleaning business. Although they knew some English, their conversational skills were weak. They found they had serious difficulty speaking with their children's teachers at school and, when in the hospital for treatment, communicating with the staff.

As a family, they discuss mutual concerns, such as dating and schools. Helena enrolled at University of Waterloo in mathematics and business, and Daniel went to Sheridan College for graphic animation. Helena, who received two thirds of her education in Korea, is more traditional. Daniel, who received two thirds of his education in Canada, is more acculturated to Canadian ways.[49] His Korean Canadian girlfriend greeted his family by saying "Hi" instead of bowing in the traditional manner that shows reverence for the elders. She sprawled across the furniture in a Canadian way, unlike the formal posture expected of Korean women. Canadian professors Kim and Berry point out that young Koreans in their high school years assimilate readily to Canadian ways, but later on, when at university, become aware of their "Koreanness" and recognize the importance of retaining their identity.[50] Theresa and Paul expect the children to marry Korean Catholics. Helena says that she hopes to choose a Catholic marriage partner. As a family, they honour annually their deceased grandparents on the day of their death. Yet it is the first son who is primarily responsible for this act of reverence, whereas the other children are not strictly obliged. The family celebrates together the Korean Lunar New Year and Independence Day. Paul and Theresa keep up with Korean events by visiting Korean friends, reading Korean newspapers, and attending Korean seminars at church. Although they work long hours and have little time for entertainment, they do enjoy North American films. By contrast, their children search for information on the Internet, on TV, and in magazines.

Koreans pray regularly and enjoy prayer. Theresa and Paul say morning and evening prayers and the daily rosary. They are members of the Third Order of St. Francis and, like St. Francis, read the Bible as the foundation for their imitation of Christ. They also pray in groups, go to seminars, and attend Bible study. They are members of the neighbourhood prayer group, which visits the homes of Korean newcomers to Canada and invites them to church socials and prayer groups. The members of prayer groups visit the aged in retirement homes and street people in hostels. Seeing their compatriots in need, Koreans have a great sense of urgency and solidarity.[51]

Service to the Canadian Church: The Story of Andrew Kim and Catherina Seung Ja

Andrew Kim and Catherina Seung Ja completed high school in Korea in 1958. Andrew was a designer for heating, ventilation, and air conditioning systems. Andrew and Catherina married at Seoul in 1965 and over the next few years had three children. In 1973, Andrew decided to take his family to Canada, believing his children would get a better education there. After arriving in Toronto, Andrew went to George Brown College for six weeks and then was able to find employment in a Canadian engineering firm. When the children were old enough for school, Catherina attended George Brown College for six months, where she enjoyed improving her English and learning computer skills.[52]

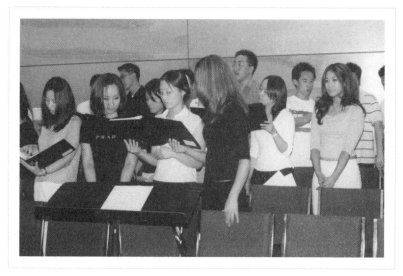

Korean Canadian young people sing at Mass
at St. Andrew Kim church, Surrey, British Columbia.

Andrew and Catherina raised their children, Yong Im, Min Ki, and Yong Hi, to speak Korean at home. During the week, the children learned English at school, but on the weekend they attended Korean Heritage School to maintain their Korean fluency and to read and write. They now work in English, but have retained their Korean culture and language. They performed Korean dancing at Toronto's annual Caravan festival of cultures and at military memorials at Ottawa. Yong Im completed her bachelor's degree in music at the University of Toronto and then entered religious life. She is now Sister Mary Theresina Kim of the Missionary Sisters of Charity, working in Washington, DC. While working on his master's degree in biochemistry at the

University of Toronto, Min Ki visited Honduras as a medical missionary and realized his call to become a Catholic priest and serve the larger community. He was ordained to the priesthood and is now known as Father Alexander Kim of the Legionnaires of Christ. Julianna Yong Hi completed her studies in French at the University of Toronto and is now working full-time in an office.

When the children were small, the parents made the decision about "Korean things," including that the children should learn Korean and study the culture. The children responded by doing this. While they were growing up, the children avoided incidents of generational conflict. Yet in regard to "Canadian things," as they grew older, the children made their own decisions in regard to university education and the career they would follow. The family continues their Asian respect and care of elders, meet for family gatherings at Christmas, Korean New Year, and birthdays, and enjoy Korean food and fellowship. On these occasions, as is the custom, they ask God to bless the food and those gathered around the table. The Kims practise their faith in a conscientious and intentional way. The Kims live in Toronto and expect to live out their lives in Canada.

News, sports, and Internet information are mainly gleaned from the English media. Yet Andrew and Catherina look to Korean videos for drama and entertainment. The Catholic newspapers from publishers in Toronto and the United States are available to them in the Korean language.

Andrew and Catherina say morning and evening prayers at home and attend daily mass at an English-speaking church near their home. Their prayers at home include the rosary and meditation on the Scriptures. They supplement their prayer by reading the Bible, spiritual books, and lives of the saints. They attend a Korean charismatic prayer group on Thursday evenings. As members of the Legion of Mary, they visit the sick in nursing homes and act as translators. Legion of Mary members also visit air terminals to welcome new arrivals from Korea and hand out literature welcoming newcomers to St. Andrew Kim Catholic church. Learning English is a major ministry for Korean Catholics. They help newcomers find ESL classes and various other services, such as Catholic schools for children. Despite being reluctant to accept Western medicine, they assist newcomers in procuring Ontario coverage for the health care of their families.[53] Korean Canadian Catholics have integrated into the Canadian Catholic church by generously inspiring their adult children by a lifetime of service in the Church and by performing the local ministries of visiting the sick, the poor, and the homeless.[54]

Conclusion

Koreans immigrate to Canada for various reasons and encounter numerous surprises when they arrive. The hardship of gaining "Canadian work experience" and accommodating to the Canadian lifestyle may reduce middle-class newcomers to working class until they can use their education and skills in a better way.

Older Korean Catholics make every effort to maintain their religious and ethnic cohesion. By this positive program of language maintenance, they deepen their personal identity as Korean Canadian Catholics. By contrast, many third-generation Korean Canadians adopt Canadian ways and are willing to limit their assimilation of Korean culture to the taste of Korean foods and the sharing of Korean memories, such as celebrating Korean Christmas and New Year, and remembering the dead. The diminishment of Korean language occurs among the second and the third generation, and they continue to delight in the Korean culture of music, dance, and food.

From our sample of 21 people, nine were soon employed by a Canadian company and twelve became self-employed. David Ley writes that self-employment is touted to be "a preferred occupational strategy," but what it means in reality in North America is that governments and businesses fail to take seriously their responsibility to assist struggling newcomers to fit in. This blindness "informalizes" the economy by creating marginal jobs that permit the avoidance of regulations and sharpen the competitive edge. Ley contends that ethnic economies are marginal and generate only fragile benefits, and reports that Koreans have "the highest level of self-employment" in both Canada and the United States.[55] They avoid an exclusively ethnic economy, which limits business opportunities, and they refrain from transnational business enterprises, which seldom prosper. Although the average rate of failure of self-employment is 50 per cent, Koreans have been exceptionally successful in their enterprises because they have a higher than average education and extend their business activities into mainstream Canadian markets.[56]

Since their credentials are not always recognized, Korean Canadians, to gain Canadian experience, must change their job expectations, open their own business, or take work that is offered to them. Their middle-class status in Korea is lowered to working-class status in Canada for a time. In some cases, Canadians take advantage of Korean Canadians, which is the unfortunate price newcomers pay for being in a strange land. Korean Canadian Catholics learn that forgiveness and starting their life again is the best route to avoiding the isolation that can afflict them.[57] They discover that they must put aside their Asian reserve and become more articulate and outgoing in the Canadian marketplace.

In search for Canadian support groups, Korean Canadians look to the Christian churches for help and guidance. They seek links to Canadian life and try to find meaning in their religious communities. In their search for meaning, they may begin attending Protestant churches, since these are smaller and more available. But for some, making this search leads them to one of the two Catholic churches, which have larger congregations and broader fellowship. Despite the dominance of English-language churches, Catholic churches of visible minorities thrive in

Toronto. Korean Catholics, through their church groups, plan to retain their Korean Catholic culture.

The intense faith of the members of the Korean Catholic community helps them draw closer to God so that in their new rootedness they feel more a part of the Canadian environment. Korean Canadians express their faith in regular prayer, devotion to Mother Mary, and a desire to go on pilgrimage. Yet it is the weekend Eucharistic celebrations in their churches that spiritually unify the parish and gather parishioners together. They learn that prayer helps them to adjust to the demands of Canadian life, offers hope during periods of immigration darkness, and is a bright light at the end of the conflictual cultural maze in which they find themselves. Although the language barrier impedes full integration into the Canadian Church, they are given enough space to expand and thrive as visible minorities, and in time, will contribute their ethnic cohesiveness and strong faith to Canadian Catholicism. The Korean Catholic community is endowed with energy, which desires to contribute to Canadian life.

Tamil Canadian youth at a charismatic meeting at St. Boniface church, Scarborough

6

Tamil Catholics:
A Search for Canadian Identity

Tamil Catholics from south India and northeastern Sri Lanka have arrived in Canada over the last 40 years. Although Tamils are predominantly Hindu, the Christian culture in India can be traced back to St. Thomas the Apostle in the first century,[1] to Syrian missionaries at Kerala in the fourth century, and to the later Catholicism of the Portuguese Franciscans and to the Jesuit St. Francis Xavier in the sixteenth century.[2] Some Tamils migrated from India to Sri Lanka, which was partly Christian, in the seventeenth century. Further Christian evangelization in subsequent centuries came from Dutch Protestants and the Church of England. Over one million Catholic Tamils live in Sri Lanka today. In Canada, 12 to 15 per cent of Tamils are Christian.[3] Catholic Tamils in Canada seek out parishes that provide Tamil liturgy and culture. In religious devotion, Tamils tend to be conservative and relish traditional Catholic ritual. At Christmas, most Tamils, including Hindus, celebrate the religious events of the holiday season in their homes.

Tamils from south India arrived in Canada in the late 1960s and first settled in Montreal. From cosmopolitan families, they arrived in Western dress and assimilated easily into Canadian society.[4] They were young, single, and well educated, and they spoke Western languages easily. These new Canadians found professional, technical, and administrative jobs and quickly slipped into Canadian society. Once they had families of their own, they encouraged their children to excel in school, seek a university education, avoid distractions, and enter the professions.[5]

By the 1980s, the Sinhalese (the majority of the population in Sri Lanka) were using their numerical majority to support Sinhalese language usage and Sinhalese settlement in Tamil areas. Quotas were established limiting Tamil access to teaching positions and other professions, and legislation was passed restricting Tamil access to jobs and prosperity.[6] A long-running civil war began in 1983. To escape the increasing political, religious, and language discrimination, as well as racial violence, many Tamils migrated to Canada. They represented a broad cross-section of Tamil families, many of whom were not English speaking and whose women continued to wear the traditional sari. The large numbers arriving in Canada during the 1980s[7] found English or French difficult, and the Canadian culture and weather demanding major adjustment. Jobs were difficult to find, incomes were below the poverty line, and Tamil unemployment at one point was at 22 per cent. Nevertheless, like other Asian entrepreneurs, Tamils opened restaurants, small stores, car dealerships, computer shops, insurance businesses, real estate firms, and travel agencies.[8] The Tamil community proved that it could be successful in this new land, composing the "World's First Business Directory for Tamils," an impressive 832-page listing of Tamil-operated enterprises in the Toronto area.[9] Along with achieving material affluence in Canada, Catholic Tamils also sought their vision of God and the freedom to live it out.

Catholic Tamils in Toronto can be found at Our Lady of Good Health Mission at St. Joseph's church and Our Lady of Lourdes parish in downtown Toronto, St. Wilfrid's in North Toronto, the Tamil charismatic prayer group at St. Boniface church in Scarborough, St. Sylvester elementary school north of Highway 401, and in Mississauga at St. Charles Garnier school.

Tamil Practicality and Flexibility

Political Escape: The Story of Anton Sinnarasa

Anton Sinnarasa went through seminary education with the Jesuits in Pune, India, and at the National Seminary in Kandy, which is affiliated with the Urban University in Rome. He earned two bachelor's degrees in philosophy and theology. He was ordained in 1980 and lectured at the major seminary in Jaffna for two years. During the Sri Lankan civil war beginning in 1983, Anton, because he was an articulate spokesperson, was detained under the notorious Anti-Terrorism Laws and accused of supporting the Tamil Tigers, a militant separatist organization that aimed to create an independent Tamil state in the northeast of the country. During racial riots in 1983, Sinhalese criminals in prison killed 53 political prisoners; Anton, along with seventeen others, escaped the massacre. After two months, he broke out of prison and fled to India. In absentia, he was tried before the law courts in Sri Lanka in 1984 and acquitted of all charges.

For two years, Anton worked with refugees in India, then left for Norway, where he pursued a master's degree in organization and management at the Norwegian School of Economics and Business Administration. The next year, in 1987, he was dispensed from his clerical commitment and married Debbie Philip; they have two children. For seven years he remained in Norway working as a document specialist for a number of human rights organizations. As independent immigrants, he, Debbie, and their two children came to Canada in 1992. His Asian and other academic credentials were not recognized in Toronto, so Anton, a gifted social animator, became a community organizer. He was active in Ontario politics as special assistant to a member of the legislature but, when overly cautious intelligence agencies discovered false reports about his Tamil Tiger involvement, he resigned his position. He continued to maintain strong contact with Toronto politicians and still works for them during election campaigns. Although active in Canadian politics, Anton's attention is focused on the physical needs and human rights issues of Tamils in Sri Lanka.

At home, when dealing with illnesses in their children, the Sinnarasas use both Tamil home remedies, composed of spices and herbs to expel colds and fevers, as well as Canadian medicines. They also use the Canadian medical system for more serious illnesses. Psychiatry is new to Tamil culture and, as Anton points out, Tamils need to be educated about its strengths and weaknesses. Although the Sinnarasas arrived in Canada together as a family, Anton says that the Tamil husband generally is the pathfinder. He arrives in Canada first; then, when a home is established, he sends for his wife and family.

As active Catholics, Anton and Debbie help regularly at the Mission of Our Lady of Good Health at St. Joseph's church. The Mission offers three weekend masses in Tamil. The Sinnarasas' commitment to Catholic liturgy in the Tamil language is the centre of their spiritual life. Anton published a quarterly Catholic journal in Tamil which was discontinued after four years due to lack of funds. He believes that priestly leadership is the key to the well-being of Catholic ethnic communities. Such leadership serves to guide the Tamil community, integrating it gradually into the Toronto Catholic parish and archdiocesan structure. Currently, when Catholic Tamils arrive in Canada, they are evangelized aggressively by born-again Christian communities, and large numbers succumb to these overtures. At present, the Tamil Mission feels cut off from the larger Catholic world. In an effort to break out of their isolation, the parish elders sponsored a Tamil Outreach Saturday in the fall of 2003 whereby they invited delegates from Asian and African Catholic communities to share their mutual experiences of accommodating to Canada.

The Tamil Mission in Toronto rented space at St. Maria Goretti church, and according to Anton, their rent was raised by 100 per cent. Even so, they were not allowed to hold meetings at the church after 7 p.m. and were not full participants in the parish. They would like to dialogue with a bishop who could help them deal with their ecclesial problems, but they felt excluded from episcopal contact. Anton and Debbie have raised their teenage children to respect Tamil cultural and Catholic values. Debbie's family includes dance and music teachers who are rich in the resources of Tamil culture. With the collaboration of the Tamil community of Toronto, Anton and Debbie have sponsored the dance troupe of the Kalai Kaveri Colleagues of Fine Arts from Tamil Nadu in India to perform in Toronto, Ottawa, Montreal, and Cornwall. Their son, Edward, has been schooled in classical violin, guitar, and piano. Their daughter, Patricia, does traditional dancing and singing and has entertained audiences in the Markham Theatre Centre at graduation exercises. The family relationship between parents and teenagers in their home is warm, cooperative, and without conflict. The question of multicultural dating and marriage still lies in the family's future. Their accommodation to Canadian ways and their fashioning of a Tamil Canadian identity are still in process.[10]

Adjustment: The Story of M. J. Augustine Jeyanathan

M. J. Augustine Jeyanathan was a council member at Our Lady of Good Health Mission at St. Maria Goretti in Toronto. He completed his Bachelor of Arts in Sri Lanka by writing the examinations for the University of London. He was a bank officer in Sri Lanka and is bilingual in Tamil and English. Leaving behind the unstable conditions caused by the civil war in Sri Lanka during the 1980s, he and his wife, Angela Rosalin Simon, came to Canada in 1988 to provide a good education and secure future for their children. Their eldest daughter, Marina Albert, who had already arrived in Toronto as a political refugee, was the family pathfinder. She gained landed immigrant status and then sponsored her mother and father to come to Canada.

For Augustine, who was semi-retired at 60 years of age, it was time to leave Sri Lanka and to bring his family to Canada. Augustine and Angela gradually sponsored their remaining six children, who were teenagers. When Sri Lanka became enwrapped in a civil war, the conscription of young men and women was a very real threat. When Augustine arrived in Canada, he sought employment in Toronto to offset the expense of moving his family halfway around the world. As he submitted job applications, he heard the embarrassing question that many immigrants face: "Canadian experience?" He eventually found a part-time position keeping books for a dance company.

Upon coming to Canada, family relationships were restructured, including family discussion, part of the parental direction of the children. The Asian style, which does not welcome consultation between parents and children, was left behind, and the new Canadian parents sought dialogue with their adolescent children. The parents found it unsuitable to dictate decisions to their children: it was more useful to work out mutually agreeable solutions. Nevertheless, cultural continuity was preserved as their four daughters and three sons speak Tamil, as do their grandchildren. Through discussion on Canadian marriage, the family realized the importance of marriage based on personal love. Mutual understanding between marriage partners, for the Jeyanathan family, was more important than having an arranged marriage. Thus, the children were permitted to choose their own life companions, bring them home to meet their parents, and thus share in the process of mutual approval. As it happened, all their children married Catholics who are regular churchgoers and continue the custom of family prayers. One daughter lives in England; the other six children are permanent residents in Canada. The family retains the Tamil custom of gathering for Christmas mass and dinner, for Easter time, and for birthdays.

In religious practice, Augustine believes that the Toronto Tamil community is mistakenly preoccupied with maintaining too many Sri Lankan customs in Canada. Historically, Christianity did not attempt to remake Tamil society but accepted its mores as they existed. As young Catholics in Sri Lanka, says Augustine, his generation was very "committed" to avoiding sin and gaining a place in heaven as a reward for a life well lived.

Since the Second Vatican Council and the stresses and strains of the Sri Lankan civil war, the Tamil community has been changing rapidly, whereas the Tamil community in Toronto seeks to avoid change and preserve the remnants of the pre–Vatican II church they remember. For instance, the Second Vatican Council stressed the importance of Christian ecumenism, yet the Toronto community sees little need for becoming ecumenically involved. In an archdiocese of almost 1.9 million Catholics, the Tamils in Toronto, he reasons, suffer from the lack of a Tamil auxiliary bishop to speak for them directly to the archbishop of Toronto.

The Jeyanathans were long-term members of the Legion of Mary at St. Maria Goretti parish. This membership composed the only Tamil presidium (branch) in Toronto and was founded before the Mission of Our Lady of Good Health (1994) was established. The Tamil Mission and the Legion of Mary do not recruit newcomers, but allow them to seek prayer communities in their own way and their own language. Little is done to meet newcomers, as Tamils are highly individualistic and self-reliant. Augustine asserted that Tamils are from a poor and dry country and are used to expending great energy in the struggle for life. Having taken maximum advantage of educational opportunities offered by Christian missionaries, they are always eager to work hard and learn. In Toronto, Canadian Tamils make good use of job opportunities and are not found at the food bank or in the welfare line. Tamils have not burdened the Canadian taxpayer, but for themselves demand a unique type of leader to guide strong-willed individuals toward a common goal.

The Jeyanathans have made their home in Toronto a centre where their children can relate to them, and they see Canada as their permanent home. They appreciate the strengths of the Canadian medical system, which relies on scientific diagnosis, but also value the benefits of Asian healing, such as Aayurveda, which is of Chinese origin and which attempts to balance the various elements of the body. While he and his family accept

Western psychiatric practice, he points out that many non-Christian Tamils have a strong belief in evil spirits that possess and destroy people. One reason for this belief in evil spirits, he continues, was the contagious nature of tuberculosis, which was not understood but greatly feared. Prudent persons guard their family against such contagion in any way they can. Tamils would not consider psychiatry an effective tool for dealing with such problems. Augustine believes that Tamils are slowly changing their attitudes to Western psychiatric medicine and its obvious benefits.[11]

Formation of Tamil Community: The Story of Christi Joachim Pillai

As a good student in Sri Lanka, Christi Joachim Pillai joined the Oblates of Mary Immaculate in 1949, becoming a Catholic priest and religious scholar. Leaving Sri Lanka to study in Rome, he enrolled at the Angelicum University and was ordained in 1956. He completed his doctorate of sacred theology at the Gregorian University in 1961, enrolled for further studies at the Biblical Institute, and spent a year at the École Biblique in Jerusalem. He returned to teaching and formation work at the Sri Lankan National Seminary. As a priest and university professor involved in priestly formation, Father Pillai came to Canada in 1971; he joined the faculty of Saint Paul University in Ottawa and, later, St. Augustine's Seminary in Toronto. As a Catholic academic, he found it easy to move from one continent to another because there was no racial discrimination in Catholic circles, and academic degrees from distant universities were readily recognized. While there is an absence of racial discrimination in ecclesial life, Father Pillai contends that there are glass ceilings in academia that oppress scholars and circumscribe their teaching and publishing. These glass ceilings are rooted in one's theological and social views that are judged as being either safe or dangerous. Secular society, he believes, is more tolerant than the Church in rewarding innovation, competence, and intelligent attitudes. For him, the Tamil culture is ancient, precious, and worth preserving. It includes family values, love of nature, openness to other faiths and cultures, and a genuine pride in the Tamil language and literature. He points out that Tamil newspapers and journals are published in Canada, and that Tamils have their own radio and TV programs. [12]

As a spiritual counsellor, Father Pillai observes that Sri Lankan parents in Canada are over-protective of their traditions, while children struggle to integrate the old with the new. Often, in the process, the young are drawn toward the superficialities of contemporary Canadian culture and forget the deep roots of their own culture. It causes genuine strain for young Tamils to work out their new identity. When Tamils gather on ceremonial occasions, they enjoy the taste of their own cooking, the sound of their music, the presentation of the garland, and the wearing of the pottu (the coloured dot on the forehead). The young try to preserve their relationship with their parents and elders, but find it difficult after having been educated in Canadian schools. After mixing with Canadian children, Tamil children begin to see themselves as Canadian, and seek their own autonomy. They creatively modify the Asian cultures of dance and art to accommodate Western tastes. Intergenerational conflict inevitably follows when sons and daughters attending university ask their parents questions they cannot answer. The young people discover that they have been uprooted from their Sri Lankan culture and are fighting for a soft landing in North America. Too quickly, young Tamils overthrow traditional boundaries without having time to develop new critical instincts and personal balance.

Like most ethnic groups, the great majority of Tamils would prefer marrying persons of their own culture and religion. Intermarriage with other ethnic groups in a multicultural society is a consideration, but for Tamils there is less tolerance for interfaith marriage. Catholic will generally marry Catholic, and Hindu will marry Hindu. When leaving their home country, Tamils continue the tradition of using herbal remedies and home care. Some, however, switch overnight from Asian health care to Canadian health care. In this transition, new Canadians switching too quickly to Western medicine do not fully understand its strengths and weaknesses and are inclined to overuse the system for minor illnesses until they adjust. It takes time to realize that traditional home care is still beneficial for minor health concerns. Running to the emergency room for minor ailments and seeing specialists too quickly is something the newcomers learn from Canadians without fully understanding the limits of the system.

Both lay and clerical Tamils tend to resist the acceptance of psychiatric help. The common Tamil assumption is that people are mentally healthy and do not need therapy. To the question "How are you?" the common Tamil response is "No problem!" Father Pillai jests that East Indians may seem chaotic, but the people are functional, while North Americans may appear efficient, but the people are dysfunctional. Coming to Canada as a family, Tamils would never send a young daughter ahead as the pathfinder, as the Irish or the Filipinos do. Women are protected. Once the family arrives in Canada, however, the wife very often finds work more quickly than her husband, and she supports the family. This upsets the family gender balance, which is built around the patriarchal authority of the husband as the breadwinner and natural head of the family. According to Tamil custom, the wife brought her dowry to the marriage and her family paid for the wedding. In contrast, the husband's job provides income for the future of the family. The dowry is decisive for the couple's financial future and may underwrite a business venture. Thus, in family decisions, the wife in the home has power, and often the upper hand, while outside the home the husband has control. Family decisions are especially planned to provide for the success of the children.

Tamils, like other Asians, have active prayer groups, and many are inspired by the North American charismatic movement. The groups are organized and ministered by lay people. Participants gain their identity by being members of the group and having their special spiritual gifts recognized, such as being baptized and slain in the Spirit, praying over others, speaking in tongues, and witnessing healing. These charismatic activities can broaden to be narcissistic, as if one were to wrap oneself in a shroud of holiness for an identity, and then desire others to follow. Scripture is studied in a fundamentalist way, and piety guides members when a greater sense of social justice is needed. For newcomers, an evening of prayer is a social occasion that costs the family little money and adds to family values and sharpens the sense of Tamil Canadian identity. In some ways, Catholic organizations like the Legion of Mary, St. Vincent de Paul Society, and social service groups are helpful for parishioners and, as Father Pillai believes, offer the broadening experience of international Catholic organizations.

Tamils have an elaborate network of both secular and religious organizations that perform good works in the community. Hindus and Christians work together to assist newcomers and others needing help. Tamil groups organize around their former membership in Sri Lankan colleges and parishes to foster devotional, social, and fundraising events. In Toronto, many of these organizations plan pilgrimages, outings, and religious and social events. Father Pillai advises that Tamil centres of worship are necessary during the transition stage, until the newly arrived feel comfortable in Canadian parishes. He believes that Our Lady of Good Health Mission at St. Joseph's church in Toronto is a temporary expedient, and perhaps not the best model for the future. Tamils attend church services on a regular basis, are community centred, and feel the need to be actively involved in Church matters. They are faithful Catholics desiring a Catholic education for their children. At times, hyperactivity within the Tamil community serves as a substitute for its outreach to the wider community and the challenges that result.

Since the 1980s, as large numbers of Tamils have arrived in Canada, there has been no need for churches to recruit. New arrivals are normally welcomed by families, who look after them until they locate a home, a church, schools, and shopping areas and learn about Canadian money and credit cards. The Tamil Eelam Society looks after newcomers and helps them with social and legal matters. Lawyers and doctors who are close to the Tamil community are always available. Language, says Father Pillai, can be a difficulty for the older generation, who did not learn English in school; some newcomers attend English as a Second Language instruction at Msgr. Fraser College or similar institutions.

The Tamil Catholic community in Toronto has shown a flexibility to adapt to Canadian life and form itself into a community. The Tamil Eelam Society is an umbrella organization registered in Ontario that has been able to plan gatherings for special celebrations and occasions. While Tamil Catholics are encouraged to attend local parishes, they need centres where they can come together to be themselves, eat, talk, and worship in their own way.[13]

Canadian Tamil Identity

Preserving Tradition: The Story of Joseph Andrews Arulappan and Nalini Daniel

Joseph Andrews Arulappan completed his degree in commerce in 1988 and, after post-graduate studies, was employed by a multinational trading company in India. Nalini Daniel completed post-graduate work in commerce in 1996 and was employed as an accountant with an American multinational company. The parents of Joseph and Nalini arranged their marriage in Madras, India, for May 6, 1991. As a married couple, they had adequate income, but decided to move to Canada in search of new economic opportunities, a better standard of living, and more educational opportunities for their children. Joseph looked forward to working for a Canadian trading company and, as the pathfinder for his family, arrived in Toronto in November 2000. After establishing a home in Toronto, he called for his wife Nalini and son, David, to come to Canada. They arrived in March 2001.

Not finding opportunities in commercial trading in Canada, Joseph began work as a part-time insurance sales representative for a Canadian bank in Toronto. Two years later, he passed the examination to become a licensed insurance broker for an international brokerage firm. Fluent in English but recognizing the cultural misunderstandings that can happen, he worked on his Canadian vocabulary and diction to be more clearly understood in the Canadian environment. After arriving in Canada, Nalini hoped to fine work as an accountant, but was turned down because she lacked "Canadian experience" – even though in Madras she worked for an American multinational company. She accepted the fact that, while raising their family, she had to be content with temporary work in a Canadian bank.

Joseph and Nalini speak Tamil at home, cultivate a rich family life, and attend the Catholic Eucharist each Sunday in English. Their children, David and Catherine, attend Catholic schools and deepen the quality of their Christian faith. David, a good student, often serves mass. The thought of conflict between the generations in Canada was a surprise to Joseph and Nalini; in India, it would not happen as parents do not explain issues. Extended families live together in large homes and maintain close family cohesion by respecting elders and doing as they ask. When parents speak, they are carefully listened to, and their advice is implemented without further delay. Joseph and Nalini discovered that children educated in Canadian Catholic schools ask questions that demand time and energy to answer. Whereas the parents like the idea of discussion with their children, they find it is an approach to be learned. The possibility of their children marrying non-Tamils is something that Joseph and Nalini are considering for the future.

As Joseph and Nalini plan their future life in Canada, they find Canadian medicine very helpful, especially for their family. They also bring home remedies from Madras, finding them helpful for colds, flu, and fevers. Although they would accept psychiatric help if it were needed, they do not find such care a priority. They find the spiritual inspiration of Our Lady of Lourdes parish more relevant to them and more helpful to their young family. The mission statement of Our Lady of Lourdes attracted them: "We are a Spirit-filled Catholic Community of Pilgrims gathered from different lands and different cultures. ... Our ministry and hospitality embrace all." Nalini has attended meetings of the Catholic Women's League and an interfaith group. Joseph and Nalini look for other Tamils arriving in Toronto and help them integrate into Canadian life. They enjoy attending Our Lady of Lourdes church because among the choice of seven weekend masses is a Tamil mass with Carnatic singing (classical East Indian music from Tamil Nadu). Tamils often have festivals and socials connected with the Mass. A friendly people, they welcome such social occasions. Joseph and Nalini have demonstrated flexibility in adjusting to Canadian expectations, but cherish their Tamil Catholic roots and wish to pass them onto their children.[14]

Family Loyalty: The Story of Peter Gitendran

Peter Gitendran completed his bachelor of theology degree at the Sri Lankan National Seminary in the capital city, Colombo. After doing parish work in Sri Lanka for eleven years, he migrated to the United States, where he served in a parish for twelve years while enrolled in a program in Clinical Pastoral Education to qualify as a hospital chaplain. In September 1996, for both family and ethnic reasons, Father Gitendran immigrated to Toronto, where he accepted a position as chaplain at the Toronto General and Sick Children's hospitals. Father Peter found no discrimination in Canada but believes in the religious virtue of accepting the good and the bad. He will remain in Canada and travels on a Canadian passport.

He learned in his religious training to be detached from people and places, ready to live anywhere in the world, and endure adversity with patience. Adjusting to Canada, he observes that Tamils in Canada enjoy their home life, religious beliefs, and family festivities at Christmas, Easter, and the feasts of the saints. Like their parents, they understand the importance of caring for the sick and elderly. In attending Canadian schools, the young learn spontaneity, creativity, and how to speak in English and share their views. The elders find youthful openness abrasive and hard to deal with. Interfaith and inter-ethnic marriages among Tamils are tolerated in Canada, but are more likely to happen among the university educated.

As a hospital chaplain, Father Peter believes that Tamils find the Canadian medical system excellent, providing great help to families. At the same time, the Tamil community as a whole is wary of psychological therapy because they fear the social stigma attached. But he believes that these attitudes will change in time. Migrating to Canada, the husband or oldest son will come first to check out the living environment, and then gradually bring their family. With both the husband and the wife working in Canada, career decisions are made to protect the husband's employment rather than the wife's.

Spiritual groups for Tamils are of two types: Marian devotional groups of Tamils devoted to the saints, and charismatic prayer groups inspired by Scripture. The former groups prefer Marian celebrations, processions, and devotions on Marion feasts. They believe in going to Jesus through Mary. Their faith echoes the processions and colourful devotion of the Portuguese; they find English piety introspective and dull. Charismatic groups, in contrast, have lay leadership and lay preachers, music groups, and engage in communal prayer based on the Scriptures. The charismatic movement believes in going directly to Jesus through Bible study and prayer. Embracing both these Tamil religious traditions as a Catholic priest, Father Peter came to Canada to be with his family members, to serve the Tamil community in Toronto, and to deepen the sense of a Tamil Canadian identity.[15]

Community Dialogue: The Story of David Thomas

David Thomas graduated in engineering from the Polytechnical Institute of Sri Lanka in 1972 and, after being twice elected to political office, left to work in Singapore for political reasons. It was there he met his wife, Jeyamani Victor, who was Singapore born and worked in a bank. After their marriage, David and Jeyamani moved to Malaysia, where he sought a position as a pastoral worker at a local Catholic church. Desiring a better political and economic future for his family, David came to Canada as the pathfinder in 1988; the next year, Jeyamani followed with their daughter, uniting their family in Toronto.[16]

David completed a degree in business administration at Ryerson University in 1992 and got a job at a Canadian bank. Jeyamani, who upgraded her banking skills in Toronto, became a part-time bank employee while raising their children. They have one boy and three girls who attend Catholic schools, are Tamil speaking, and receive the Catholic sacraments. The children and parents attend the Tamil mass at Our Lady of Lourdes and share in the social activities there. They are enriched by Tamil culture and learn Tamil dance and song. Feeling at home in Tamil, the children are able to speak with their grandparents and relatives and relate with young people of their own age when visiting Sri Lanka.

Generational conflict within the family has been limited by the children's young age and natural preference for Tamil culture and customs. Family discussions are held twice monthly to head off the stresses and strains of family life. By Tamil tradition, teenage girls are not allowed to go with a girlfriend unescorted to a movie. Adjusting to Canadian mores, Thomas family members dance together at weddings despite the community elders' prohibition of mixed-gender dancing. Because of their custom of open family discussion, their oldest daughter has become a "corridor" counsellor for her school friends. Yet, within the Tamil community, generational conflict within family life is percolating and cannot be prohibited.

David and Jeyamani do not object to inter-ethnic dating and marriage for their children, but both they and their children prefer Tamil Catholic friends. They accept their children choosing their own marriage partners rather than following the Tamil custom of prearranged marriages. They plan their future in Canada, and David has become politically involved in provincial election campaigns. He commits time and effort for electioneering in Canadian public life to deepen the Tamil sense of Canadian identity. For their family, they find Canadian medicine "good and advanced," and psychiatry very helpful to new Canadians striving to cope with the new cultural environment. Jeyamani believes that newcomers often have a poor understanding of Canadian culture; for example, they do not see why they should not spank their children. She feels that newcomers need guidance to know how to dress appropriately in the Canadian climate, how to find housing, where to shop, and where to find the services they need. Readily available information would assist puzzled newcomers to adjust to their new environment.

David and Jeyamani were determined to form a Tamil religious community in downtown Toronto to inspire Sri Lankan newcomers who were acclimatizing to their new surroundings. They tried forming a Tamil community at St. Peter's church, then at Holy Name, St. Helen's, and St. Anthony's. They finally settled at Our Lady of Lourdes. David felt that a number of pastors treated him as if he were a business person founding an enterprise and wishing to rent space in their buildings. It took a year of working with the pastor of Our Lady of Lourdes, Father Robert Foliot SJ, for David to form the downtown Tamil community. He found Tamil priests studying at the University of Toronto to act as chaplains at the parish. Since then, other Tamil priests have served the downtown Tamil community. Father Peter Gitendran, the Catholic hospital chaplain described earlier in this chapter, became the regular priest for presiding at the weekend Eucharist in Tamil and offering the other sacraments. The community provided the distinctive Tamil Carnatic singing to enhance communal participation in the liturgy. The Tamil Sunday collection at Our Lady of Lourdes went toward the maintenance of the church, although Tamil Catholics, who compared the solid construction, carpeting, and regular maintenance of Canadian churches to the inexpensively built Sri Lankan churches, did not see the need for much support of Canadian churches. By special arrangement, three times a year— on Christmas, New Year's, and Easter—a second collection was taken up for the needy in Sri Lanka.

The archdiocese then assigned Father Peter to be administrator of a relocated Tamil community at St. Joseph's church on Leslie Street in Toronto. Some Tamils followed Father Peter to St. Joseph's, while others continued to attend the sacraments at Lourdes in English. Still other parishioners were drawn to the 33 Protestant churches in Toronto that offer Sunday services in Tamil. After two years, a youthful priest from Sri Lanka, Gabriel Arulnesan, replaced Father Peter. Meanwhile, at Our Lady of Lourdes, Paskaran Selva Razali, along with David Thomas, led the Lourdes Tamil community through English-language liturgies. The Tamil Community at Our Lady of Lourdes numbers about 75 persons and does not actively recruit new members. The downtown Tamil community is concerned with the welfare of new arrivals, to whom they give assistance in finding employment, homes, schools, welfare, translation help, and immigration information, but is reluctant to recruit newcomers who are labouring through their first months in the city. By contrast, the Pentecostal churches aggressively recruit Catholic Tamils in this transitional stage.

The Tamil laity are proud to be full participants in Our Lady of Lourdes parish and at the same time active in reaching out to newly arrived Tamils. They feel very much part of Canadian Catholic life. David and Jeyamani conjecture that Tamils do not need their own church, as there are many churches in Toronto, but they need a Tamil community centre to share fellowship. Tamil Catholics are pleased to share their strong Christian faith with Catholics in Canada but struggle to find a new authentic Tamil Canadian identity. As the Second Vatican Council has asked that liturgy be performed in the vernacular, the Tamil Catholic Community at Our Lady of Lourdes hopes that in the future, the Tamil liturgy will be allowed to them again.[17]

Inter-ethnic Marriage: The Story of Philip S. and Merina Soosaithsan

Born in Sri Lanka, Philip S. Soosaithsan received his adult education in England and Wales. In 1959, he completed a bachelor of arts degree at the University of London, then returned to Sri Lanka and married Merina, who had graduated from the Franciscan convent school. They established a home and started a family. Philip went back to Wales for studies, and became a chartered accountant there in 1965. Returning to Sri Lanka, he operated his own accounting firm until he received an offer of a position in Zambia. Living apart from his family, he would vacation during the holiday seasons with them in Sri Lanka. At the height of the civil war in 1989, Philip came directly to Canada to scout the possibility of moving to Toronto after being threatened by insurgents. He found work as an accountant for a year and a half until he received a permanent position as auditor with Revenue Canada. He found a home in Our Lady of Lourdes parish in downtown Toronto and prepared for the arrival of his family. Merina brought their five children to Toronto two years later.

Integration into Canadian society was begun, and two of his youngest children were enrolled in Canadian schools. Although educated in England, Philip found that Canadian pronunciations and idioms were different from the English he knew; he had to listen carefully to Canadians, who spoke quickly. Canadian accounting methods were often the reverse of the English method, which put assets to the right and liabilities to the left. In Canada, driving and walking were done on the opposite sides of the street from the English way. Winter snow and cold seemed to inhibit work and social activities. In time, the family found that the centrally heated homes and buildings made the winters manageable. The children adjusted and eventually went to university; four of the five are working in the professions in Canada. The eldest son returned to Sri Lanka, where he still lives and works. The children are fluent in Tamil and enjoy frequent visits to Sri Lanka. They have learned Tamil dancing and music, and feel comfortable in the Tamil milieu.

The family members are regular churchgoers at St. Timothy's parish, where Philip is on the pastoral council. He was one of the founders, in 1990, of the Tamil Catholic Community of Toronto, and both he and Merina are members of the Legion of Mary. As a family, they have retained their Catholic values and continue to attend the parish church nearest them.

Their third son, Rajan, a lawyer, did not feel comfortable introducing his Sinhalese Buddhist girlfriend to his parents. After she became a Catholic, they married without informing his parents. Inter-religious continuity of a Catholic-Catholic wedding was maintained in the marriage, yet the inter-ethnic mixing of a Tamil and Sinhalese demanded cultural adjustment. Although goodwill existed on both sides, wounds still linger from this Canadian-Tamil accommodation.

The political and economic environment has recently stabilized in Sri Lanka, and Philip and Merina, now retired, look forward to living once again in rural Sri Lanka, where life is more relaxed, more traditional, and less expensive. They retain their Canadian passports, have enjoyed their years in Canada, and may well return to Toronto someday. They especially like the Canadian health-care system and would feel comfortable accepting Western psychiatry if it were necessary. Observing the patriarchal system, they believe that the husband's career is central in making family decisions, but learned to make accommodations for life in Canada.[18]

Religious Tradition: The Story of George Antony and Regina Sinnathurai

George Antony worked as a checker at Cement Corporation. When the civil war in Sri Lanka intensified after 1983, the Sinhalese government nationalized Tamil businesses and closed them down. Among the companies closed was the Cement Corporation. Because of warfare and fear for his life, George decided it was necessary to leave Sri Lanka. He travelled first to India and then to Spain and Cuba before arriving in Canada in 1987. He settled in Toronto and found work as an electronics tester. Regina Sinnathurai was a secretary in Sri Lanka. Once George had established a residence, Regina came to Canada, and they were married in 1988 at St. Anthony's church in Toronto.

Tamil Canadians: seminarian Francis Salasiar, Father Lazar Savarimuthu SJ, Charles Delan, Father Ahilaraj Sivarajah SJ, Paskaran Selvarajah. Mass servers are standing at the rear.

George and Regina have two children: Christina, 13, and Dunstan, 11. Born in Toronto and attending Catholic schools, the children prefer to speak English as their peers in school. Although they understand Tamil, which is spoken at home, they do not respond in Tamil. The children have an appreciation for Tamil culture, which includes watching Tamil videos and being involved in Tamil songs and dances. They also have a keen respect for Catholic family values, and have high regard for their elders. George and Regina expect their children will enter into arranged marriages, as they did, which means the marriage will be determined within the Catholic Tamil community.

The Antonys intend to spend the rest of their life in Canada. Their children find Canada attractive as it is peaceful, orderly, and home to them. George relishes cool weather and prefers Canada in the wintertime. George and Regina like the Canadian health-care system and would use psychiatric counselling were it helpful to them or their family. When making family decisions, the relevance of both their jobs is considered, but at times the husband's position is given preference.

Tamil Canadian children at a charismatic meeting
at St. Boniface church, Scarborough

George and Regina find attending mass and religious devotions in Toronto are much like attending mass and religious devotions in Sri Lanka. The culture and language remain the same; only the geographical location has changed. They joined the Tamil Charismatic Prayer Group when it was founded in 1993 at St. Boniface church. The group meets on Friday evenings and is directed by the laity with clergy support. Through a commitment to Jesus Christ, the prayer group's goal is to bring about a personal conversion of life. The Tamil Charismatic Prayer Meeting is an inexpensive Friday night of singing and speaking in Tamil and having access to Tamil preachers and videos. Members enjoy the meetings fully and seek out new members who want to be part of a loving, prayerful, faithful community. They support each other in finding jobs and suitable housing. They encourage their children to consider seriously the Lord's call to them to commit their life to the church as a priest or religious sister or brother.[19]

On Friday nights, the Tamil Catholic New Life Good News Prayer Group gathers Tamil Catholics together from across metropolitan Toronto at St. Boniface church, 142 Markham Road, in Scarborough. The evening begins with an English-language mass in the church and is followed by charismatic prayer in Tamil. Brother Jesu Thavarajan leads the 200 participants through responsorial prayers, petitions, and songs. The mixed choir, singing Tamil and English songs, provides the music leadership. Young men from the group supply keyboard accompaniment backed by recorded Tamil music. The effect of the repetitive prayers and the Tamil songs is deeply devotional and almost hypnotic. Participants raise their arms and hands, chanting prayers and singing praise. Other leaders of the group are the secretary, Bastian Patrick, and the public relations advisor, Rasarayagam Aseer. Priest professors Joseph Chandrakanthan and Christi Pillai OMI are available for Tamil Eucharistic celebrations, yet this charismatic group is inspired and well guided by the Catholic lay community.

Tamil Canadian altar servers at Our Lady of Lourdes, Toronto

The number of recent Tamil university graduates has multi-plied the number of Tamil professionals and enhanced the image of Tamils as an educated and professional workforce. These professionals guide social events and help the community find acceptance in Canada. The Tamil Catholic leaders of Toronto organize events such as a yearly pilgrimage to Martyrs' Shrine at Midland, Ontario, which can attract 5,000 Tamils. Similar pilgrimages are planned to Mary Lake on Marian feast days. As Tamils go through the pain of Canadianization, pilgrimages inspire them with the comforts of familiar food, conversation, and moral support. The Tamil Catholic community of Toronto arranges seminars and conferences to discuss questions that arise about family, community, and acculturation. Tamil members re-cruit volunteers to serve those in the community who need help. Tamil Catholics bring strong faith and their energetic lifestyle to Canadian churches.[20]

Accustomed to adversity, Tamil Canadian Catholics are hardworking, quick learning, and have a sense of adventure about life. Upon arrival in Canada, they seek whatever work they can find. They run gas bars until they are able to buy the gas bar, are low-paid office workers until they open their own business, or work in a restaurant until they become the chef or owner. Other Tamils get Canadian experience by doing commercial cleaning, plumbing, electrical work, or foundation and renovation work. Being adventurous, Tamils often open their own businesses in related areas of restoration, cleaning, restaurant, and new product sales. Tamils are willing to take a chance in business. Sixty per cent of parents expect their children to go to university and look for a bright future.

In Montreal, the Tamil Mission of Notre-Dame-de-la-Délivrance can be found at Saint-Iréné on Henri-Julien Avenue. Father Andrew Thuraisingam, on loan from the Jaffna diocese, is responsible for directing the Mission, which has 220 families. During Holy Week, the Tamil Catholic community observes an evening vigil on Maundy Thursday and on Good Friday for the reading of the Johannine Passion and the communal Stations of the Cross. Carnatic singing, *Bharata Natyam* dance, and instrumental music provide continuity and inspiration to Tamil Catholics.[21]

The British educational and parliamentary systems influenced the Tamil culture. The strong anglophone input in their culture helped prepare Tamils for the encounter with Canadian ways. Tamil culture gives priority to close-knit families and thus is endogamous in its marriage customs. Canadian Tamils arrange marriages for their children within their class and caste and pay a suitable dowry to the groom's family. Young men have a moral obligation to provide a dowry for their sisters.[22] Tamils will often marry a second cousin or sponsor a marriage partner from home to strengthen family bonds. The husband is expected to dominate the family, while his wife is to play a subordinate role, not even calling him by name. The woman's self-concept is based on her

Dharma (virtue), her loyalty to her family as a homemaker, and her role as mother of her children. Her personal satisfaction comes from fulfilling her life role rather than seeking individual career aspirations for herself.[23] This does not mean that Tamil women do not exercise authority, but rather that they exercise it in a subdued and unobtrusive way.[24] In Canada, these customs are softening as younger couples work and share family responsibilities. Like other Asians, Tamils value family life more than single life and treasure their children as gifts from God.

The pathfinders for Tamils were the well-educated middle class who were immediately welcomed to Canada as professionals in the 1970s. Tamils, like other Asians, prefer to locate in major Canadian cities.[25] Upon arrival, they will reside for a time in the Tamil neighbourhood that reproduces traditional culture and their social network.[26] Eventually, with greater affluence, the family will move into mixed suburbs when suitable housing becomes available. Recent Tamil arrivals enjoy a high level of literacy in their own language, but may lack fluency in spoken English. Most have a high school education, with 30 per cent having the advantage of post-secondary education. In university attendance, men have exceeded women two to one, but women are rectifying that imbalance.[27] Catholic Tamils send their children to Catholic schools, which educate them in Canadian culture and heritage programs. The latter includes the Tamil language, Carnatic vocal skills, and *Bharata Natyam* dance. Carnatic music provides Catholic liturgy with a particular contribution in sacred music and provides Tamil Catholics with a unique identity. They read Tamil newspapers and magazines, listen to Tamil radio, and watch Tamil videos. Sri Lankan musicians and artists tour communities across Canada to keep the oral language and culture alive.[28]

As the civil war in Sri Lanka died down for a time, political interest among Tamils has shifted away from the Sri Lankan conflict to Canadian provincial and federal politics.[29] Tamil politics are traditional, but the concern for the struggle in Sri Lanka preoccupied Tamil attention and provoked the younger generation to challenge authority as they perceived government as an oppressor. Young Tamils "are extremely vocal against discrimination of any form and are not afraid to fight back."[30] In Canada, young Tamils are active in social work among their colleagues and are members of political parties. Like other Asians, they have learned to deal with discrimination in their life, move on, and support others who are facing similar difficulties.[31]

Christian Service

Accounting Service: The Story of Francis Joseph and Mary Anne Anthony

Francis Joseph completed his B.A. in 1969 at the University of Percideniya in Sri Lanka. As part of his work in government administration, he was sent to St. John's, Newfoundland, for six months to study cooperatives in the fishing industry. Mary Anne Anthony completed her B.A. at the University of Sri Lanka in 1970 and began her teaching career. In 1973, Francis and Mary Anne married and began raising their family. Francis went to England in 1978 to complete a three-year program to become a Chartered Management Accountant. Although he had intended to return to Sri Lanka in 1981, he was offered an accounting position in Nigeria. After three years in Nigeria, he gave up the position and returned to his family in Sri Lanka. He wanted to start an accounting practice, but the civil war left the political and economic stability of the country in doubt. Francis and Mary Anne decided to immigrate to Canada with their three small children, as Canada offered them a compassionate and stable society with an excellent education system.

Arriving in Canada, Francis found a position as an accountant and worked for a number of firms until he opened his own business in 1994. When speaking English in Canada, he discovered he was not always understood. He had to learn Canadian idioms and pronunciation and adjust to Canadian social customs.

He found that he was socially too direct and had to learn Canadian indirectness. Mary Anne, who had taught in Sri Lanka, decided after making inquiries that it would be too complicated to requalify as a teacher. She accepted a job in a bank, which proved to be easier than teaching and offered regular employment, limited hours, and a better salary. Their children were educated in Canadian schools; they have a passive knowledge of Tamil, but are not active in speaking it. Like their father, who plays tennis and swims on a regular basis, the grown children also play sports. They are now completing university degrees, or are professionally employed. The Tamil custom of arranged marriages was out of the question once the children went to Canadian universities. Francis and Mary Anne have learned that in interfaith and inter-ethnic marriages, couples need to share similar values. For instance, their eldest daughter, Venetia, is married to a New Brunswick Acadian who teaches physics at the University of Moncton. As a family, they retain the values of going to church together on Sunday and celebrating family events such as birthdays, Mother's Day, Father's Day, Easter, and Christmas.

Although they no longer carry Sri Lankan passports, Mary Anne and Francis still enjoy extended visits to their family in Sri Lanka, but their permanent home is in Canada. They find the Canadian health care system very useful and do not object to psychiatry were it necessary for them. Living in the modern world, they appreciate the benefits of Western science, and as Catholics have learned to reconcile science and religion. Following the Tamil custom in family decision making, Francis makes the career decisions but in consultation with his wife and children.[32]

Intellectual Achievement: The Story of Joseph Chandrakanthan

Born in Sri Lanka, Joseph Chandrakanthan completed a master's degree in philosophy and a master's degree in theology in 1980 at the Jesuit university in Pune. He then taught Christianity and Islamic studies at the State University of Jaffna. At Saint Paul University in Ottawa, he completed a doctorate in philosophy in 1986 and a doctorate in theology in 1988. Returning to Jaffna to teach, he became associate professor and head of the department. To broaden his academic environment and for reasons of personal security, he returned to Canada in 1991 and was appointed professor of theology at Concordia University in Montreal. When better opportunities became available in Toronto, he moved there in 2000 and began teaching in the Christianity and Culture Program at the University of St. Michael's College at the University of Toronto. He later moved to the Toronto School of Theology, teaching for St. Augustine's Seminary. Father Joseph is also a bioethicist in the Centre for Clinical Ethics at St. Joseph's Hospital. On weekends, he is busy with priestly ministry among Sri Lankan Catholics at Our Lady of the Annunciation church. Father Joseph believes that Sri Lankans exude the values of family, hospitality, and religious commitment. When migrating to Canada, Tamils come as a family unit of one, two, or three generations. The family is patriarchal, and according to Father Joseph, the husband, or the eldest son, makes the principal decisions. Initiating employment in Canada, Tamils often accept work in food services or initiate catering services in major cities. They firmly believe that young people should pursue higher education and that elders should be respected. In fact, elders and youth live in different languages and different worlds. The young live in Canadian English and cannot fathom the environment from which their grandparents came and in which they still live. As Canadian-educated youth have not experienced the Tamil cultural matrix from which they spring, they do not share the Asian language and geographical experiences of their grandparents. In their crowded Toronto apartments, Father Joseph observes, the young no longer share the village experience and the broad vistas of a rural community in Sri Lanka. In small villages, everyone is known and expected to conform to the norms of local Tamil culture. Tamil grandparents would like to share their culture with their grandchildren so the young can learn to imitate their elders' lifestyle, but in Canada, the young disappear into the high-rise canyons of the amorphous city and do what they like. Generational misunderstanding is spurred on by two different life experiences and expectations. Marriages with non-Tamils are always a possibility, but as Father Joseph points out, such marriages are only for the strong-hearted, as they halt the identity growth of these young people and cut short a sense of their place in the world.

Father Joseph has made his home in Canada. He observes that the Canadian health-care system concentrates its resources on healing the sick rather than keeping the healthy well. Tamil herbal medicine is designed to maintain good health and to extend the life of the sick. Existing for more than 3,000 years, the herbal medical approach has proved its value. For instance, bitter gourd taken twice a day can provide natural insulin, kill germs, and purge worms from the body. Proper food and beverages are provided to the sick to nourish them with minerals and vitamins to renew their health. Western psychiatry is not readily accepted, as it is considered a stigma on the family's name. Rather, says Father Joseph, dealing with mental illness in the Saivite religious way is more acceptable for Tamils, where society invites the temple and village community to be sympathetic caregivers.[33]

Tamil Outreach

Tamils wish to overcome their self-preoccupation, and thus, in the fall of 2003 sponsored a "Tamil Outreach" to other Asian Catholics. Anton Sinnarasa, Deacon Joseph Savundranayagam, and Francis Joseph, under the inspiration of Father Christi Pillai OMI, planned the conference theme "That They May Be One" and proceeded to invite the Chinese, Malayalee, African, and Korean communities. Forty-five delegates from various Toronto parishes arrived on November 22, 2003, to present the Canadian vision and their strategies for retaining their own ethnic identities. Stephen Young Huh and Sister Rita Kim represented the Korean community; Augustine Jeyanathan, the Tamil community; Father Paul Varghese Moonjely, the Malayalee community; Tony Chow, the Chinese community; and Father Michele Meunier, the African community.[34]

Father Pillai emphasized the theme: that all—families, people, and humanity from all nations—may be one. Father Joseph Chandrakanthan demonstrated that Tamils emerged from an East Indian multicultural society to migrate to multicultural Canada. He stressed the importance of a Canadian society that is open to Jew and Gentile, men and women, rich and poor. The Canadian ideal of unity in diversity, he explained, is exemplified in the city of Toronto, home to ethnic groups that speak 111 languages. He believes that family values, which are strong among Asians, must be respected.[35]

Augustine Jeyanathan explained to participants that the first Tamils to arrive in Toronto in the 1970s spoke English well and integrated into Canadian society without difficulty. After 1983, for political reasons, the large influx of Tamils arriving from Sri Lanka were less proficient in English. They needed help in learning English and assimilating Canadian culture. The Tamil Mission of Our Lady of Good Health was established under the leadership of the Tamil priest Father Patrick at St. Maria Goretti. Tamil priests at this time in Toronto were numerous, but it was Father Patrick who was designated the pastor of a Tamil parish. Tamil communities, Augustine said, would like to buy property for their own community church and centre, but thus far have not been able to do it. The Tamil laity are active in social work in the community. He quoted the advice of Father Robert Foliot SJ that God has called the Tamils here for a special purpose: "You have to go beyond your own ethnic group to other groups." Augustine asked the Tamil community what the program for youth was, and challenged them to respond to a brief question: "Just our old values, or a new understanding?"[36] From the St. Thomas the Apostle Malayalee Mission, Father Paul Varghese Moonjely cmi stressed that those present were from many countries, speaking many languages, but were all one in the spirit of God.[37]

Tony Chow spoke on behalf of the pastor of Chinese Martyrs parish, Father Peter Leung. The parish has 5,000 families registered. On weekends, seven masses are celebrated for 4,000 congregants. Their RCIA program of Christian instruction has been extended to eighteen months, and the parish baptizes over 400 people per year. They have choirs for each of the seven masses, and 250 altar servers. Their active prayer groups include social justice, Marriage Encounter, Bible study, vocational witness, and First Friday devotions. Tony's presentation revealed the Chinese genius for organization.[38]

From the African French community, Michele Meunier, a missionary from Africa, pointed to the fact that francophone Congolese began arriving in Toronto in the early 1970s as refugees and immigrants. They came from a multicultural continent of 53 countries with over 1,000 languages and as many cultures. African Catholics in Toronto number over 300,000 people, of which about 10 per cent are Catholic. Father Meunier said that Africans are a faithful people and have a great ability to bounce back from disaster. Yet, for Africans, blood is thicker than water. Africans attend the church where they find relatives and friends, where they feel welcome, and where they can sing and dance. The African experience of racism among church people puts them down. Catholic Africans in Toronto are located principally at Assumption church in Forest Hill and Sacré Coeur in the downtown. It is sad, however, that Africans often have to work on Sundays and therefore cannot attend the Sunday masses they prefer. Given the diversity of languages and cultures, Father Meunier recommended that churches "let people express their faith the way they want."[39]

Stephen Young Huh and Sister Rita Kim, representing St. Andrew Kim Korean church, pointed out that Korean Catholicism was initiated by laity, who first learned about Christianity while on a trip to China in 1784. St. Andrew Kim in Toronto has three adult masses and two family masses for its 5,000 members. Sister Rita spoke of the hunger and the need Koreans have for spiritual nourishment. They are very staunch Catholics and parishioners.

Concluding the Tamil Outreach program, I spoke as a Canadian historian to the diverse group about my interests in Asian and African Catholics. I believe that the religious commitment of these newcomers enhances the identity of Canadian Catholics. Asian Catholics bring to Canada a deep sense of religious devotion, family values, and cohesive community. To back up Asian Catholics, the Asian bishops meet in Asian cities periodically to update the third-world theology of collegiality, subsidiarity, concern for the poor, and interfaith dialogue. The personal and theological gifts of Asians enrich and influence the Canadian Catholic Church.[40]

Conclusion

Tamil newspapers, radio, television, and video reports stir up interest in the homeland. Civil conflict has separated Canadian Tamils from the Sinhalese-run Sri Lankan government. In Canada, financial assistance is collected among Tamils for the rehabilitation of Tamil areas in Sri Lanka. Many Tamils are very concerned about family members left behind and how to help them. Concern with the struggle in Sri Lanka and the lack of English-language fluency in Canada can be barriers for Canadian Tamils to link with the larger Canadian community. The intermarriage of Canadian Tamils with cousins and Sri Lankan spouses reinforce the strong internal ties of the Tamil community. But many Tamil Canadians, especially those who attend university, become leaders in their family and community; for them, arranged marriages are less imaginable.[41]

Tamil Canadians are concerned about reviving Tamil culture and creating strong families.[42] Tamil Catholics, by entering daily into the Passion of Christ through the church's liturgy during Lent, strengthen their family bonds and come to an understanding of the suffering they are going through. Novenas, charismatic prayer, passion plays, pilgrimages to Marian shrines, Carnatic music, and festivals, such as that of St. Anthony, awaken a deep sense of a Tamil-Catholic interconnectedness.

When suffering from ill-health, Tamils employ eastern home remedies as well as utilizing western medicine. Tamils also welcome the intervention of medical doctors and will be docile to their recommendations.[43] Asian culture demands that the emotions of hurt, anger, and frustration be repressed and not exposed. One who discusses their private feelings and past experiences, as in Western psychiatry, is not looked upon favourably and is not socially acceptable. In a case of extreme necessity, parents may look to a psychiatrist to provide an instant diagnosis and immediate treatment. Prolonged treatment is considered a family embarrassment and reduces the family status.[44]

"Coming to Canada is a cultural shock to a lot of newcomers," says Dushy Gnanapragasam. "People are caught between two cultures. Parents have to struggle with two, three jobs and don't get to see their wives and children. Families are not functioning as they did back home."[45] Yet according to Norman Buchignani and colleagues, "South Asians have made a successful attempt to integrate themselves socially and culturally into the mainstream of Canadian society." Tamils have avoided becoming a subordinate minority group and have pulled their weight economically. Their salaries are "higher than the average immigrant arriving in the same year."[46]

Tamil Catholics bring with them a strong sense of their own identity, enjoy stable familial ties, are educated, and want a university education for their children. Recently arrived Tamil Catholics are rooted in a traditional and patriarchal society that remains focused on the preservation of Sri Lankan culture. Their children attend Catholic schools, where they learn religion in the Canadian context; at home, children receive Tamil culture from their parents. Both parents and children struggle to integrate their new Tamil Canadian identity. On Sundays, they participate in the Carnatic singing of the Catholic mass. Industrious, hardworking, family-oriented people, Tamils add much piety, faith, and energy to Canadian Catholicism. If immigration trends continue, they will become a large, important, and cohesive Catholic community.[47] They are active church members who embrace the transcendental vision of the Catholic religion and the freedom of Canadian democracy. They seek the freedom to enjoy family life, speak Tamil along with English, educate their children, have access to adequate health care, and give praise to God for the blessings they have received. The ultimate value they seek is the Tamil Catholic vision of God and the freedom to live out this vision.

Our Lady of La Vang
at the Church of Holy Martyrs of Vietnam in Montreal

7

Vietnamese Canadians:
Religious Ties Deepen Integration

After the French withdrew from North Vietnam in 1954, 600,000 to 800,000 Vietnamese Catholics emigrated to South Vietnam and France.[1] Many North Vietnamese left everything to move south and start all over again. The Vietnamese who gathered in the south were from many cultures and did not always agree about political issues. After the Americans withdrew from South Vietnam in the mid-1970s, 850,000 Vietnamese left their country and its 4,000-year history to take up residence in the United States, Canada, and China.[2] They carried with them Buddhist, Confucian, and Catholic traditions, teaching a humanism that moderated the relations between parents and children, husband and wife, and teachers and students, and presumed male dominance of the family.

Professor Peter Phan points out that the Catholic religion has a long history in Vietnam, starting with Catholic missionaries in the sixteenth and early seventeenth centuries. The Jesuit Alexandre de Rhodes arrived in 1624. He learned Vietnamese, integrated into Vietnamese culture, and trained Vietnamese converts to be Christian catechists. Speaking in Vietnamese, he and his catechists had great evangelical success. At the same time, Rhodes set the Vietnamese language to the Roman alphabet and, with the help of diacritical marks, distinguished the tones that the Vietnamese used in their speech.[3] "The planting of the church in Vietnam," according to Professor Samuel Moffett, "was one of the finest achievements of seventeenth-century Catholicism in Asia, a model of courage and Christian endurance for all Asia."[4] Despite efforts over 400 years by Christians to indigenize, Vietnamese nationalists depicted Christianity as a foreign religion. Nonetheless, Catholics, in spite of periodic persecutions, have consistently numbered about 10 per cent of the Vietnamese population and are well-established members of Vietnamese society.[5]

Intellectual Integration

Vietnamese Students and Professors in Canada

When arriving in Canada, Vietnamese Catholic immigrants discovered that since the 1950s, French-speaking Vietnamese students had been studying at Université Laval, Université de Montréal, and Université d'Ottawa. Grants from Catholic sources and the Colombo Plan provided financial assistance to these students.[6] In the mid-1960s, the number of Vietnamese students in Canada increased, and small Vietnamese communities sprang up around francophone universities in Quebec City, Montreal, Ottawa, Sherbrooke, and Moncton.[7] Some Vietnamese university graduates from the United States and other Western nations, afraid to return to Communist-dominated Saigon, migrated to Canada to attend graduate school at English-speaking universities, such as the University of Toronto. These students often went on to professional positions as professors, scientists, engineers, and administrators. They married and settled down in Canada.

More than 7,000 Vietnamese made their way to Canada after the collapse of the South Vietnamese government in 1975. Later, between 1979 and 1981, more than 53,000 boat people escaped the rigours of Vietnamese Communist rule. Despite efforts during the 1980s by the Vietnamese government to stem the flow of migrants, an additional 79,000 Vietnamese left the country; many came to Canada. During the sixteen years from 1975 to 1991, a total of 141,133 immigrants of Vietnamese extraction came to Canada: two-thirds were Vietnamese, while the remaining third were Sino-Vietnamese (Chinese Vietnamese).[8] Fleeing for political and religious reasons, they landed principally in Toronto, Montreal, Vancouver, Calgary, and Edmonton.[9] The newcomers were predominantly young, numbering more males than females.

The first arrivals in the 1950s were from elite families. They earned Canadian university degrees and easily assumed well-paying professional and managerial positions. "Université Laval in Quebec hired 21 Vietnamese Canadians as professors and senior administrators, and several Vietnamese men and women worked for the provincial government as high-ranking civil servants."[10] Those who arrived after 1975 had to learn English, find work, and requalify in their professions; they were forced to accept lower-paying, less-skilled jobs, such as those in the service industry and factories. Alberta was one province that accepted Asian degrees and welcomed into the workforce the highly qualified professionals coming to Calgary and Edmonton. Alberta accepted medical, legal, and scientific degrees, which made it easy for professionals to migrate to that province.[11]

Some Vietnamese and Sino-Vietnamese became entrepreneurs and tradespeople upon arriving in Canada. Others opened grocery, video, and jewellery stores, restaurants, garages, and travel agencies, and law, dentist's and therapist's offices. These stores and offices provided decentralized places for Vietnamese socialization.[12]

Vietnamese Canadians maintained student associations and networks of contacts for economic, religious, social, and political purposes. "Charismatic" Buddhist monks and Catholic priests inspired the creation of religious organizations.[13] Buddhists monks in Toronto helped Vietnamese newcomers adjust to Canadian society, and opened ten temples for them. Vietnamese Catholic priests were slower to arrive, but before long opened two Toronto parishes to assist their faithful with cultural integration. Student associations were formed in Quebec City in the 1960s, and in Ottawa and Toronto in the 1970s. Most, but not all, of the student associations were anti-Communist. Ethnic Vietnamese and Sino-Vietnamese congregated in separate networks. After 1978, mutual help organizations for women, seniors, single mothers, children, and athletes flourished. These various groups formed into the Canadian Vietnamese Federation to represent Vietnamese Canadian interests to the government. The Federation, which represented the majority of Vietnamese Canadians, was against the Communist regime in Vietnam. A minority, represented by the Congress of Vietnamese in Canada, had contact with and supported the Communist regime. Overall, "in Montreal, for instance, the number of Vietnamese voluntary associations grew from one in 1965 to sixty-three in 1990, and in 1993 Toronto had at least forty different associations, and Edmonton fifteen."[14]

Rediscovery of Catholic Roots: The Story of Jasmine Nguyen

Jasmine Nguyen was born in Saigon in 1952 to a Buddhist mother and a Catholic father. Her father had entered a seminary as young man. He would have become a priest, but his only brother died at the age of eleven, and their heartbroken father died shortly afterwards. His mother was left alone, with no means of support. Living in a country in which filial duties took priority due to Confucian influence, Jasmine's father left the seminary to take care of his mother. Except for the three-year period when he was jailed by the Communist government, he stayed with her until her death at age 100. He married and had a family; Jasmine was the fifth child, with four sisters and four brothers.

Since her father did well in his construction business, Jasmine and her siblings were sent to French Catholic schools. Jasmine earned the Baccalaureat issued by the French Consulate in 1970; she applied to a French-speaking university for further studies, as did many of her fellow students. Upon obtaining her visa to study in France, she joined her older sister, who had emigrated there a few years earlier. During her two years in France, Jasmine travelled through Europe extensively and completed a course in computer studies in Paris. She returned to Saigon in 1972.

Leaving behind her dreams of living abroad, Jasmine enrolled at Minh Duc University, a private Catholic university, for a degree in business administration. Although she completed the program before the fall of Saigon, she did not obtain the diploma, since the new regime ordered that all private educational institutions be amalgamated with public ones. Jasmine and her fellow students attended meetings organized at the law school at the University of Saigon in the hope of receiving their diplomas. However, the meetings turned out to be designed to distribute Marxist-Leninist propaganda and to hold demonstrations supporting the new government. Disheartened, Jasmine decided to stay home and help with the family business, which employed about 300 workers and was involved in a dozen construction projects across the country.

After 1975, Jasmine's father enthusiastically reacquainted himself with former fellow combatants who had been part of the Resistance against the French Colonialists in the years prior to 1954. He moved south and settled in Saigon, while the former soldiers joined the Northern Army of Liberation in Hanoi. He believed that these rediscovered colleagues might protect him from political harassment, especially since after 1975 he regularly gave financial assistance to President Thieu's united Vietnam. He spoke openly for the government and against corrupt members, and avoided any kind of contact with Americans. He was allowed to finish his construction projects in the south. He also volunteered to lead a delegation of architects and builders to Hanoi to rebuild the diplomatic enclave. Nevertheless, during a roundup of capitalists in South Vietnam at the end of 1976, he was arrested and incarcerated. As a result, Jasmine was made the signing officer of the family business and, with her mother and brother, ran it under the close watch of a district security officer.

By 1978, her father had still not been released. Along with many ex-officers, civil servants, and other capitalists of the old regime and their families, Jasmine and her family started realizing—slowly, painfully, but clearly—that they were undesirables under the new regime. While the heads of the families were sent to re-education camp or kept in prison, undesired families were sent to remote and undeveloped areas of the country to produce food. Being city dwellers all their life, they knew that this relocation would be their death sentence, given the lack of food and medical facilities in the country at that time. Their only hope for survival was to flee the country, even if they had to risk their lives to do so. They devised plans to escape Vietnam on fishing boats of various sizes. For Jasmine, the opportunity to leave came in 1978.

Her mother opted to remain in Vietnam to await the return of her husband and children. Jasmine broke with tradition, left her family behind, and withdrew from her home with a few friends. Thirty people, among whom were two physicians, sailed for seven days on the China Sea before landing in a Malaysian refugee camp. She applied to go to Canada because it was bilingual and, according to the UN Commissioner for Refugees in Malaysia, for whom she worked as an interpreter, it had the highest standard of living in the world.

Jasmine waited in the refugee camp for a few months. During that time, she was traumatized by the stories of women being raped by pirates, of boats being endangered by storms and the passengers having to be rescued by passing ships, and of boat people stranded on desert islands for months and having to eat the flesh of their dead companions. In the camp, desperate people occasionally committed suicide or mourned for many days and in loud voices over the deaths of loved ones. Medical facilities were sadly lacking. Jasmine wished to help, but was unable to offer assistance as a refugee herself. While awaiting her departure, she tried to put the heartbreaking stories aside and enjoy the beautiful island where the camp was located, with its coconut trees and white sand beaches. She made excursions around the island and into the spectacular undersea world of fish and coral.

Arriving in Canada in the summer of 1978, Jasmine had time to adjust to her new country before winter snows covered the landscape. She began to learn English, her third language, as well as discovering Canadian culture and customs. In 1979, she married a Vietnamese Canadian and gave birth to a daughter, Verona. When the marriage fell apart a few years later, she resolved to raise Verona alone, with some financial support from her ex-husband. She worked as a secretary for various insurance companies for fourteen years, after which she took courses in psychology and obtained a degree from the University of Toronto. Subsequently, she finished her master's degree in psychotherapy and opened a private practice.

Verona attended Catholic schools, finished high school, and graduated from York University with a degree in computer studies. She then worked full-time, married a Caribbean Canadian, and had a son. Verona was reared in Vietnam's Confucian tradition to respect the hierarchy of relations, protect family honour, respect the elderly, and assist family members in need. However, being born and raised in Canada, she also assimilated Canadian mores, such as openness to multiculturalism and resistance to parental authority. Verona learned to integrate the strengths of Asian and Western cultures. Her husband is a practising Catholic, and they are raising their son in this religious tradition.

As for Jasmine, she was not baptized until a few minutes before her wedding ceremony in a Protestant church, although she practised Catholicism when she was young. After the breakdown of her marriage, she drifted away from the Catholic Church for nine years. At a retreat, she rediscovered her faith and made Jesus the focus of her life. She became a regular practising Catholic, observed Sunday obligations, and participated in parish activities. She belongs to a Vietnamese Christian Life Community prayer group, organizes retreats, and helps Vietnamese newcomers find lodging and clothing. In the 1980s, she took part in a pilgrimage to Rome to attend a ceremony to canonize 117 Vietnamese martyrs and joined a political group proclaiming religious freedom for Vietnam. She maintains close contact with her siblings around the world and financially assists her elderly parents in Vietnam. Catholic teaching, practice, and fellowship in Vietnam and Canada have helped her to open up to the Western world and integrate her more fully into Canadian life.

At the age of 52, Jasmine bought a house in the suburbs. She intends to spend her retirement in Canada, unless circumstances allow her to relocate to a warmer climate. She is grateful to Canada for a second chance away from persecution, warfare, and poverty. She is glad to contribute her life skills to Canada and proud to maintain Canadian citizenship. She enjoys her grandson and her many friends from diverse cultural backgrounds. [15]

Attuned to Western Culture: The Story of Bao Van Pham and Le Tham Huang Yen

Bao Van Pham was born in Northern Vietnam to a Catholic family. In 1954, when the Communists took over, his family moved south to Saigon, as did Le Tham Huang Yen and her family. She completed a bachelor of arts and a bachelor of law at the university in Saigon in 1965. She then worked as the assistant director at the foreign exchange department at the National Bank. It was there that she met Bao, who was the director of research at the bank. Yen was baptized a Catholic, and, in 1967, she and Bao married. [16]

Bao went to the United States on a student visa and received his MBA from Western Michigan University in 1974. The next year, while still in Michigan, he initiated proceedings to immigrate to Canada. Bao sought a neutral country to which he could move his family and where his children would receive a good education. Landing in Toronto in 1976, he sponsored his wife and family to come to Canada. They have two children, Mary Thanh-Tam Pham and John Y-Nhan Pham, who were ages 11 and 8, respectively, when they arrived in Canada in 1979.

As a newcomer, Bao resolved to take any work he could find. At the same time, he enrolled in the master's program in library science at the University of Toronto and was employed by the Toronto Public Library. Yen looked for employment in French and found it as a claims adjuster, working at this job for nineteen years. She did not have difficulties fitting into the French-language position, but Bao found that he had what he describes as a "foreign accent," which caused him problems. In addition, he had been raised to be discreet, traditional, and humble, but found in North America that he was expected to assert himself and verbally sell his skills. Nonetheless, the French education he and his wife received in Vietnam attuned them to Western culture and made the adjustment in Canada easier than it might otherwise have been.

The adjustment period in Toronto proved to be helpful for family dialogue. Family members explored Canadian life together and discussed their discoveries. They went to museums and visited universities to prepare themselves for English-language education, with Bao asking the children, "Are you ready for university studies?" They discussed possible universities and professional careers. The parents told their children that arts are for native-born Canadians but that science and technology are for newcomers who must make their way in a competitive society. The parents stressed the importance of fitting into Canada, along with the family bonds of attending mass, celebrating holidays, and eating Vietnamese and French foods. As the years went by, the parents had less and less time to spend with their children. They learned to propose ideas to the children and then step back, knowing that the young are assertive, "independent and proud of what they could do." Eventually, however, Bao realized that he wanted to be a teacher for his children and, changing his approach, became in the dialogue both "a listener and a contributor."

Bao and Yen's daughter, Mary, while studying to be an optometrist in Toronto, benefited from the Newman Centre, the Roman Catholic campus ministry at the University of Toronto. The students there were "like brothers and sisters," says Bao, and they learned to balance religious emotions and rationality. Mary married a Vietnamese who became a Catholic; she and her family attend mass in an English-speaking parish. John, who was three years younger than Mary when they came to Canada, is more Canadian and more independent, and has caused his family acculturative stress. He married a Scottish Canadian woman from a non-churchgoing family, and they do not attend church. Mary and John still sing Vietnamese songs on festive occasions, and John clothes his baby girl in Vietnamese dress on the Lunar New Year.

Mary, the optometrist, now lives in Maryland, and John is an engineer elsewhere in Canada. For Bao and Yen, their adult children moving away was difficult. For Vietnamese with a keen sense of family, children moving away is always painful. Psychiatrists have commented that "for Vietnamese who live in [North] America, one of the biggest changes has been the loss of the extended family structure .... Many Vietnamese parents were shocked to see their children moving away for better job opportunities after finishing their education."[17] Success in transition to Canada for Vietnamese brings unexpected joys but also painful changes in the cherished family structure. Bao points out that disruptions within the family began when the family arrived in Canada. Often what happens is that women are inclined to get jobs right away and to become the family breadwinner. Having neither work nor a pay envelope humiliates the husbands. Some Vietnamese Canadians who bring over Vietnamese wives who are unprepared for North American life and try to live a Vietnamese lifestyle in Canada often find themselves in conflict with their wives. With religious motivation and contacts, Bao and Yen work unofficially with Vietnamese couples to help them get jobs, housing, and integrate into Canadian life.

Bao and Yen have Vietnamese- and Canadian-born friends, and they communicate with them in English, French, and Vietnamese. They intend to remain in Canada, but if they were able to assist Vietnamese people in the rebuilding their lives and their country, would be tempted to return to Vietnam. They could financially manage life in Vietnam, since the cost of living is less than in Canada. With a similar mind for helping others, Bao's youngest sister is a Catholic religious and a nurse working in the Congo.

When Bao and Yen and their children first arrived in Toronto, they attended Joan of Arc church and enjoyed the lively parish, interesting homilies, and good relationship between the parishioners and clergy.

In Vietnam, Bao and Yen had been very impressed with the Catholic missionaries who had a great influence on the people. The missionaries lived in poverty, assisted the needy, and won over a number of Buddhists. In Toronto, Bao asked Archbishop Philip Pocock for his support in founding a Vietnamese Catholic mission. The archbishop, in turn, directed Vietnamese Catholics to meet on Sundays in the crypt of St. Basil's church on the campus of St. Michael's College in downtown Toronto. Many knew by heart the Vietnamese hymns and prayers, and sought to worship in Vietnamese. With the help of a $2,000 donation from St. Catherine of Siena parish, Bao and others collected and printed a 300-page Vietnamese prayerbook. Bao believes that "to maintain a good spiritual life the religious devotions need great understanding and mature assimilation to bring the religious sentiment up to their rational conviction." In other words, when people understand devotions properly, they will not fall into magical belief in ritual; religious ritual without understanding borders on magic. Most Vietnamese Canadian families read short prayers in the evening. Their spiritual groups are informal and include both Catholics and non-Catholics. They gather for dialogue over mutual problems and to share fellowship. They learn to balance sentiment with rationality, and the activities they engage in are efficient and helpful to the Vietnamese community, Bao says.

Bao believes that Vietnamese spirituality combines the old and the new, the emotional and the rational, and must be guided by Christian prayer and discernment to grow toward mature understanding of Vietnamese Canadian identity. Vietnamese Canadians are searching for their own inspiration to lead them to the kingdom of God, and are sympathetic to those around them who are suffering as they have suffered. For instance, at St. Joan of Arc church, parishioners reached out to sponsor Kenyan immigrants to Canada. Reflection on and the search for a new Vietnamese Canadian identity will embed the Vietnamese Canadians in the Canadian Church. [18]

Vietnamese Volunteers:
A Free University: The Story of John Do Trong Chu

An example of Vietnamese volunteerism is John Do Trong Chu, who was born into a Catholic family in a small northern village 44 kilometres south of Hanoi. He studied law at the University of Indochina in Hanoi and, later, went to St. Thomas College in St. Paul, Minnesota, where he completed his bachelor of arts in 1951. He attended graduate school at the University of Minnesota and worked as a Vietnamese language instructor in Washington, DC. In 1954, he was one of four Vietnamese who picketed the White House to protest the partition of Vietnam by the Geneva Agreement. During the ten months following July 1954, there was a mass migration of North Vietnamese to the south to escape the oppressive Communist government. John's two sisters, along with their husbands and children, left Hanoi on the last French airlift to Saigon, where they resettled with the help of U.S. humanitarian aid.

Shortly afterwards, John, along with five other Vietnamese from American and European universities, returned to Saigon in 1954 to participate in the new government of Prime Minister Ngo Dinh Diem. In the same year, he and his friends opened a free university, the Popular Polytechnic Institute. In the evening, the school offered vocational, language, business, and secretarial courses. No fee was charged, since all instructors were volunteers. More than 7,000 applied for admission, but only 1,700 were accepted. John donated his services as an English-language instructor and as dean of studies.

John then worked for the government as assistant to the Vietnamese high commissioner for refugees and a promoter of tourism. He left Refugee Affairs to promote tourism among North Americans and Europeans to stimulate the Vietnamese economy. He wrote tourist booklets, taught English to tourist guides and taxi drivers, attended international tourist conferences, and sought to attract American hotel chains and tour boat operators. After three years, he joined the Ministry of Foreign Affairs and was sent on diplomatic postings to New Delhi, Jakarta, Phnom Penh, Canberra, and Bangkok.[19]

A Community Organizer: The Story of Thérèse Tran Thi Mau and John Do Trong Chu

Thérèse Tran Thi Mau was born to a Buddhist family in South Vietnam. Her father was a primary school principal in Giadinh. She studied at a convent school and at the Collège des jeunes filles in Saigon, and spent four years in Paris for further education. She returned home to Saigon to work for Air Vietnam and afterwards was baptized a Catholic. Both Therese and her husband, John Do Trong Chu were deeply involved as volunteer community organizers in adult education and in assisting war victims when they married in the Cathedral of Saigon. They had six children: Christine, Michelle, Tom, Theodore, Robert, and Katie. As a young adult, Christine was sent to the United States to study at the College of St. Catherine in St. Paul, Minnesota. Michelle attended the University of Heidelberg in Germany.

At age 30, Thérèse was elected to the Vietnam parliament, the youngest member at that time. John and his brother Do Manh Quat, a well-known lawyer, also ran, but only his brother was elected.

One year after the Paris Agreement of January 1973, when the South Vietnamese government faced imminent collapse due to the massive invasion from North Vietnam, John and Thérèse's eldest daughter, Christine, who had completed her studies in the United States and established herself in Canada, sponsored her parents and her four younger siblings to immigrate to Canada. They arrived in Toronto in 1975 as landed immigrants. The younger children were enrolled in school, and the search for employment and accommodations began. After five weeks of intensive searching, John and Thérèse found a job that also provided living accommodations for the whole family. At noon on April 30, 1975, the day John and Thérèse moved in as superintendents of an apartment building in Etobicoke, west of Toronto, North Vietnam tanks rolled into Saigon.

John and Thérèse worked as a superintendent team for four years, until May 1979. Thanks to John's previous work with refugees, the Vietnamese Association of Toronto, funded by the Ontario and Canadian governments, hired him as senior co-ordinator to settle the Vietnamese boat people. Six years later, in May 1985, John was suffering from deteriorating health due to stress. He resigned from his job and took a position as a property caretaker in Jackson's Point on Lake Simcoe. There he supervised the country estate of a rich land developer, who appeared only on weekends. Recovering after a year, John applied to Mississauga's community legal services office, which was looking for a community worker to provide legal counselling to Vietnamese and Canadians. John was hired and continued this work for ten years beyond his official retirement. Being trilingual, he then worked as a freelance court interpreter for city, provincial, and federal courts. For his public service, John received the Ontario Bicentennial Award in 1984 and the Ontario Medal of Citizenship in 1994. Thérèse, meanwhile, received an award from the Catholic Children's Aid Society in 1990.

In most Vietnamese families, parents make the family decisions until the children reach university age. Once in university, the children make their own decisions. Yet for Vietnamese, "kinship relations, family networks, and personal memories," writes Louis-Jacques Dorais, "appear to be much more meaningful than community organizations and collective discourses .... Most Vietnamese appear to be interested primarily in family affairs and in transmitting traditional family values to their children."[20] In Vietnam, families retain Vietnamese Catholic traditions, but in Canada both Vietnamese and Catholic traditions are softened, owing to the pressure to integrate into multicultural Canada. When the first Vietnamese arrived in Canada, there was little Vietnamese media available, and many distractions existed to disrupt Vietnamese customs. The older Chu children retained their Vietnamese language and culture better than did the younger ones. Some retained their Catholic religion, while others did not. Some married Vietnamese Catholics, and others did not. Some of the grandchildren are baptized Catholics, going to Catholic schools, and others are not. Generally, the marriages of Vietnamese Catholics to other Vietnamese Catholics endure better than mixed marriages. Vietnamese prefer endogamous marriages, and Vietnamese Catholics prefer Vietnamese Catholic marriages, but with few choices available in a multicultural society this is not always possible.[21]

Although the Chu family came as sojourners to Canada, no one now talks of returning to Vietnam. Canada has become the permanent residence for this family, which currently comprises two lawyers, two court interpreters, one accountant, one retired navy lieutenant-commander, one registered nurse, and one real estate agent.

John and Thérèse were among the founding members of the Marriage and Family Enrichment Program at Mission of the Vietnamese Martyrs parish. At home, they occasionally share daily prayers, say the rosary, and read the Bible. They have been active in a group to sponsor Vietnamese seminarians preparing for the Catholic priesthood. Their group has funded 167 seminarians, sending them each $400 yearly for their education. Over ten years, 21 seminarians have been ordained for Vietnam. A Vietnamese Capuchin priest, whom the Chu family had sponsored to come to Canada, died in Toronto eight years ago; they are now sponsoring a young man in Vietnam in his third year of seminary. Thérèse is involved in the Legion of Mary, and John in the Society for the Propagation of the Faith, to attract non-Catholic Vietnamese to the Catholic community. A number of non-Catholics in interfaith marriages have been prepared for baptism. The strong faith of the Vietnamese community has contributed priests to dioceses across Canada and in Vietnam, as well as sisters to serve Vietnamese- and Canadian Catholic communities.[22]

Recruiting Vietnamese Clergy for Canada

Professor Peter Phan comments on the large number of North American Vietnamese vocations, writing that

Vietnamese American Catholics have already visibly transformed the American church in the number of priestly and religious vocations they have produced .... The large number of vocations could be attributed to the high respect in which priests and religious are held among Vietnamese (which has, of course, its own negative side), but certainly it has roots in the devout faith of Vietnamese American families.[23]

Archbishop Adam Exner of Vancouver commented that Vietnamese clergy and laity who share the same bonds of faith as Canadian-born Catholics fit easily into the Canadian parish environment. Vietnamese priests have proven to be excellent pastors. Vietnamese, according to the archbishop, want to fit into Canada and Canadian parishes, and strive to learn English and cope with Canadian culture.[24] Professor Jonathan Tan writes that, for Vietnamese North Americans, the "Catholic parish is often the most important ethnic institution, serving various sociocultural roles in addition to the usual religious functions ...."[25] The Vietnamese have sacrificed much for their faith and have deepened it in the process, but they are not put off by what they see as Canadian softness and laxity. [26]

Vietnamese laypersons process in the relics of the Vietnamese martyrs at St. Cecilia's church in Toronto.

Archbishop Exner says that Vietnamese Catholics have enriched the diocese, as have individuals from countless other cultures. More than half of the parishioners in the Archdiocese (57 per cent) speak a language other than English at home. Of this group, 30 per cent speak Chinese, while the other 70 per cent speak 138 other languages, of which Vietnamese would be one.[27]

There are twelve Vietnamese priests in the Archdiocese of Vancouver and two Vietnamese congregations, one in Vancouver and the other in Port Moody. Father Peter Pham OP is the pastor of the 6,100 parishioners at St. Joseph parish in Vancouver, where three of six weekend masses are celebrated in Vietnamese. In this large parish, Father Pham's associate pastor is Peter Tran OP. Father Joseph Hieu Nguyen is the pastor of St. Joseph's 2,700 parishioners in Port Moody, including a number of Vietnamese. Speaking of Vietnamese American parishes, Peter Phan comments that "Vietnamese Catholics are deeply attached to their Vietnamese churches and hold their pastors in high esteem. They spare no resources to have their own churches and their own priests so as to be able to worship in their mother tongue and to preserve their religious and cultural customs."[28]

Edmonton has one congregation of Vietnamese Catholics at Queen of Martyrs (Vietnamese), whose pastor is the Vietnamese-born Father Peter Tran OP. In Calgary, there are a number of Vietnamese parishes and Vietnamese priests. Fathers Ignatius Thu Tran is pastor of Ascension church in Calgary. Father Peter Hung Tran OP is chaplain of the University of Calgary Catholic Community. Father Dominic Phamvanboa OP is pastor of Holy Trinity parish, which caters to Vietnamese parishioners, and Father Paul Dzung Tran OP is pastor of St. Vincent Liem parish, which offers mass in Vietnamese.[29]

Language Maintenance

The greater majority of Vietnamese in Canada speak their language at home, but Canadian-born youngsters, once they have learned English in school and on the playground, resist speaking Vietnamese. To counter this difficulty, Catholic churches and Buddhist temples encourage the enrollment of Vietnamese children on weekends for language study, receiving widespread

parental support. Vietnamese newspapers, magazines, and jour-
nals are available in Canada, providing a vehicle for the adver-
tisement of Vietnamese companies and agencies. Distribution is
through Vietnamese stores, doctors' offices, and meeting places.
Magazines and journals discuss Vietnamese identity abroad,
Canadian-Vietnamese adaptations, life in Vietnam after 1975,
Taoism and the harmony of the universe, Buddhism and the seek-
ing of inner peace. Vietnamese authors write of the Canadian-
Vietnamese experience in English, French, and Vietnamese.
Vietnamese music, radio, and television are available, along with
Vietnamese videos and cassettes. Vietnamese-speaking priests
and religious sisters serve Vietnamese Catholic parishes across
Canada (15 to 20 per cent of Vietnamese Canadians are Catho-
lic), including the first parishes, which were in Montreal, and
those in Quebec City, Ottawa, Toronto, Hamilton, Winnipeg,
Calgary, and Vancouver.[30]

Urban Integration

Acculturation in Winnipeg

Father John Te Nguyen began his education in Vietnam but,
for political and religious reasons, left his country via a refugee
camp in the Philippines and landed in Canada in 1982. After
settling in Winnipeg, he enrolled in an English as a Second
Language course. He was attracted to the Vietnamese Catholic
community, which had been meeting since the 1980s in St.
Boniface, an area of Winnipeg. He asked to join the Archdiocese
of Saint Boniface in 1992 to begin studies to become a priest.
With the approval of the Archdiocese, he enrolled in St. Peter's
Seminary in London, Ontario, and was ordained a priest in 1997.
He became pastor of St. Philip Minh parish in St. Boniface,
which serves 450 parishioners, including 100 children. (He
was recently replaced by Father Joseph Tran.) As a priest in the
Archdiocese, Father Nguyen says he was treated as an equal by
his fellow priests and with respect by his parishioners.[31]

The Vietnamese Catholic community knits together Vietnamese culture and the Catholic religion. St. Philip Minh parish offers regular language and culture classes to children whose parents speak Vietnamese at home. Parents teach their children to honour and respect their elders. In contrast, the young attending Canadian schools are taught Canadian culture, which includes questioning things they do not understand and being open to talking about taboo topics. To Vietnamese parents, according to Father Nguyen, their children's open and inquisitive minds lead them to experimentation and promiscuity, and to the loss of Vietnamese tradition. Vietnamese conversation, in the view of the elders, avoids topics such as pregnancy, gays, HIV/AIDS, and pre-marital sex. If the young talk openly about these topics, they provoke tension between themselves and their elders. Yet parents doing shift work have little time to supervise and educate their children. The children learn by themselves how to survive socially and academically in the Canadian environment. Parents would prefer their children to marry other Vietnamese, but have learned to accept their children's choices. Vietnamese who are Buddhists and then become Catholics find the transition easy since Buddhists are concerned with honouring ancestors, as Christians are.

Father Nguyen likes his work in Canada and carries a Canadian passport, and yet in retirement might seek a warmer climate in Vietnam, or in Victoria. He likes the medical and social welfare systems, which include nursing homes and old-age pensions. He would not hesitate to take advantage of psychiatric services, as he looks upon psychiatry as a "useful tool."

When migrating, Vietnamese generally send a son to Canada to look for work, establish a residence, and then sponsor their family members. Father Nguyen believes that, following Vietnamese custom, protecting the career of the husband is the principal concern of the family decision-making process. Yet in Canada, wives tend to find work more quickly than their husbands; thus, husbands learn to accept the leadership and advice of their wives. Nonetheless, Vietnamese men struggle to accept in Canadian society that women are the equal of men in the workplace.

The arrival of Vietnamese professionals in Canada provided volunteers for the Archdiocese of Saint Boniface. In 1998, these volunteers renovated the empty diocesan-owned junior seminary and turned it into a church and community centre. They rebuilt the chapel into a church, dining room into a parish hall, bedrooms into classrooms, and convent into a rectory.

Vietnamese newcomers brought Vietnamese devotions with them. For example, Vietnamese Catholics have a strong devotion to Our Lady of La Vang, whose eighteenth-century shrine is in a mountainous area in central Vietnam near Hue. From 1798 through the nineteenth century, the shrine was a refuge from government persecution for Vietnamese Catholics.

The seventeenth-century Vietnamese martyr St. Philip Minh is the namesake for the parish in Winnipeg, which is the centre of devotional life for Vietnamese Catholics there. Prayer groups, such as the Holy Family Movement, aim to deepen family bonds. Group ministries include sponsoring Vietnamese families as new arrivals to Winnipeg. New members to the Vietnamese Catholic community are recruited by word of mouth. A Vietnamese, Sister Marie Joseph Doan Bich Hong, instructs Vietnamese neophytes in the Rite of Christian Initiation of Adults. At regular periods, elders gather for prayer in the Vietnamese way. The youth group studies social justice, and children are part of the Eucharistic Movement. Activities and devotional groups are offered to parishioners of all ages. Celebrating the Tet (New Year) in a traditional way is the major event of the year. In parish devotions in Vietnam, Father Nguyen observes, men are more involved in church activities than women, whereas in Canada, the reverse is true.[32]

Vietnamese came to Winnipeg following others from their family and village. Many of the new arrivals arrive with professional skills but soon discover that their skills are not recognized in Canada. Instead, they must find work in restaurants, doing maintenance, or on assembly lines.

Filled with Hope: The Story of Hien Duc Tran and Nguyet Nguyen

The parishioners of St. Philip Minh are full of hope in their new land. For instance, Hien Duc Tran was a naval officer in South Vietnam until 1975. When he and his wife, Nguyet Nguyen, arrived in Canada in 1990, he hoped to be a math teacher, but found it was necessary to finish Grade 12 at Red River College and then accept employment with a health food company. Nguyet, who had finished Grade 12 before they moved to Canada, was a merchant in Vietnam, but now works as a leather cutter. Hien and Nguyet came to Canada for a better life, but both found it difficult adjusting to Canadian languages and customs. At language school, Nguyet experienced discrimination by other students. Their child, Tin, was educated principally in Canada, but he also speaks Vietnamese and is familiar with Vietnamese culture. Belief in God and respect for elders is part of that culture. In the view of the parents, the young maintain about half of the Vietnamese traditions when they move to Canada. Parent-child conflict arises from a range of minor and major issues: for example, when Canadian-raised children do not like the cooking oil odours of Vietnamese foods, or when parents want to chose their child's marriage partner. Vietnamese children in Canada want to choose whom they marry, regardless of whether the chosen person is Vietnamese.

Since their arrival in 1990, Hien and Nguyet have put down roots in Canada. Apart from winter visits to Vietnam, they will spend the rest of their lives in St. Boniface. They find the Canadian health-care system useful and would welcome psychiatric help if it were necessary. They continue to make family decisions in the patriarchal Asian style.[33]

Committed to Canada: The Story of Kim Nguyen

Kim Nguyen was a student in Vietnam. After fleeing her country, she ended up in a refugee camp in the Philippines before travelling to Canada in 1985. She took English as a Second Language for a year in junior high and completed high school. Unlike Vietnamese schools, which operate under the strict rule of the teacher and with the full support of the parents, she found Canadian schools welcoming, friendly, and pleasant for students. At the University of Manitoba, she earned a bachelor of science in chemistry and is now employed in Winnipeg. From her early years in Vietnam, she has retained her ability to speak Vietnamese and her sense of the importance of family cohesiveness. As a young woman, Kim feels that young people will maintain traditions when they can participate in community activities that reinforce their ethnic culture. Generational conflict, she believes, is inevitable between elders who were brought up in Vietnam and youth brought up in Canada. She hopes to marry a Vietnamese Catholic and fully integrate into Canadian society. Even though she has found Winnipeg winters a difficult adjustment, Kim is committed to a future life in Canada and is appreciative of Canadian health care.[34]

Adjusting to Canadian Life: The Story of Dao Lieu

Dao Lieu arrived as a Vietnamese refugee to Canada in 1985. She had taught school in Vietnam and had hoped to do the same in Canada; however, she found she could not qualify to teach without returning to school, and instead accepted a job as a nurse's aid. Adjusting to the Canadian language and culture was difficult for her. Her four children are Canadian raised and educated, but they still use their mother tongue. They all have jobs in Canada. Coming from a tropical climate of Southeast Asia, Dao finds the Manitoba winter a challenge and hopes one day to move to the milder climate of Vancouver or Toronto. As a mother, she believes that the young maintain about half of the

Vietnamese traditions; she has been able to soften generational conflict by readily adjusting to Canadian life. For instance, she has learned to accept intermarriage of Vietnamese with members of other ethnic groups. Her family appreciates the Canadian medical system, particularly since psychiatric services, which are not acceptable in Vietnam, are available in Canada. Breaking the Asian stereotype, Dao believes in shared family decisions between husband and wife.[35]

Dao belongs to St. Philip Minh church in Winnipeg, where parish life is the centre of her social activities and religious commitment. Parish groups include the Eucharist Youth Society, the Holy Family, Legion of Mary, and several choirs for children and adults. The men are active in mass and devotions, yet, according to Dao and her young friend Tia Pham, who came to Canada in 2002, women seem more comforted by prayer and meditation. Children make up 25 per cent of the parish and give special hope for the future. Newcomers arriving through the help of family and friends in Winnipeg are welcomed by parishioners and drawn into parish life. The Vietnamese of St. Philip Minh parish see themselves as good-humoured and spirited Canadian Catholics.

Acculturation in Toronto:
Two Vietnamese Congregations Show the Way

Toronto has two Vietnamese congregations. Mission of the Vietnamese Martyrs parish, which was erected in 1986 at St. Cecilia's church, was led by Father Dominic Bui. A second Vietnamese congregation emerged in Mississauga at Ss. Salvador do Mundo parish, where Father Peter Ba has a congregation of 600.

Father Bui relates that he began his seminary education in Vietnam, escaped with the boat people, was marooned in a refugee camp for nearly five years, and finally completed his priestly education in Toronto, being ordained at St. Michael's Cathedral in 2002. The following year, he was appointed pastor of

Vietnamese Martyrs parish. The congregation has 3,000 members, who attend one of the three weekend Vietnamese masses. Three other masses are held in English for parishioners of Italian and Portuguese descent.[36] In 2005, a second Vietnamese priest, Father Joseph Tap Van Tran, succeeded Bui as pastor.

Vietnamese spiritual organizations, including the Legion of Mary, the Family Enrichment Forum, three Vietnamese choirs, the pastoral council, and a language school, are busy in the parish. The Legion of Mary fosters spiritual growth, group prayer, and ministry among parishioners. The Family Enrichment Forum leads families in regular prayer and in reflection on the Scriptures. Parents initiate their membership by making a weekend retreat at the Regina Mundi centre in Sharon, Ontario. Families organize themselves into prayer groups for weekly meetings, mutual enrichment, and social support. Choirs lead the singing at each of the three Vietnamese masses on the weekend. The pastoral council supports Father Tran as he spiritually directs the parish. Saturday afternoon language classes teach the Vietnamese language to 300 students from grades 1 to 12 for regular school credit.

Seeking Religious Freedom: The Story of Michael Huynh and Agnes H. Tran

Born a Catholic in Vietnam, Michael Huynh came to Canada with his family in 1983 in search of political freedom and a better economic future. He completed an engineering program at Seneca College in Toronto. Also born a Catholic is Agnes H. Tran, who escaped from Vietnam as a boat person and was sponsored by a Catholic group to come to Toronto, where other family members already lived. She came to Canada in the hope of political and religious freedom and a good education. Agnes went to a Toronto high school to learn English and then entered the University of Windsor to do a bachelor of science in community nursing. Completing this program in 1997, she began nursing at a North York hospital. In the same year, Agnes and Michael were married in Toronto.

Michael experienced linguistic difficulties when he first came to Toronto; Agnes admitted having similar problems. She believes that the hospital where she worked discriminated against her. She relates that her comments were not listened to with the same seriousness as those of Euro-Canadian nurses. In her view, these nurses received privileges that she did not. For instance, Euro-Canadian nurses were more likely to receive day-shift assignments, whereas Asian nurses were expected to work both day and night shifts.

At home, Michael and Agnes like to discuss family decisions and come to a resolution, but, in the end, Agnes says she lets Michael make the decision. Both agree that they hope to teach their children the Vietnamese language and the Catholic religion. However, they are aware that when children reach their teens, they follow the fashions of their peers, and may stop speaking Vietnamese or even cease going to church.

Michael and Agnes point out that elderly Vietnamese rely on textbook prayers and the rosary, and when they pray, "they pray loud and long!" By contrast, Michael and Agnes meditate at home quietly, reflect on the Scriptures, and say short prayers. They also attend Sunday mass at Vietnamese Martyrs and go to prayer groups. They have participated in the Family Enrichment Program and regularly attend one of the 30 Vietnamese neighbourhood subgroups. An average of 30 couples take the Family Enrichment Program yearly, and 600 Vietnamese Catholic couples have completed the weekend, one third of whom continue to be active in the movement. Through these weekends, 20 non-Catholic spouses have become Catholics and feel more unified with their partners in their religious faith.[37] For Vietnamese, the extended family "constitute[s] the most meaningful component of overseas Vietnamese communities" and "the family—and religion" are the most important institutions.[38]

Acculturation in Montreal:
Mission of the Vietnamese Martyrs Parish

In Montreal, Father J. B. Thanh Son Dinh is pastor of the well-established Mission of the Vietnamese Martyrs at Saint-Philippe in Rosemont. Ten Vietnamese families arrived in Montreal in 1975; Vietnamese have continued to flow into the city. Since that time to 2003, 35 young men have entered the seminary, seeking ordination to the priesthood.

Father Dinh was one of nine children. He completed his minor seminary education in Vietnam. After the Communists took over, his family came with the boat people to Montreal in 1979. The following year, he attended a government school for new Canadians, and in 1981 entered the seminary. After ordination four years later, Father Dinh sponsored his parents and sisters, who came to Canada in the late 1980s.

Vietnamese Martyrs has a daily mass in Vietnamese and three on the weekend. Three thousand parishioners are registered in the parish, but 1,000 fill church pews for weekend Masses. The rest go to their local Montreal parishes, which are often closer to where they live and have more parking. Father Dinh is impressed with the strength of the many Vietnamese devotional groups, which include the charismatic movement, Legion of Mary, Army of Mary, Small Souls of St. Theresa, Eucharist Crusade, and the Third Order of Franciscans for Families. Fifteen weddings occur yearly in the parish; newly married couples are invited to Family Life Enrichment weekends.

Family Life Enrichment is a Vietnamese creation to support married couples. It was founded in Vietnam by Father Caiu Quang Minh SJ (see more on Father Peter-Minh Quang Chu in Toronto below), who travels 300 days a year animating the 245 Vietnamese groups throughout the world. In Montreal, eighteen groups gather on a regular basis and welcome the annual visit of Father Minh. The weekend is composed of instruction on family psychology, reading and explanation of the Word of God, and prayer on the Word. Twenty couples participate in the weekend as an initiation to become full members of prayer groups. Ten families belong to a group, which meets in a home every other month. Group members have been married from three weeks to 42 years. As a result of the weekend, couples are strengthened and reconciled, and one divorced couple remarried. For example, during the weekend, a husband of 45 years learned to say to his wife for the first time in his life, "I'm sorry." Father Dinh reported that the members of these groups attend mass with their families, offer marriage preparation programs, and give social strength to Vietnamese Martyrs parish.

Members of the charismatic movement meet weekly to pray the Bible. They emphasize the coming of the Holy Spirit and God's forgiveness. They are very faithful in attending the Eucharist, recite the rosary, and participate in divine adoration. They look for intimate sharing with God and celebrate God's goodness with singing and praise. Their enthusiasm for the Gospel brings converts to the parish.

Vietnamese Catholics do not look for handouts from the Canadian government. They are hard working, finding employment and living within their means. When necessary, they help one another with food, clothing, and lodging. Vietnamese secular and religious societies look after the aged and infirm. Of the 30,000 Vietnamese in Montreal, about 10 per cent are Catholics.[39]

The first and second generations of Vietnamese now living in Canada speak their language at home, embrace their traditions with affection, and attend church faithfully. Yet Father Dinh admitted that the children who are born in Canada and attend local schools do not wish to speak Vietnamese, except at home, nor do they have the same desire as their parents to attend church weekly.[40] Recent research has shown that the children of Vietnamese Canadians "are much less involved than their parents in transnational family networks and Viet Kieu [Vietnamese foreign] organizations."[41]

Family Adjustment

Family Life

Vietnamese family life in Canada tends to be traditional and has great reverence for elders. It is in the family that the young are schooled in Vietnamese politeness and obedience. On account of this family training, Vietnamese Canadian children are considered more polite, obedient, and shy than their Canadian peers. In fact, Vietnamese children suffer from living in one culture at home, which demands reticence, and in another at school, which requires assertiveness. Although the young want to be independent as Canadian youths are, they find they are not ready to be so, having been raised in a protective atmosphere.[42] The father is expected to play the role of the spokesman, provider, and protector of the family, although in Canada it is often easier for women and teenagers to get work. While mothers, in fact, control the purse strings and family finances, children lead the family's contact with the outside world. Surplus money is frugally saved for a future house, private schools, and remittance to relatives in Vietnam. These factors modify the Vietnamese family system to meet Canadian exigencies.[43]

In Vietnam, people avoid living alone, preferring to dwell with family. Single Vietnamese men in Canada have a difficult time finding a traditional Vietnamese wife, who must be obedient and submissive. Part of the difficulty lies in the fact that single men outnumber women here, in contrast to the situation in Vietnam. Some Canadian males return home and, with the help of relatives, marry Vietnamese women who are willing to immigrate to Canada. Father Bui points out that such an arrangement generally requires the bride's family to make wedding payments, which can be costly. In addition, the newly married couple will have expenses to meet and may have debts to settle upon their arrival in Canada. A Vietnamese spouse in Canada without suitable preparation for Canadian ways can put the relationship under severe strain. Thus, choosing a spouse from Vietnam is less and less of an option for Vietnamese Canadian men.

Living together and experimental marriages are not acceptable to Vietnamese, who deem marriage necessary. After seeking family permission to marry, a couple must raise a family of three to five children to honour family ancestors.[44] The eldest son is to gather members of the family at Tet (New Year's) celebrations and on ancestors' special memorial anniversaries, which include family events.

Vietnamese clergy in Toronto celebrate the Day
of Andrew Dung Lac and the Vietnamese martyrs

The Confucian culture has great respect for intellectuals, teachers, and religious as persons who make singular contributions to society and thus deserve societal respect. Catholic young people who wish to become priests or religious sisters fall within this cultural tradition. Their families look favourably on their son's or daughter's vocation to serve the church, considering it a great honour to have a child in religious life. The parents of such children receive great respect and reverence from their community.[45]

Family Support: The Story of Joseph Tap Tran

Father Joseph Tap Tran succeeded Dominic Bui as pastor of Mission of the Vietnamese Martyrs parish in Toronto in 2005. Joseph was born in South Vietnam in 1954. He attended Catholic schools, then entered the seminary, but the Communists took control of the south and closed the seminary when he was 18. By 1975, his parents decided that the family should relocate to Canada, but it was up to Joseph and his younger brother Viet to initiate the move. Canada had a good reputation as a country that accepted newcomers, was prosperous, and offered a good education and excellent health care. But in the final analysis, the main attractions of Canada were its freedom of religion, civil rights, educational opportunities, and political stability. The Tran family relatives who preceded them to North America advised them not to wait but to emigrate immediately. Joseph and his brother Viet escaped to Indonesia in 1980 and arrived in Canada in 1982. In 1986, they sponsored their siblings Duc, who came with a bachelor of commerce degree, and Agnes (Huong), who became a registered nurse after moving to Canada.[46]

Joseph arrived in Toronto wishing to pursue seminary studies, which meant he must learn to speak English. A Dominican priest in Ottawa advised him to bypass English as a Second Language and attend the five-year Ontario high school program. At age 28, Joseph enrolled in an Ontario public high school and attended it for five years. Receiving government support as a refugee, he was able to learn English well. These five years of learning the English language and Canadian culture eliminated the language barrier for him and for his two brothers and sister who followed the same path. Joseph's grandmother arrived in Canada in 1991 and became a Canadian citizen at the age of 101. Joseph entered St. Augustine's Seminary in Toronto in the autumn of 1995. He completed his master of divinity degree in

2000 and was ordained a Catholic priest. Speaking English with facility, Joseph did not encounter discrimination in the seminary or in the archdiocese.

The Tran family's decision to come to Canada was a shared decision. Vietnamese decisions are family decisions, with advantages and disadvantages. One advantage is that all the members of the family share in each other's future; one disadvantage is that the parents can use these decisions to control their children. Joseph's family completely supported his decision to become a priest, just as the family would have supported other siblings to be doctors or to follow other professional careers. The whole family, as Father Tran explains, got behind his career decision, prayed for him, and encouraged him. Yet, this type of support always presumes that decisions can be recast when necessary, and he would be supported if he left the seminary. Vietnamese families are extended families; cousins are treated as brothers and sisters. When grandparents retire, their children want to keep them in their homes to provide them with Vietnamese food, traditions, and religious devotions. Catholic grandparents know the hymns and prayers in Vietnamese and are consoled by being able to sing them in their own language. Father Tran estimates that 70 per cent of younger Vietnamese Canadians do not know how to speak Vietnamese.

When considering marriage partners, the priority for Vietnamese Canadian Catholics is that they be Catholic first and Vietnamese second. Courting takes at least one year, in order to win parental agreement for marriage. As 10 per cent of Vietnamese Canadians are Catholics, interfaith marriages are a real possibility, and 60 per cent of interfaith marriages end up with the non-Catholic partner converting to Catholicism.

Canadian Buddhists, feeling isolated from the dominant culture in Canada and admiring Catholic schools, often become Catholic to live and die in the warmth of Catholic fellowship. Christian communities offer a blend of culture, language, and religious values that are a definite attraction for Asian Canadians.

Father Tran estimates that 80 per cent of his parishioners attend mass weekly. In their homes, Vietnamese Canadian Catholics say grace at table along with the Our Father. In the evening, they say prayers, including the rosary. In church and at home, they enjoy making novenas to Mary and devotions to Joseph. Parishioners mark the feast days of the Church with public processions and celebrations. Speaking of American-Vietnamese faith, Peter Phan explains that "this fervent faith is nourished no doubt not only by the sacraments but also by popular devotions. Indeed, the cultivation of popular devotions is a distinguishing characteristic of many Vietnamese American communities and constitutes an important contribution that Vietnamese American Catholics make to the American church."[47] Many Vietnamese Canadians are members of the third order of Franciscans or Dominicans, or are members of the Legion of Mary. The monthly charismatic mass at St. Cecilia's is held in the Vietnamese language, which facilitates overt devotional practice. Four hundred couples have taken the Marriage Enrichment Program, which is led by the Vietnamese Jesuit Father Peter-Minh Quang Chu. Those who have completed the Marriage Enrichment Program in Toronto are divided into seventeen geographical zones; participants meet regularly to share their spiritual progress and renew their spiritual energy. The Vietnamese Canadian Catholic Women's League is responsible for celebrating feast days and other events at St. Cecilia's church and preparing food and decorations for the community.

When Vietnamese newcomers arrive in Toronto, parishioners invite them to lunch with Father Tran, so they can meet the Catholic community and know they are welcome. Parishioners introduce the newcomers to members and help them find homes, schools, hospitals, and shops. The Catholic community also attracts new members through weddings and funerals. Buddhists attend these events as well; some decide to join the Vietnamese

Catholic community so they, too, might take part in the sacramental events of the Catholic community.[48]

Vietnamese are proud of their ability to fit in, make a living, and not seek financial help from others. Street begging would embarrass them and other Vietnamese. Vietnamese Canadians do not come to church to receive help but to give help. St. Cecilia's church opened up a food bank to assist newcomers, but closed it down because it didn't get any business. The Vietnamese Catholic community hopes to contribute to the Canadian Catholic church by sharing its firm faith and strong family life. The concrete manifestation of their presence in recent years is that they have contributed eight young men to serve the Church as priests and a number of young women to serve in religious orders.

Family Enrichment: The Story of Hien and Phuong Nguyen

Hien Nguyen was born to a Catholic family and, when in his late teens, attended university in Vietnam for three years. As an oppressed Catholic seeking political and religious freedom, he escaped from Vietnam, became a refugee in Thailand, and came to Canada in 1980, settling first in Victoria. Phuong Nguyen, also a Catholic, was educated as a registered nurse, and worked in a hospital in Saigon. To safeguard her Catholic faith, she escaped by boat from Vietnam to a Malaysian refugee camp. She came to Canada in 1980. As her nursing degree and hospital experience from Vietnam were not recognized in Canada, she began work as nurse's aid in a nursing home in Victoria. During this period, she met Hien. The two were married in Victoria in 1981 and moved to Toronto in 1985. Phuong got a job as an electronic inventory administrator and Hien found a position as an inventory analyst.[49]

Mastery of English was a difficult barrier to cross. Hien and Phuong felt discriminated against in the workplace. Hien believed that to overcome workplace discrimination, he had first to do well on the job and second make sure his peers liked him.

Hien and Phuong are active at Vietnamese Martyrs in the Family Enrichment Program, which encourages family dialogue and teaches forgiveness and healing. Their family dialogue included their children, discussing issues first and making decisions later. The skills of dialogue were very useful for Hien because, as a musician and composer, he works with choir members and on special occasions conducts the music program at Vietnamese Martyrs. Through their involvement in church organizations, especially through the format of Family Enrichment, he and Phuong have learned to share themselves with others.

Hien and Phuong have two adult children, Alphonse and Anton, who were raised and now work in Canada. At home, the parents spoke Vietnamese. On Sundays, they took the children to Mass at Vietnamese Martyrs. Alphonse and Anton speak English but are functional in Vietnamese. In religion, they have gone their own way, but occasionally attend Sunday mass. The issues of church, heterosexual dating, and mixing with non-Catholics or non-Vietnamese caused family friction. The parents admit that the number of possible Vietnamese Catholic brides in Canada is limited, but no one is talking of importing a Vietnamese bride. For the Nguyens, public information comes mainly through the English media. Older Vietnamese, say the Nguyens, rely on Vietnamese newspapers, magazines, and an hour-long program on TV. Most interesting are the online Vietnam news programs, newspapers, and magazines.

Religion is very important for Hien and Phuong. They and most Vietnamese Catholic families take ten minutes in the evening to say evening prayers in Vietnamese and English, which includes singing a hymn or two and praying the Our Father, Hail Mary, Glory Be, a Bible reading, and a brief reflection. They also say the rosary daily, read the Bible, attend Mass weekly, and are active members in the Family Enrichment Program. The latter involves working with subgroups to be available to offer counsel when marriage problems emerge. The Family Enrichment groups make a point of celebrating wedding anniversaries of members.

Hien and Phuong attend daily Mass whenever they can because it helps "to bring their lives together with understanding and happiness." An annual weekend retreat is offered to new members of the parish to help them reflect on and fashion their new Vietnamese Canadian Catholic identity.[49]

Conflictual Dialogue: The Story of Kim and Buuran Huynh

A baptized Catholic, Kim Huynh earned her bachelor of arts in Saigon in 1974 and taught high school until 1980. She married Buuran, a Vietnamese lawyer, in 1976; they have two children, Anne and Peter. She and her family in 1980 decided to strike a blow for freedom and join the boat people leaving Vietnam for Palawan in the Philippines. At the same time that Kim and Buuran came to Canada, her siblings and her mother moved to California. Arriving in Toronto, Kim completed a diploma in computer science at Centennial College and is a project manager for a computer company. She has continued her education; currently, for her own academic interest, she is studying for a master of theology degree at St. Augustine's Seminary at the Toronto School of Theology. Her daughter Anne finished university and now works in a bank, while her son Peter will go to university next year.

Being the new person in a workplace where peers talk in half-sentences and conversations are interrupted, Kim found English words and phrases difficult to catch. Learning English on the job, she found it difficult to get people's attention, to get anyone to listen. She felt ignored, and not heard or understood. She believes the discrimination she encountered was "more personal than racist."

At home in Toronto, Kim and Buuran included their children in discussions and came to a consensus before making family decisions. On reflection, Kim wishes she had included her children on more decisions, such as about family vacations. She guided her children in the practice of the Catholic faith, love of education, respect for elders, and speaking Vietnamese. When at home, the children keep the Vietnamese Catholic traditions, but once they go to university, she admits, it is difficult for the young to continue in these ways. Upon being told that Vietnamese girls do not whistle, her daughter Anne retorted, "Why can't I whistle? Boys do!" When she went to university, Anne asked why go to church, and challenged the shortcomings of the Church. However, as time passed, Anne worked through her skepticism and reached a new level of maturity, recognizing that nothing is perfect or without shortcomings. Another point of conflict for Kim will be the possibility of her children marrying non-Catholic Vietnamese. Kim says that she would accept the choice of her children, but "with great concern."

The Huynh family enjoy prayer alone, gathered together, and at Sunday Mass, and take part in weekend retreats. They participated in the Family Enrichment Program and made weekend Cursillos. The weekend retreats of the Family Enrichment Program are a good occasion to recruit new members for the Legion of Mary, Bible study groups, and the Catholic Women's League. Providing for newcomers to Canada was a concern fifteen years ago, but it is not a concern now, as Vietnamese immigration has all but ceased. The only newcomers are those arriving as part of the family reunion program, and relatives look after them. Kim believes that Vietnamese bring to the Canadian Church their love of artistic activities, such as dance, music, drums, incense, and church processions for Mother Mary in May and for the Vietnamese martyrs in November. Vietnamese Catholics also bring personal sensitivity to family dialogue and a love of colourful drama to the Canadian Church.[50]

Family Conflict and Healing: The Story of Dac Dung Ho and Kim-Anh Vu

Dac Dung Ho and his family, seeking political freedom from Vietnam, escaped as boat persons to a refugee camp in Hong Kong and arrived in Canada in 1979. Dac completed a degree at Mohawk College in Hamilton in 1987 and works as an assistant material manager in Brampton. He was baptized Catholic in 1990. Kim-Anh Vu, a member of a Catholic family, escaped from Vietnam as a boat person to a refugee camp in Indonesia. She came to Canada in 1984 seeking religious freedom. Arriving in the Toronto area, she completed a degree at Mohawk College in computer technology in 1990 and works as a computer analyst. Dac and Kim met at Mohawk College and were married in Toronto in 1991. They have two boys: Peter is 13 years old and Martin is 10. Dac's parents live with them, and Kim's parents live with her sister nearby. Upon arrival, both Kim and Dac had difficulty with the English language. Kim, working at a Canadian bank, discovered that the bank officers assigned her the tasks that were least likely to bring her opportunities for advancement in her department.

Dac and Kim imbue their children with love of the Catholic faith, respect for others, and concern for their neighbour. For five years, the boys were sent to Vietnamese language school on Saturdays. The parents have discovered that their children have great difficulty maintaining these traditions when their friends do not keep them. Flare-ups can occur between parents and children over the preservations of these traditions. Once the children become independent, they do not want to go to language school on Saturday or to church on Sunday. Rather than being considered weird or gay, they want to date the opposite sex. The parents accept interfaith marriages, but they hope their boys will marry Catholics. Looking to the future, the parents accept inter-ethnic marriages as they realize the next generation will be without preferences and Canadian culture will have won. For daily information, the family uses both the English and Vietnamese language media. After Dac and Kim retire from their jobs, Dac would like to return to Vietnam, but Kim wants to remain in Canada.

Kim prays alone, with other members of her family, and with the Vietnamese community at Sunday mass. Dac regularly attends Sunday mass with the family. They have made the Cursillo, attend the Family Enrichment Program, and pray for familial healing and unity. Family Enrichment is self-perpetuating, in that those who complete the weekend are asked to recruit the same number of couples for next year. Next year's enrichment group will recruit another group for the following year, and so on. The Family Enrichment Program has brought great benefits to their family and offers Canadian Catholics the gift of strengthened family life in their neighbourhoods.[51]

Integration into Canadian Society

The Search for Integration: The Story of Peter Tran

Peter Tran was born into a Catholic family in Vietnam and graduated from the University of Saigon with a master of linguistics, then completed a second master of linguistics at the University of Cardiff in Wales in 1964. He returned to Vietnam to become a lecturer of linguistics at the University of Saigon and to marry Bernadette Nguyen, a pharmacist. They have three children. Canadian missionaries in Vietnam at that time praised Canada as a country to live in. Peter scouted out Canada for the quality of its democracy and its freedom of religion. In 1975, the Tran family joined the exodus of Vietnamese who landed in Thailand. Canadian embassy staff came to the refugee camp, and Peter worked for them as an interpreter. He asked to go to Canada, his family was accepted, and they were among the first Vietnamese to immigrate to Canada.

Arriving in Toronto, Peter Tran did not expect to get a professional job but resolved to take the first job he was offered. He began as a dishwasher at a Chinese restaurant, earning $95 a week, then advanced to kitchen helper, waiter, and bartender. Although he was trilingual, he did not speak Chinese and felt the barrier of discrimination. In 1985, he became an employee of the Ontario government as a counsellor at Ontario Welcome House, where he received boat people who needed help. From 1980 to 1983, he appeared many times on CBC-TV and CBC-

Radio, and the *Toronto Star* published articles about his exodus from Vietnam and his initial employment in Canada as a dishwasher. His experience was not an uncommon one for Vietnamese newcomers to Canadian shores.[52] Peter resolved to write a series of monthly articles about his experiences. Two years later, he published a book of his articles in Vietnamese. Since then, he has written ten volumes on how Vietnamese adjust to Canadian life. He includes the lighter side of Vietnamese adjusting to Canadian life and crisply contrasts the different Vietnamese and Canadian mores.

At home, Peter and Bernadette made decisions for their children until they reached university. They encouraged their children to pursue Vietnamese culture, and taught their children Vietnamese, gratitude to their ancestors, belief in God, keeping the tradition of the Vietnamese New Year, and seeking parental approval of their weddings. Vietnamese language classes were not available for their children in the early years, and in religion the children were eclectic. They believed in God but not necessarily in the Church's teaching. Despite parental nurturing in their early years, the children, who were educated in Canada, proved to be very Canadian, mixed with Canadian friends, and went their own way. Their two daughters became medical doctors, and their son became a lawyer. What would never happen in Vietnam happened in Canada: as soon as their daughters got jobs, they moved out of the family home. The parents love living in Canada, but grieve that their children have lost much of the civil and religious heritage of their ancestors.

When it comes to prayer, Peter prefers not to pray in ready-made formulas but to talk to God freely as his loving Father. He prays for help to the Father of All. At St. Pius X parish, he serves daily mass. In contrast to his own experience, he finds many Vietnamese prefer to recite written prayers. He believes Vietnamese Canadians would like to learn more about God in order to be more comfortable with God. Peter says Vietnamese Catholics require leaders who are firmly rooted in God and will lead Vietnamese Canadians into the freedom of the sons and daughters of God. In the past, Peter has made the Cursillo, but now his priorities are daily mass, his grandchildren, helping his wife at home, and his own reading and writing. Peter Tran believes that the gift of Vietnamese Catholics to the Canadian Church is their strong belief in God. He sums up his vision of Vietnamese Canadian Catholics as having a strong devotional life, obeying the Church's teaching, and being active in their parish.[53]

Conclusion

Diaspora Vietnamese grieve that the Communist regime is destroying their home country. Many Vietnamese believe that by remaining faithful to Vietnamese customs while abroad, they will one day support the restoration of Vietnamese culture in their homeland. They debate whether Canadian government and business contacts with Vietnam will assist in opening Vietnam to democracy and human rights, or just prop up a decadent and oppressive regime.

Forced to migrate to Canada, Vietnamese had to seek new employment, which generally meant lowering their work expectations. In Canada, they can suffer from discrimination in the workplace while the choice jobs go to Euro-Canadians – discrimination that may be personal or racial. Isolated, they can feel ignored and misunderstood. A Vietnamese immigrant to the United States, Professor Peter Phan points out that being an "immigrant means being at the margin," being betwixt and between, not being American and not being Vietnamese. He continues that "American Vietnamese will never be 'American enough.'" At the same time, in Vietnam, they are no longer considered Vietnamese, but *Viet kieu* (Vietnamese foreigners). On a positive note, Phan writes that being "neither this nor that allows one to be *both* this *and* that" and in fact to transcend both cultures and be enriched by world culture.[54]

Family life is the number one priority for Vietnamese; living alone is avoided in favour of dwelling with an extended family. Mothers arriving in Canada quickly find work, providing income for the family. This situation may give them a leadership role in the family, which can inadvertently displace the father from his traditional role. Vietnamese men outnumber Vietnamese women in Canada, and brides are hard to find. Yet bringing brides from Vietnam has not proved to be a solution to such difficulties.

"For Vietnamese as for other refugees," writes Dorais, "religion plays an important role in coping with grief and stress."[55] Religious experience helps refugees restore their disjointed past by learning reconciliation with the past and present. It helps them to stabilize their lives and keep their mental balance in the midst of changing horizons. Vietnamese Catholics have a deep sense of being Vietnamese and a strong desire to follow their religious and social customs, while at the same time entering into Canadian life. In doing so, they consider themselves both Vietnamese and Canadian.

Ironically, the Communist government in Vietnam has strengthened Vietnamese Catholicism among those in the diaspora. While some, in the hurried flight from Vietnam, may have lost touch with their faith, many in Canada have regained it upon being welcomed into Vietnamese Catholic communities. Through the healing balm of Christian fellowship, sacraments, prayer groups, marriage enrichment programs, and retreats, many are restored into the Vietnamese Canadian community. The recent canonization in Rome of 117 Vietnamese martyrs stimulated the exile community to reclaim religious freedom for Vietnam and elsewhere. While Canadian Vietnamese buy houses in Canadian suburbs, they maintain close contact with their siblings around the world and financially assist elderly relatives in Vietnam. At the same time, they are glad to contribute their life skills to Canada and are proud to maintain Canadian citizenship. Christian discernment guides the emotional and rational components of Vietnamese spirituality toward integration into Canadian life. Vietnamese Catholics are searchers for the kingdom of God, yet have equal concern for others in Canada who have suffered through the disruptive experience of immigration.

Conclusion

At the beginning of this study on Asian Catholics, I stated that we in the postmodern world are writing contemporary history before it vanishes. Working from the limited oral and published material available, this study attempts to reach tentative conclusions that are reasonable and point in the right direction. I do not offer hardened conclusions fashioned to affirm an ideal model or to please the scholarly connoisseur. I do present the reader with a preliminary report from data as narrated by newcomers trying to integrate into Canadian society. This history is not written in stone, but is a first report from fresh research.

The presence of Asian Catholics in Canada, whose numbers have increased exponentially since 1970, has had an affirming influence on the Canadian Church. Their staunch faith and solid commitment give firm direction to their national churches and sweep over the devout in other Canadian churches. Their membership in prayer groups, such as Marriage Encounter, Family Enrichment, Legion of Mary, and Bible study, assist the integration of Asians into Canadian spirituality. Their prayer groups help them reflect on the cultures they have espoused and discern what to retain in these cultures and what to jettison. Sharing in prayer groups in their mother tongue helps them to sort out what is Asian Catholic and what is Canadian Catholic. Their families, having tight internal cohesion, have been the source of vocations for the diocesan priesthood and for religious life. Numerous Asian Canadians who have been ordained to the priesthood and have entered religious life make an indelible mark on Canadian Catholics. The devotional life of the parishes and missions to which they are assigned is enriched by their university education, occupational skills, and strong faith.

The employment of both historical sources and qualitative interviews allowed this study to proceed from oral and written sources. In addition to the written sources of professional history, postmodern historians recognize a network of information from new sources that depict life in all its diversity. Postmodern scholars construct narrative history without necessarily fabricating a dominant theme. Life is seen as a montage of conflicting images and diverse points of view. These historians postulate that creative works of history are produced by cultural communities that make up the languages of communication, by artists who work out the forms, and by historians who record this fresh new material. Communities shape the historical context in which artists and historians work; ultimately, new visionary products are constructed. Although individuals create artistic work, the community around them shapes the culture in which they work and the choices they are allowed to make.[1] Modern historians, unlike postmodern ones, presume that the world "is built on the assumption that knowledge is certain, objective, and good." In contrast, postmodern historians do not have these expectations and do not "search for universal, ultimate truth because they are convinced that there is nothing more to find than a host of conflicting interpretations or an infinity of linguistically created worlds."[2]

Television, in many ways, illustrates the postmodern montage: images of ads, news, sitcoms, documentaries, and dramas are spun across the screen as if they all have equal veracity.[3] There is no rational priority for these images except their ability to weld viewers' attention to the screen. Postmodern history as presented here does not read like traditional history, but deliberately juxtaposes personal stories with historical and analytical commentary. The postmodern techniques of qualitative analysis link the traditional techniques of historiography to produce an integrated narrative combining personal storytelling with general historical analysis. The textual style may puzzle those used to the smooth narrative charm of traditional history, but it must be said that an integrated text combining the two scholarly techniques offers a doubly enriched history to the perceptive reader.

The ethnic groups examined in this volume experience the ever-present need to search their own culture in order to retain what they find valuable and discard what they consider unnecessary. From their arrival and their confrontation with Canadian culture, ethnic groups strive to purge the unimportant areas of both cultures and hold fast to the essentials of their culture and religion. Asian Canadians are working out their own unique identities by sorting through Asian and Canadian traditions. They are effectively doing postmodern history by searching their roots and avoiding the superficialities of Asian or Canadian cultural norms. Each group passes through the similar defining experience of integration into Canada, but in its own unique way.

Whereas former generations of Asians Canadians chose the path of stoic silence in the face of unfairness, and did not confront inequity, today's young professionals are self-confident, multilingual, and able to challenge discriminatory practices.[4] But with regard to Canadian multiculturalism, one Chinese Canadian, Professor Peter S. Li, raises the question of whether Canada has the political maturity for genuine multiculturalism, or remains pluralistic. He wonders whether Canadians have created a multicultural society guaranteeing equality, or whether they settle into a series of competing cultures in a vertical mosaic, allowing charter groups more access to resources and rewards.[5]

Canada committed itself to multiculturalism in 1970; the mission of the Catholic Church in Canada fully embraces this vision. The influx of Chinese, Filipino, Korean, Tamil, and Vietnamese Catholics completes the multicultural image of Canada and the Canadian Catholic Church. These ethnic groups are now integrated into a Catholic history that began with the French, Irish, and Scottish, and continued with the Germans, Polish, Ukrainians, Hungarians, Italians, Portuguese, and Lebanese. Canadian Catholics welcome new Canadian Catholics of all ethnic backgrounds from around the world, offering to help them integrate into Canada and into the Canadian Catholic Church. This account of Asian Canadian Catholics allows me to complete the study of Canadian Catholics begun in 2002 in *A History of Canadian Catholics: Gallicanism, Romanism, and Canadianism.*

Appendix

Interview Guide: Asian Canadian Catholics

Date: _____

1. Name (maiden): _____
Phone: _____

2. E-mail Address: _____
Parish: _____

3. Age group: (1) ____under 35; (2) ____35 to 60 years;
(3)____ 61 to 80 years

4. List your academic degrees, with institution and dates: _____
_____

5. From Catholic family? _____
When were you baptized? _____

6. When and where married? _____
Maiden name of your spouse _____
Highest education: _____
Occupation:_____

7. Names and ages of children:_____
Canadian raised? _____
Functional in parents' language? _____
Work in Canada?_____

8. In what country do your parents live? _____
How are they cared for? _____

9. Who initiated immigration proceedings?_____

10. When and how did you come to Canada? _____
Why did you come to Canada?_____

11. Employment in Asia: _____

Hoped-for employment in Canada: _____

Employment in Canada: _____

12. Experience of linguistic difficulties or discrimination in Canada:

_____

13. How are family decisions made? _____

14. What traditions do you retain?_____

15. Do the young maintain these traditions? _____

16. Does this result in generational conflict? _____

17. Do you accept dating or intermarriage with other religious and ethnic groups? _____

18. How do you connect with Canadian life, clubs, radio, television, newspapers? _____

19. Do you plan to spend your life in Canada? _____

20. How do you pray? _____

21. Spiritual groups: _____

Goals: _____

22. How are new members recruited? _____

23. How does your group respond to needs of new Canadians? ___

_____

24. How do your ethnic qualities fit into the Canadian Church? __

_____

Notes

Introduction

1   Statistics Canada 2001, Ottawa, Ontario, Canada K1A 0T6, March 2005, http://www.statcan.ca/english/freepub/91-541-XIE/91-541-XIE2005001.pdf (accessed 13 March 2008).

2   Jonathan Y. Tan, *Introducing Asian American Theologies* (Maryknoll, NY: Orbis Books, 2008), 57.

3   Thomas C. Fox, *Pentecost in Asia: A New Way of Being Church* (Maryknoll, NY: Orbis, 2003), 31.

4   These figures are derived from *Statistics Canada 2001*, Religion (95) and Visible Minority Groups (15) for Population, for Canada, Provinces, Territories, Census Metropolitan Areas and Census Agglomerations, 2001 Census – 20% Sample Data, 97F0022XCB2001005.

5   Fox, *Pentecost in Asia*, 29.

6   Tan, *Introducing Asian American Theologies*, 59.

7   Tan, *Introducing Asian American Theologies*, 60–61.

8   Archdiocese of Toronto, Personnel Office, 2009.

9   Catherine Kohler Riessman, *Narrative Analysis* (Thousand Oaks, CA: Sage Publications, 1993), 1–7.

10 Stanley J. Grenz, *A Primer on Postmodernism* (Grand Rapids, MI: William B. Eerdmans, 1996), 39.

11 D. Jean Clandinin and F. Michael Connelly, *Narrative Inquiry: Experience and Story in Qualitative Research* (San Francisco: Jossey-Bass, 2000), 1–10, 54–55; N. K. Denzin and Y. S. Lincoln, eds., *Collecting and Interpreting Qualitative Materials* (Thousand Oaks, CA: Sage Publications, 1998).

12 Juanita Johnson-Bailey, "Dancing between the Swords: My Foray into Constructing Narratives" in *Qualitative Research in Practice: Examples for Discussion and Analysis*, edited by Sharan B. Merriam and Associates (San Francisco: Jossey-Bass, 2002), 323–25.

13 Norman K. Denzin and Yvonna S. Lincoln, eds., *The Landscape of Qualitative Research: Theories and Issues* (Thousand Oaks, CA: Sage, 1998), 80.

14 "The *Tri-Council Policy Statement: Ethical Conduct for Research Involving Humans* describes the policies of the Medical Research Council (MRC), the Natural Sciences and Engineering Research Council (NSERC), and the Social Sciences and Humanities Research Council (SSHRC) .... The Councils believe that this policy statement will benefit research through addressing the paramount need for the highest ethical standards." (http://www.ncehr-cnerh.org)

15 Spiritual Statistics for the Years 1999–2007, Archives of the Roman Catholic Archdiocese of Toronto (ARCAT).

Chapter 1

1   Jin Tan and Patricia Roy, *The Chinese in Canada* (Ottawa: Canadian Historical Association, Booklet 9, 1985), 6–7.

2   Peter S. Li, "Chinese" in *Encyclopedia of Canada's Peoples*, edited by Paul Magocsi (Toronto: University of Toronto Press, 1999), 355–7.

3   Li, "Chinese," 355–57.
4   David Chuenyan Lai, Jordan Paper, and Li Chuang Paper, "The Chinese in Canada: The Unrecognized Religion," in *Religion and Ethnicity in Canada*, edited by Paul Bramadat and David Seljak (Toronto: Pearson Longman, 2005), 103–04.
5   Edgar Wickberg, ed., *From China to Canada: A History of the Chinese Communities in Canada* (Toronto: McClelland and Stewart, 1982), 123.
6   Wickberg, *From China to Canada*, 172, 257–58.
7   Wickberg, *From China to Canada*, 151.
8   Wing Chung Ng, *The Chinese in Vancouver, 1945–80: The Pursuit of Identity and Power* (Vancouver: UBC Press, 1999), 45–47, 104–06.
9   Wickberg, *From China to Canada*, 151.
10   *Hong Kong Catholic Church Directory 2002* (Hong Kong: Catholic Truth Society, 2001), Educational Institutions, 239–335, 597.
11   Rosario Renaud, *Le Diocèse de Süchow (Chine): Champ apostolique des Jésuites canadiens de 1918 à 1954* (Montréal: Les Éditions Bellarmin, 1982), 13–14.
12   *Taiwan Catholic Church Directory, 2001* (Taipei: Catholic Archdiocese of Taipei, 2001), 213–28, 439–44, 563–70, 590–91, 630–33.
13   These figures are derived from *Statistics Canada 2001*, Religion (95) and Visible Minority Groups (15) for Population, for Canada, Provinces, Territories, Census Metropolitan Areas and Census Agglomerations, 2001 Census – 20% Sample Data, 97F0022XCB2001005; Li, "Chinese," 367.
14   *Religion and Ethnicity in Canada*, edited by Paul Bramadat and David Seljak (Toronto: Pearson Longman, 2005), 103–04.
15   Religion (95) and Visible Minority Groups (15) for Population, for Canada, Provinces, Territories, Census Metropolitan Census – 20% Sample Data, Census 2001, *Statistics Canada*.
16   Madge Pon, "Like a Chinese Puzzle: The Construction of Chinese Masculinity in *Jack Canuck*," in *Gender and History in Canada*, edited by Joy Parr and Mark Rosenfeld (Toronto: Copp Clark, 1996), 88–100; Peter S Li, "Racial Supremacism under Social Democracy," 27:1 (1995), 3–4, 7 and "The Place of Immigrants: the Politics of Difference in Territorial and Social Space," 35:2 (2003), 3–5, *Canadian Ethnic Studies*.
17   *The Precursor* (Montreal), November–December 1943, 337–38; Deborah Rink, *Spirited Women: A History of the Catholic Sisters in British Columbia* (Vancouver: Sisters' Association, Archdiocese of Vancouver, 2000), 166–68.
18   Ng, *The Chinese in Vancouver*, 46–7; Rink, *Spirited Women*, 170–71; Vincent J. McNally, *The Lord's Distant Vineyard: A History of the Oblates and the Catholic Community in British Columbia* (Edmonton: University of Alberta Press and Western Canadian Publishers, 2000), 302–03.
19   Wickberg, *From China to Canada*, 172–73.
20   *St Francis Xavier Parish, 1933–1988: Golden Jubilee.* Vancouver ca. 1988.
21   Interview, Father Aloysius Lou, Vancouver, 17 July 2003.
22   Ng, *The Chinese in Vancouver*, 30–36; Thomas C. Fox, *Pentecost in Asia: A New Way of Being Church* (Maryknoll, NY: Orbis, 2003), 118.
23   *St Francis Xavier Parish, 1933–1988: Golden Jubilee.* Vancouver ca. 1988.
24   Curriculum Vitae of Frederick C. Wong, Archives of the Scarboro Foreign Mission Society, Scarborough, Ontario; Father Aloysius Lou, Vancouver, 17 July 2003.

25   Peter S. Li, "Ethnic Enterprise in Transition: Chinese Business in Richmond, B.C., 1980–1990," *Canadian Ethnic Studies* 24:1 (1992), 131–38.

26   Doreen Chau's testimony of June 2002 and interview with Joseph and Doreen Chau, Vancouver, 20 July 2003.

27   Doreen Chau's testimony of June 2002 and interview with Joseph and Doreen Chau, Vancouver, 20 July 2003.

28   *Taiwan Catholic Church Directory, 2001*, Overseas Chinese Parishes and Communities, 657–63, and Vancouver, Calgary and Edmonton diocesan websites.

29   *Sharing the Harvest: The Tenth Anniversary of the Chinese Catholic Parish: Planning the Future, 1987–1997.* Edmonton ca. 1997, 34–35.

30   Interview, Philip Lee, Blessed John XXIII church, Winnipeg, Manitoba, 1 June 2004.

31   John Zucchi, *A History of Ethnic Enclaves in Canada* (Ottawa: Canadian Historical Association, Booklet No. 31, 2007), 18–20.

32   *Directory of the Archdiocese of Toronto* (2000), Section VI, 1.

33   Spiritual Statistics for the Years 1999, 2000, 2001, Archives of the Archdiocese of Toronto.

34   Shun-hing Chan and Beatrice Leung. *Changing Church and State Relations in Hong Kong, 1950–2000* (Hong Kong: Hong Kong University Press, 2003), 30–45.

35   Interview, Father Peter Leung, Pastor of Chinese Martyrs Mission with the Care for Souls, Markham, Ontario, on 23 December 2002.

36   Interview with Father Thomas Tou, Holy Spirit church, Montreal, 11 September 2003.

37   *Toronto Chinese Catholic Centre, 20th Anniversary, 1967–1987*, 34.

38   Notes of Archivist Leo Ng, 2002, Archives of Our Lady of Mount Carmel, Toronto; *Toronto Chinese Catholic Centre 10th Anniversary*, 1977, 42–3; *Toronto Chinese Catholic Centre, 20th Anniversary, 1967–1987*, 9.

39   Tan, *Introducing Asian American Theologies*, 63–64.

40   Peter S. Li, "The Consumer Market of the Enclave Economy: A Study of Advertisements in a Chinese Daily Newspaper in Toronto," *Canadian Ethnic Studies* 31:2 (1999), 49–51.

41   *We Are the Church: The Blessed Chinese Martyrs Catholic Mission* (Scarborough: Chinese Martyrs, 1992), "Major Events of the Church Building Project."

42   *The Blessed Chinese Martyrs' Catholic Church: Dedication of the New Church, October 15, 1994.* (Toronto: Blessed Chinese Martyrs, c. 1994).

43   *The Blessed Chinese Martyrs' Catholic Church: Dedication of the New Church, October 15, 1994.* (Toronto: Blessed Chinese Martyrs, c. 1994).

44   Edmond Lo, "Catechesis at the Chinese Martyrs Church from the Time of its Founding to the Present." Archives of Chinese Martyrs church, Toronto. (Unpublished paper, 2002), 5–8.

45   Au, *The Blessed Chinese Martyrs' Catholic Church*.

46   Au, *The Blessed Chinese Martyrs' Catholic Church*.

47   Interviews, Father Bosco Wong and Deacon Peter Fan, St. Basil's parish, Ottawa, 3 June 2009.

48   *50th Anniversary of the Priestly Ordination of Father Thomas Tou* (Montreal: Chinese Catholic Mission, ca.1998), 12.

49   *Growing with God, 75 Years: The 75th Anniversary of the Montreal Chinese Catholic Church, 1917–1992* (Montreal: Private publication, ca. 1992), 7–8.

50   *From China to Canada*, 91–92, 236–37.

51   *50ᵗʰ Anniversary of the Priestly Ordination of Father Thomas Tou*, 13.

52   *Growing with God*, 9; *50ᵗʰ Anniversary of the Priestly Ordination of Father Thomas Tou*, 14–15.

53   Wickberg, *From China to Canada*, 122–28.

54   *The Precursor* (Montreal), March–April 1943, 80–81; *Growing with God*, 75 *Years*, 4–5.

55   Wickberg, *From China to Canada*, 172–73.

56   Sister Huguette Turcotte MIC, Proposal for the CCHA Annual Conference, 15 January 2003.

57   Denise Helly, *Les Chinois à Montréal, 1877–1951* (Montréal: Institute québécois de recherche sur la culture, 1987), 165–66.

58   *The Precursor* (Montreal), May–June, 1943, 145–9; *50ᵗʰ Anniversary of the Priestly Ordination of Father Thomas Tou*, 13.

59   Turcotte MIC, "Hospitals for Chinese in Canada," 1–2.

60   Turcotte MIC, "Hospitals for Chinese in Canada," 5.

61   *Growing with God: 75 Years: The 75ᵗʰ Anniversary of the Montreal Chinese Catholic Church, 1917–1992*, 12-13, 43, 50, 64-65.

62   *From China to Canada*, 91–92, 193, 236–37.

63   *Growing with God*, 13–4.

64   Interview, Father Thomas Tou, retiring pastor of Holy Spirit church, Montreal, 30 December 2002.

65   *Growing with God*, 44–45, 55–56, 57–58, 73–74.

66   Li, "Chinese," 367–68, 370.

67   Pauline Longtin, "Mother Mary of the Holy Spirit and the Immigrants," *Precursor*, June 1977, 13.

68   Li, "Chinese," 369.

69   Joint University Chinese Catholic Community websites: http://come.to/lccc2000; http://utccc.sa.utoronto.ca; http://hello.to/qccc; http://hello.to/wccc.

70   John Zucchi, *A History of Ethnic Enclaves in Canada*, 8–9, 16–17; Li, "Chinese," 371–72.

71   Maria Castagna and George J. Sefa Dei, "An Historical Overview of the Application of the Race Concept in Social Practice," in *Anti-Racist Feminism: Critical Race and Gender Studies*. edited by Agnes Calliste and George J. Sefa Dei (Halifax: Fernwood, 2000), 28.

72   Vivian Ligo, *Singing the Lord's Song in a Foreign Land: Reclaiming Faith in a New Culture* (Ottawa: Novalis, 2002), 138–44.

73   These figures are derived from *Statistics Canada 2001*, Religion (95) and Visible Minority Groups (15) for Population, for Canada, Provinces, Territories, Census Metropolitan Areas and Census Agglomerations, 2001 Census – 20% Sample Data, 97F0022XCB2001005.

Chapter 2

1   Similar studies using the technique of qualitative analysis to collect data on Chinese Canadians are available. Hong Zhu used qualitative analysis to interview 44 participants and found that the determining factors of successful

integration into Canadian culture were language ability, social skills, corporate cultural competence, and socio-cultural knowledge. Hong Zhu, "Capital Transformation and Immigrant Integration: Chinese Independent Immigrants' Language and Social Practices in Canada," Ph.D. Diss., University of Toronto, 2005, 261.

2   Chinese have always had high regard for education, and newcomers to Canada hope to establish their family home near the best schools. Victoria Yip relates in *Jin Guo: Voices of Chinese Women*, edited by Momoye Sugiman (Toronto: Women's Press, 1992), that "I liked high school, but I found studying very hard. I liked it because, like my father and uncle, I believed that education was the most important thing. I wanted to learn as much as I could." (129) In Charlottetown, Rosemary Ling wrote in 1996 that "My parents emphasized the value of education and the need to respect elders." In *Enduring Hardship: the Chinese Laundry in Canada* by Ban Sen Hoe (Ottawa: Canadian Museum of Civilization, 2003), 72.

3   Tony and Lydwine Ma as newcomers fulfilled the model laid out by some Canadian psychologists. The psychologists believe that the personalities of both husband and wife were essential to the proper development of their children. While they considered the mother the most important person during the early years of the children's development, nevertheless the father was to be a calming influence as he played with them, read them stories, and took interest in their lives. The father's presence would avoid the "inherent dangers" of a woman-dominated home. Mona Gleason, "Psychology and the Construction of the 'Normal' Family in Postwar Canada, 1945–60," *Canadian Historical Review* 78, no. 3(Sept. 1997): 472–73.

4   Chinese-Canadian parents do not attempt to arrange marriages, but today in Canada "marriages [are] preceded by romantic love." Evelyn Lee and Matthew R. Mock, "Chinese Families" in *Ethnicity and Family Therapy*, 3rd edition, edited by Monica McGoldrick et al. (New York: Guilford Press, 2005), 306.

5   *Statistics Canada*, Census 2001, Religion (95) and Visible Minority Groups (15) for Population, for Canada, Provinces, Territories, Census Metropolitan Census – 20% Sample Data.

6   Interview, Tony Ma, Chinese Martyrs church, Toronto, 12 May 2005.

7   Wei-Chin Hwang, "Acculturative Family Distancing: Theory, Research, and Clinical Practice," *Psychotherapy: Theory, Research, Practice, Training* 43, 4 (2006), 397, 400.

8   Interview, Joe Chan, St. Justin Martyr church, Toronto (Unionville), 12 May 2005.

9   David Ley, "Explaining Variations in Business Performance Among Immigrant Entrepreneurs in Canada," *Journal of Ethnic and Migration Studies* 32 (5) (July 2006), 758–59.

10   A popular option for Chinese young people is to become a hyphenated Canadian, that is, a "Chinese Canadian," as they believe that becoming a "Canadian" is only open to "British immigrants" after several generations. Chinese youths, as they incorporate into Canadian culture, will choose to become bilingual, bicultural, and binational. As Chinese Canadians, they are "transnationals" with multiple homes and cultures and are linked to a culturally and economically resourceful Chinese community. Emi Ooka, "Growing up Canadian: Language, Culture,

and Identity Among Second-Generation Chinese Youths in Canada," Ph.D. diss., University of Toronto, 2002, iii, 204–206, 216–220.

11 Statistics Canada, Religion (95) and Visible Minority Groups (15) for Population, for Canada etc., 2001 Census. Chinese-Canadian Catholics number 120,420 among a Chinese-Canadian population of 1,094,700.

12 Interview, Father Peter Leung, Chinese Martyrs parish, Toronto, 20 May 2005.

13 Hwang, "Acculturative Family Distancing," 400–01.

14 Interview, Dr. Theresa Chiu and Dr. Augustine Cheung, Chinese Martyrs and Blessed Trinity parishes, Toronto, 27 May 2005.

15 *Jin Guo: Voices of Chinese Women* (Toronto: Women's Press, 1992), discusses cultural adjustment, in the words of Velma Chan, as "bending with the tide, [and] going along with the Canadian ways." Velma goes on to say that the "Chinese Canadians of my generation were all evolving, becoming Canadianized" (165).

16 Interview, Patrick Yeung and Nancy Chung, Chinese Martyrs parish, Toronto, 27 May 2005.

17 Interview, Tony Chow, Chinese Martyrs parish, Toronto, 16 June 2005.

18 Chinese Canadians were not alone in cautioning against mixed marriages. Canadian psychologist Samuel Laycock warned against mixed marriages as "apt to cause trouble." He continued that mixed marriages were discouraged because they often ended in divorce. Gleason, "Psychology and the Construction of the 'Normal' Family in Postwar Canada, 1945–60," 460.

19 The founder of Buddhism, Siddhartha Gautama (563–483 BCE), was born in northern India about 500 years before Jesus Christ. Buddhism, a reform movement, offered egalitarianism as an alternative to the Hindu caste system, which placed the Brahmins at the top of the hierarchy and marginalized their inferiors socially and religiously. Buddhism eventually spread from South Asia to China, Tibet, and Vietnam. By contrast, the Chinese philosopher Confucius (551–479 BCE) was born in north-central China in Shantung during the same period. Confucius considered himself the transmitter of teaching about sincere human and social behaviour. The conscience, he taught, is inborn and a gift from heaven. Although not a religion, Confucianism invites the sense of religiosity in "self-cultivation, soul-searching, and the practice of sincerity." In the seventeenth century, Jesuits in China converted three of the principal Chinese Confucian philosophers to Christianity. The Confucian philosophy is considered compatible with Catholic teachings, as both communities seek universal truth in self-transcendence. *A Dictionary of Asian Christianity*, edited by Scott W. Sunquist, David Wu Chu Sing, and John Chew Hiang Chea (Grand Rapids, MI: Eerdmans, 2001), 98–104, 208–11.

20 Interview, Dr. Theresa Hum, Chinese Martyrs parish, Toronto, 17 June 2005.

21 Sun Yat-sen (1866–1925) was a Chinese leader and statesman who fought to establish the Republic of China in 1912. Sun is generally called the father of modern China, yet was considered too idealistic to be an effective political leader. His three principles—nationalism, democracy, and socialism—became the guiding principles of the Chinese republic.

22 Interview, Anthony Sun, Chinese Martyrs parish, Toronto, 27 June 2005.

23   Canadian psychologists in the postwar period, according to Mona Gleason, argued that marriage had "become a more democratic institution .... Ideally, nonetheless, modern marriage was no longer based on the sole authority of the husband." The profession considered the authoritarian patriarchal type of marriage obsolete. "Psychology and the Construction of the 'Normal' Family in Postwar Canada, 1945–60," 457–58.

24   John Ling at Charlottetown in 1996 affirmed the importance of "hard work" for Chinese: "I realize how hard my father actually worked and there was never a lot of money in it .... I've always worked most of my life ... I guess that comes from my Dad." In Ban Seng Hoe, *Enduring Hardship*, 72.

25   Interview, Edmond Lo, Chinese Martyrs church, Toronto, 28 June 2005.

26   Many Chinese feel very strongly about ethnic marriages. In *Jin Guo: Voices of Chinese Women*, May Cheung says about her children: "I certainly would not be pleased if my children married 'foreigners.' It's definitely better for us Chinese to marry Chinese. Those *gui* [Euro-Canadians] don't know anything (laugh)" (194).

27   Interview, Paul Yeung, Chinese Martyrs church, 5 July 2005.

28   Since 1970, the Chinese have opened and funded four Chinese-speaking churches in the Archdiocese of Toronto. Our Lady of Mount Carmel was taken over from the diocese in downtown Toronto and opened as a Chinese parish in 1970. Three large and beautiful churches were constructed and opened: Chinese Martyrs in 1994 in Markham; St. Agnes Tsao-Kouying in 2002, also in Markham; and Saviour of the World in 2004 in Mississauga. *The Blessed Chinese Martyrs Catholic Mission: We Are the Church* (Toronto: Blessed Chinese Martyrs, c. 1993).

29   Charity in the Chinese Catholic community has many precedents, going back to the founding of the first community at Our Lady of Mount Carmel in 1970–1971. Two thousand needy newcomers were helped in 1970–1971 with food, shelter, jobs, housing, and other necessities. ARCAT, Our Lady of Mount Carmel Parish; Chinese Congregation; Parish Community File; Social Service Report, 1970 to mid-1971.

30   Interview, Robin Wilson Tham, Blessed Trinity parish, Toronto, 1 September 2005.

31   Interview, Brian Koo, Saviour of the World parish, Mississauga, Ontario, 1 September 2005.

32   Li, *The Chinese in Canada*, 120.Chapter 3

Chapter 3

1   Francisco J. Colayco, *Wealth Within Your Reach: Pera Mo, Palaguin Mo!* (Philippines, 2004), 7.

2   Interview, Francisco J. and Mary Anne B. Colayco, St. Rose of Lima parish, Manila, 14 September 2004.

3   Interview, Rodrigo C. Naquiat, Ayala Corporation, Manila, 27 September 2004.

4   Interview, Fanny R. Quimson, Jesus the Way, the Truth and the Life parish, Manila, Luzon, 22 October 2004.

5   Letter to the Council of Elders, Bukas Loob sa Diyos Covenant Community, 17 October 1990, reprinted in *Living Water,* 17 September 2004, 1, 4 and 5.

6   Interview, William J. Keyes, Executive Director, Freedom to Build, Inc., Manila, 22 November 2004.

7   Email submission by William Keyes, Manila, 14 December 2004.

8   Interview, William J. Keyes, Executive Director, Freedom to Build, Inc., Manila, 22 November 2004.

9   *The Homeowners Manual,* Manila, ca. 2002; Guidelines For House Expansion, De La Costa V.

10 Interview, Maria Elena C. Samson, Asian Social Institute, Manila, 13 September 2004.

11 Interview, Dr. Paul A. Dumol, Vice-President for Academic Affairs, the University of Asian and the Pacific, Manila, 21 September 2004; Dindo Rei M. Tesoro and Joselito Alviar Jose, *The Rise of Filipino Theology* (Paasay City, Philippines: Paulines, 2004), 38, 172–73.

12 Interview, Dr. Paul A. Dumol, Vice-President for Academic Affairs, the University of Asian and the Pacific, Manila, 21 September 2004.

13 Interview, John Schumacher SJ, Ateneo de Manila University, Manila, 19 September 2004.

14 Interview, Randolf David, University of the Philippines, Manila, 17 September 2004.

15 Interview, Albert E. Alejo SJ, Ateneo Davao University, Mindanao, 6 October 2005.

16 Albert E. Alejo SJ, "Popular Spirituality as Cultural Energy," presented at an Academic Meeting in Davao, Mindanao, ca. Spring 2004; Interview with Albert E. Alejo SJ, Ateneo Davao University, Mindanao, 6 October 2005.

17 Catalino G. Arevalo SJ has provided a summary of his thoughts on the creation of the local church in "The Rebirth of the Local Church," *Teaching All Nations* (East Asian Pastoral Institute) 16 (1976), 249–52.

18 Interview, Father Catalino G. Arevalo SJ, Loyola School of Theology, Manila, Luzon, 10 November 2004.

19 *Philippine Daily Inquirer,* 11 November 2004.

20 Catalino G. Arevalo SJ, "Filipino Theology," *Dictionary of Missionj: Theology, History, Perspectives,* eds. Karl Müüller et al. (Maryknoll NY: Orbis, 1997), 161–67.

21 Arevalo, "Filipino Theology," 161–67.

22 Interview, Jose T. Tale and Felipa Lourdes Gonzalez-Tale, San Felipe Neri, Manila, 11 November 2004.

23 Interview, Joventito B. Jongko and Jeddy Joaquin Jongko, St. Peter's parish, Manila, 13 November 2004.

24 *The Philippine Star Metro,* "Gawad Kalinga Leads Typhoon Rehab Effort," by Perseus Echeminada, 12 December 2004.

25 Interview, Antony P. Meloto (Gawad Kalinga, Couples for Christ), Manila, 25 November 2004.

26 Interview, John J. Carroll SJ, Institute of Church and the Society of Jesus, Ateneo de Manila University, 25 November 2004.

27 Interview, Denis Murphy, Ateneo de Manila University, 31 December 2004.

Chapter 4

1   Eleanor R. Laquian, *A Study of Filipino Immigration to Canada, 1962–1972* (Ottawa: United Council of Filipino Associations in Canada, 1973), 1; Ruben J. Cusipag and M.C. Buenafe, *Portrait of Filipino Canadians in Ontario, 1960–1990* (Toronto: Kababayan Community Centre and Kalayaan Media Ltd, 1993), 146.

2   Anita Beltran Chen, "Filipinos," *Encyclopedia of Canada's People*, edited by Paul Robert Magocsi (Toronto: University of Toronto Press, 1999), 502.

3   *Statistics Canada 2001*, Population by selected ethnic Origins; Religion (95) and Visible Minority Groups (97F0022XCB01005); and Visible Minority Groups (15) and Immigrant Status and Period of Immigration (11) for Population of Canada (97f0010XCB01003).

4   *Statistics Canada, 2001*, Populations by selected ethnic origins; Visible Minority Population Metropolitan Areas.

5   William H. Frey, "The United States Population: Where the New Immigrants Are," http://usinfo.state.gov/journals/itsv/0699/ijse/frey/htm (accessed 12 November 2004).

6   Frey, "The United States Population."

7   Asian & Pacific Islander Institute on Domestic Violence, San Francisco, CA, http://www.apiahf.org/apidvinstitute/GenderViolence/statistics.htm (accessed 12 November 2004).

8   Interview, Father Donald Larson, St. Patrick parish, Vancouver, 18 July 2003.

9   Geraldine Sherman, "A Nanny's Life," *Toronto Star*, September 1996, http://www.geraldinesherman.com/Nanny.html (accessed 14 November 2004).

10   Interview, Father Donald Larson, St. Patrick parish, Vancouver, 18 July 2003; Maria Elena C. Samson, "What Does It Mean to Be a Filipino?" unpublished manuscript, 7, 11.

11   Dindo Rei M. Tesoro and Joselito Alviar Jose, *The Rise of Filipino Theology* (Paasay City, Philippines: Paulines, 2004), 263–64.

12   "The Filipinos' Colonized Psyche," *PN Magazine, The Philippine Star Life* (Manila), Week of 27 September – 3 October 1995.

13   Interview, Father Donald Larson, St. Patrick parish, Vancouver, 18 July 2003.

14   John Schumacher SJ, written answers to written questions of this author, Ateneo de Manila University, 4 November 2004.

15   Frank Padilla, *Facing the Future: The Vision and Mission of Couples for Christ in the Third Millennium* (Mandaluyong City, Philippines: Flame Ministries, 2003), 15–18.

16   Interview, Father Donald Larson, St. Patrick parish, Vancouver, 18 July 2003.

17   Telephone interview, Father Mario Marin, member of the Knights of Columbus, St. Patrick parish, Vancouver, 3 February 2005.

18   Emilio Santa Rita, "Pilipino Families" in *Ethnicity and Family Therapy*, second edition, edited by Monica McGoldrick, Joe Giordano, and John K. Pearce (New York: Guilford Press, 1996), 326, 328.

19   Anita Beltran Chen, "Kinship System and Chain Migration: Filipinos in Thunder Bay," *Asian Canadians Symposium V*, Mount Saint Vincent University, 1981, edited by K. Victor Ujimoto and Gordon Hirabayashi, 204.

20   Interview, Father Donald Larson, St. Patrick parish, Vancouver, 18 July 2003.

21   Interview, Father Donald Larson, St. Patrick parish, Vancouver, 18 July 2003.

22 Myriam Bals, "Foreign Domestics in Canada: Slaves of Hope," 2, http://www.myriambals.com/en/excerpt.htm (accessed 14 November 2004).

23 Interview, Arturo (Tito) Macapinlac, St. Paul parish, Richmond, BC, 20 July 2003.

24 *CFC Newsletter* 1:1 (September 1995), 8–9, Couples for Christ Archives, Edmonton.

25 Episcopal Commission on the Apostolate of the Laity, Catholic Bishops Conference of the Philippines, "Certification of Approval of Couples for Christ," signed by Bishop Angel H. Lagdameo, 26 July 1993; Roman Catholic Archbishop of Manila, "Certification and Endorsement of Couples of Christ," signed by Teodoro C. Bacani, Jr, Auxiliary Bishop of Manila, 17 August 1993, Couples for Christ Archives, Edmonton.

26 Rouquel Ponte, Director of Couples for Christ, to Fr. Joe Hattie OMI, 26 August 1993, Couples for Christ Archives, Edmonton.

27 *CFC Newsletter* 1: 1 (September 1995), 9, Couples for Christ Archives, Edmonton.

28 Interview, Arturo (Tito) Macapinlac, St. Paul parish, Richmond BC, 20 July 2003.

29 Luis Untalan to Archbishop Adam Exner OMI, 5 February 1995, Couples for Christ Archives, Edmonton.

30 Archbishop Adam Exner OMI to Luis M. Untalan, 10 February 1995, Couples for Christ Archives, Edmonton.

31 Interview, Arturo (Tito) Macapinlac, St. Paul parish, Richmond BC, 20 July 2003.

32 Interview, Father Peter Chiang, St. Paul parish, Richmond BC, 20 July 2003.

33 Interview, Mary Anne and Francisco Colayco, St. Rose of Lima, Manila, 14 September 2004.

34 Interview, Manuelita Mejos, St. Edward's parish, Winnipeg, 11 March 2004.

35 Susan Brigham, "'I Want to Voice It Out!': Learning to Integrate in Canadian Multicultural Society," summary of her master's thesis at the University of Alberta, 1995, http:www.geog.queensu.ca/era21/papers/brigham.htm 15–16 (accessed 12 November 2004).

36 Interview, Sonia and Alberto Sangalang, St. Edward's parish, Winnipeg, 11 March 2004. 37 Telephone interview, Brian R. Massie SJ, Pastor, St. Ignatius church, Winnipeg, 31 January 2005.

38 Interview, Father Vicente Tungolh, St. Edward's parish, Winnipeg, 10 March 2004.

39 Maria P. P. Root, *Filipino Americans: Transformation and Identity* (Thousand Oaks, CA: Sage Publications, 1997), 89.

40 Interview, Father Vicente Tungolh, St. Edward's parish, Winnipeg, 10 March 2004.

41 Interview, Virginia A. Yap, Christ the King parish, Manila, 29 September 2004.

42 Interview, Father Francisco Francis (alias), St. Edward's parish, Winnipeg, 11 March 2004; interview, Randolf David, University of the Philippines, Manila, 17 September 2004.

43 Interview, Father Francisco Francis (alias), St. Edward's parish, Winnipeg, 11 March 2004.

44   H. Billones and S. Wilson, "Understanding the Filipino Elderly," *Asian Canadians: Research on Current Issues: Asian Canadian Symposium, The Eighth,* edited by K. Victor Ujimoto and Josephine C. Naidoo (Hamilton: McMaster University, 1987), 166–67.

45   Brigham, "'I Want to Voice It Out!'" 11–12.

46   E. San Juan Jr, "Filipino Bodies: From the Philippines to the United States and Around the World," http://www.boondocksnet.com/centennial/sctests/esj_97a.html, 11 (accessed 16 November 2004).

47   Interview, Father Francisco Francis (alias), St. Edward's parish, Winnipeg, 11 March 2004.

48   Telephone interview, Fathers Rodolfo Imperial and Mario Lorenzana, Blessed John XXIII, Toronto, 26–27 February 2003.

49   Spiritual Statistics for the Year 2001, Archives of the Roman Catholic Archdiocese of Toronto (hereafter ARCAT).

50   Interview, Fanny Quimson, Manila, Ateneo de Manila University, 22 and 28 October 2004.

51   Bukas Loob sa Diyos: "The BLD", www. bldworld.org, "BLD Vancouver Outreach," 18 April 2004.

52   Telephone interview, Father Paul Leblanc, pastor of Our Lady of the Assumption, Toronto, 4 March 2003.

53   Maria Elena C. Samson, "What Does It Mean to Be a Filipino?" to be published in a journal for educators and professionals in June 2005, 6–7.

54   Interview, Manuel and Elizabeth Gorespe, St. Christopher parish, Mississauga, Ontario, and Andy and Isabelle Escaño, St. Matthew parish, Oakville, Ontario, 8 November 2003.

55   Interview, Roberto and Paciencia Santos, St. Bonaventure parish, Toronto, 29 November 2003; additional e-mail letter from Roberto and Paciencia Santos, 15 October 2004.

56   Brigham, "'I Want to Voice It Out!'" 10.

57   Interview, Roberto and Paciencia Santos, St. Bonaventure parish, Toronto, 29 November 2003; additional e-mail letter from Roberto and Paciencia Santos, 15 October 2004.

58   Brigham, "'I Want to Voice It Out!'" 6–7.

59   Interview, Roberto and Paciencia Santos, St. Bonaventure parish, Toronto, 8 November 2003.

60   Yen le Espiritu writes: "Eleonor Ocampo confided, 'It's like an understood silence in my family; don't ever cross the line and marry an African American. It just saddens me because of the perception that my parents have of African Americans as being on welfare and lazy and crimes and gangs.'... they have internalized the anti-Asian and anti-immigrant rhetorics and practices that characterized so much of the culture and social structure in the United States." (187); "young Filipinos live within and in tension with a racist system that defines white middle-class culture as the norm." (192); "Part of this way of life [imperialism is diplomacy, economic necessity, and a way of life] is the 'possessive investment in whiteness' and the corresponding disinvestment in 'undeserving' groups." (211); "Filipino transnational activities must be understood in part as an act of resistance: an articulation of their deep dissatisfaction with

and anger at the contradictions between official state ideals of equal citizenship and state-sanctioned forms of subordination based on class, race, gender, and sexual orientation. It is an act of resistance against the violence of globalized capitalism, a personal resolve to provide for themselves and their families even in the wake of global reorganization of capitalism and to remain stubbornly *Home bound* even as they are flung to the 'ends of the earth' in search of work." (212); in *Home Bound: Filipino American Lives Across Cultures, Communities, and Countries* (Berkeley: University of California Press, 2003).

61 Brigham, "'I Want to Voice It Out!'" 12–13.

62 Interview, Armin Marquez and Florinda Mapa, Our Lady of Lourdes rectory, Toronto, 23 December 2003.

63 Brigham, "'I Want to Voice It Out!'" 3–4.

64 Emilio Santa Rita, "Pilipino Families," 324–25.

65 Tesoro and Jose, *The Rise of Filipino Theology*, 165.

66 Felipe M. de Leon Jr, "Beyond the Dona Victorina Syndrome," read on 25 June 2004 at the "Pagkataong Filipino: Looking for the Filipino Among Filipinos – The Theory, Practice and Value of Filipino Personhood" conference held at the University of the Philippines Film Centre, 13.

67 Interview, Manuel and Elizabeth Gorespe, St. Christopher parish, Mississauga, 8 November 2003; Yen le Espiritu in *Home Bound* finds that Filipino immigrant parents would say, "We did it for the children." In the United States, they believe, their children would have better healthcare, education, and job opportunities (179).

68 Interview, Andrew and Isabelle Escaño, St. Matthew parish, Oakville, Ontario, 8 November 2003.

69 Interview, Rosemary Abigania, Our Lady of Lourdes parish, Toronto, 10 January 2004.

70 Amendments to Regulation 285/01 of the Employment Standards Act, 2000, http://www.labour.gov.on.ca/info/minimumwage, 4 June 2009; Sergio R. Karas, "The Live-In Caregiver Program," New Delhi, November 1997, http://www.karas.ca (accessed 15 November 2004); Geraldine Sherman, "A Nanny's Life," *Toronto Star*, September 1996.

71 Ryerson University School of Journalism Diversity Watch, http://www.diversitywatch.ryerson.ca/backgrounds/filipino.htm (accessed 12 June 2009); Myriam Bals, "Foreign Domestics in Canada: Slaves of Hope," http://www.myriambals.com/en/excerpt.html, (accessed 12 November 2004); Tina liboro-Pimentel, "Caregiver law splits Filipino Canadian Community," http://www.philippinenews.com/news/view.html (accessed 12 November 2004).

72 Geraldine Sherman, "A Nanny's Life," http://www.geraldinesherman.com/Nanny.html (accessed 14 November 2004).

73 Interview, Jean Nora La Torre, St. Michael parish, Scarborough; interview, Audie Glynn F. Olano, St. Bonaventure parish, Toronto, 29 November 2003.

74 Gina Mission, writer who lives in the Philippines and writes for CyberDyaro, *The Journal of History* (Winter 2003), http://truedemocrary.net/td-9/26.html (accessed 12 November 2004).

75 Written submission by Irene G. Peralejo, Manila, 16 November 2004; collaborating view as told by Onofre Pagsanghan, Our Lady of Pentecost church, 14 November 2004.

76   The *Philippine Star*, 16 November 2004.

77   John E. Zucchi, *Italians in Toronto: Development of a National Identity, 1875–1935* (Montreal: McGill-Queen's University Press, 1988), 41–47, 53, 146. "For these sojourners, Toronto was not a permanent settlement but a labour distribution centre ...". (146)

78   Cecil J. Houston and W. J. Smyth, *Irish Emigration and Canadian Settlement: Patterns, Links, and Letters* (Toronto: University of Toronto Press, 1990), 152–62. "Whole regions of Irish were created and maintained, and the longevity of these regions ... challenges the notion of widespread rootlessness."

79   Interview, Antonio F. B. de Castro SJ, Ateneo de Manila University, 11 October 2004.

80   Laurence J Kirmayer, Morton Weinfeld, Giovani Burgos, Guillaume Galbaud du Fort, Jean-Claude Lasry, Allan Young, "Use of Health Care Services for Psychological Distress by Immigrants in an Urban Multicultural Milieu," *The Canadian Journal of Psychiatry* 52 (5) (May 2007), 301–03.

81   Jonathan Y. Okamura, *Imagining the Filipino American Diaspora: Transnational Relations, Identities, and Communities* (New York: Garland, 1998), 117–27.

82   Chen, *From Sunbelt to Snowbelt*, 57.

Chapter 5

1   Uichol Kim and John W. Berry, "Acculturation Attitudes of Korean Immigrants in Toronto," *From a Different Perspective: Studies of Behavior Across Cultures*, edited by Isabel Reyes Lagunes and Upe H. Poortinga (Lisse: Swets and Zeitlinger, 1985), 96.

2   Joseph Chang-mun Kim and John Jae-sun Chung, eds., *Catholic Korea: Yesterday and Today* (Seoul: Catholic Korea Publishing Co., 1964), 20–21.

3   Kim and Chung, *Catholic Korea*, 23–26.

4   Chul Koo Ahn, *The History of Korean Catholics: Two Hundred Years* (Seoul: Seamoonsa Publishers, 1983); Kim and Chung, *Catholic Korea*, 26.

5   Scott W. Sunquist, David Wu Chu Sing, and John Chew Hiang Chea, eds., *Dictionary of Asian Christianity* (Grand Rapids, MI: Eerdmans), 446–47.

6   Sunquist, Sing, and Chea, *Dictionary of Asian Christianity*, 446–7.

7   http://www.paulnoll.com/Korea/History/South-Korean-compare-pop.html (accessed 12 June 2009); CIA The World Fact Book: Korea, South, https://www.cia.gov/cia/publications/factbook/index.html (accessed 12 June 2009).

8   Thomas C. Fox, *Pentecost in Asia: A New Way of Being Church* (Maryknoll, NY: Orbis, 2003), 23–24.

9   Statistics Canada, Visible Minority Groups (15) and Immigrant Status and Period of Immigration (11) for Population ... and percentages taken from Young-Sik Yoo, "Koreans," *Encyclopedia of Canada's Peoples*, edited by Paul Magocsi (Toronto: University of Toronto Press, 1999), 886.

10   Telephone interview, Father Philippe Tae Koo, Holy Cross parish, Winnipeg, 21 July 2006; *Canadian Catholic Church Directory* (Montreal: Novalis, 2006).

11   Summary Parish History, Korean Martyrs Catholic Mission, Montreal.

12   Interview, Father Peter Ki Tek Sung, Montreal, 12 September 2003; Visible Minority Population, Census Metropolitan Areas, 2001 Census, *Statistics Canada*; *Canadian Catholic Directory 2006/Annuaire de l'Église catholique au Canada 2006*. Ottawa: Novalis.

13 Interview, Father Peter Ki Tek Sung, Montreal, 12 September 2003.

14 Bok-Lim C. Kim and Eunjung Ryu, "Korean Families," in *Ethnicity and Family Therapy*, edited by Monica McGoldrick, Joe Giordano, and Nydia Garcia-Preto (New York: Guilford Press, 3rd ed., 2005), 354, 360.

15 Chai-Shin Yu, "Koreans in Canada (in Toronto) and Korean Studies in Canada," *Korea-Canada in Emerging Asia-Pacific Community* (Seoul: Yonsei University, Institute of East and West Studies, 1988), 138.

16 Yu, "Koreans in Canada (in Toronto) and Korean Studies in Canada," 139.

17 Yoo, "Koreans," 886; "How Koreans Came to Call Toronto Their Home," *Polyphony: The Bulletin of the Multicultural Society of Ontario* 6: 1 (1984), 178; Mary E. Odem, "Our Lady of Guadalupe in the New South: Latino Immigrants and the Politics of Integration in the Catholic Church," *Journal of American Ethnic History* 24: 1 (Fall 2004), 27–28.

18 Interview, John Chong Kook Park and Elizabeth Hyung Za Park, St. Andrew Kim parish, Toronto, 28 June 2006.

19 Statistics Canada, Selected Education Characteristics (29), Selected Ethnic Groups (100) ..., Census 2001; Yoo, "Koreans," 886; Jung G. Kim, "Korean-Language Press in Ontario," *Polyphony: The Bulletin of the Multicultural Society of Ontario* 4: 1 (1982), 86 and "How Koreans Came to Call Toronto Their Home," 6: 1 (1984), 180.

20 Jung G. Kim writes that the first Korean-language newspaper, *Han Ka Joo Bo/Korean Canada Times*, appeared in Toronto in 1971. Seven other titles for the Korean newspaper followed during the next ten years—often a weekly, sometimes a monthly, or more recently a daily—"Korean-Language Press in Ontario," *Polyphony: The Bulletin of the Multicultural Society of Ontario* 4: 1(1982), 86.

21 Interview, Peter Yang Hwan Oh and Othilia Young Sook Oh, St. Andrew Kim parish, Toronto, 23 June 2006.

22 Jonathan Y. Tan, *Introducing Asian American Theologies* (Maryknoll, NY: Orbis, 2008) 117–18.

23 Kim and Berry, "Acculturation Attitudes of Korean Immigrants in Toronto," 104.

24 Interview, Joseph and Kathy Lee, St. Andrew Kim parish, Toronto, 21 May 2006.

25 Jung-Gun Kim, Canadian Missionaries in Korea and the Beginnings of Korean Migration to Canada, Ed.D diss., University of Toronto, 1983.

26 Yoo, "Koreans," 887.

27 Interview, Jerome Hong Kim and Margaret Ran Kim, St. Andrew Kim parish, Toronto, 6 June 2006.

28 Interview, Father Peter Choi, St. Anne's parish, Toronto, 16 May 2006.

29 Bok-Lim C. Kim and Eunjung Ryu, "Korean Families," in *Ethnicity and Family Therapy*, 354.

30 Interview, Father Peter Choi, St. Anne's parish, Toronto, 16 May 2006.

31 Interview, Cesillia Soon Ae Choi and Stephan Choi, St. Andrew Kim parish, Toronto, 27 June 2006.

32 The struggle between the Korean parents and their children is well described in "Tradition and Change" by Caroline Choi, http://www.equalitytoday.org/edition3/tradition.html (accessed 20 November 2005). For her, "Parents also

worry that their children will forget what it means to be Korean. That is why they place such a strong importance on continuing the culture through marriage. For many, who don't speak English, this is especially important because marriage within the culture breaks communication barriers. If their children's future spouses are Korean, it becomes easier to communicate with them and easier to carry on the Korean cultural traditions."

33 K. Victor Ujimoto and Gordon Hirabayashi, editors, Visible *Minorities and Multiculturalism: Asian in Canada* (Toronto: Butterworths, 1980), 234.

34 Interview, Cesillia Soon Ae Choi and Stephan Choi, St. Andrew Kim parish, Toronto, 27 June 2006.

35 Interview, Father John Jai Don Lee, University of St. Michael's College, University of Toronto, 5 June 2006.

36 Interview, Lisa Hye Young Min and Angelo Jin Yong Kim, St. Andrew Kim parish, Toronto, 11 July 2006.

37 *Korean Catholic Church Credit Union Limited: Financial Statements for the Year Ended, December 31, 2005.* St. Andrew Kim Church Archives. Koreans have been successful in founding credit unions and banks in Canada. "In Toronto there are three Korean banks – Korea Exchange, Chohung, and Hanil – branches of a number of companies such as Hyundae and Samsung, and three Korean credit unions." In Vancouver there are two Korean banks and one credit union. Yoo, "Koreans," 885.

38 Yoo, "Koreans," 888.

39 Parish History: "Kim Dae Dun Parish: Involved Laity and Solid Faith," St. Andrew Kim parish, Toronto, *Catholic Register*, 16 May 1992.

40 Chai-Shin Yu, "Koreans in Canada (in Toronto) and Korean Studies in Canada," 139.

41 Stuart MacDonald, "Presbyterian and Reformed Christians and Ethnicity," in *Christianity and Ethnicity in Canada*, edited by Paul Bramadat and David Seljak (Toronto: University of Toronto Press, 2008), 184.

42 Yoo, "Koreans," 886.

43 Yoo, "Koreans," 884.

44 Interview, Father Gregory Choi, St. Andrew Kim parish, Toronto, 22 May 2006.

45 Telephone interview, Father Robert O'Brien, Director of Lay Ministry, Catholic Pastoral Centre, 1155 Yonge Street, Toronto, 10 July 2006.

46 Lucya and Andrew Ahn were not alone in enduring the hardship of being small business owners. This was often the anxiety of other Korean Canadian owners: "Korean small-business people, who were often professionals in the homeland, are characterized by a high level of education. Overworked, they gain little financial return [in Canada]. ... Korean small businesses, especially convenience stores, face a bleak future because of their owners' unhappiness in the face of the social and economic challenges confronting them." Yoo, "Koreans,", 885.

47 Bo Kyung Kim, "Attitudes, Parental Identification, and Locus of Control of Korean, New Korean-Canadian, and Canadian Adolescents," in *Visible Minorities and Multiculturalism: Asians in Canada*, edited by K. Victor Ujimoto and Gordon Hirabayashi (Toronto: Butterworths, 1980), 239.

48 Interview, Andrew Moon Young Ahn and Lucya Jae Eun Song Ahn, St. Andrew Kim parish, Toronto, 9 July 2006.

49 "Korean-Canadian youth acknowledge the great sacrifice made by their parents. They understand their parents' dedication and the priority given to them as children. Our parents just want us to succeed in society," says David Kim in Choi's "Tradition and Change."

50 Kim and Berry, "Acculturation Attitudes of Korean Immigrants in Toronto," 102.

51 Interview, Theresa Eun Joo Lee and Helena Sun Joo Lee, St. Andrew Kim parish, Toronto, 9 July 2006.

52 Interview, Andrew and Catherina Kim, St. Andrew Kim parish, Toronto, 2 June 2006.

53 Kenneth Fung and Yuk-Lin Renita Wong, "Factors Influencing Attitudes towards Seeking Professional Help among East and Southeast Asian Immigrant and Refugee Women," *International Journal of Social Psychiatry* 53 (3): 226.

54 Interview, Andrew and Catherina Kim, St. Andrew Kim parish, Toronto, 2 June 2006.

55 David Ley, "Explaining Variations in Business Performance Among Immigrant Entrepreneurs in Canada," *Journal of Ethnic and Migration Studies* 32 (5) (July 2006), 748–49.

56 Ley, "Explaining Variations in Business Performance Among Immigrant Entrepreneurs in Canada," 754–61.

57 "The isolationist policy was further buttressed by the cultural chauvinism of the ruling class, to whom it was inconceivable that anything of value could be learned from any foreign country other than China." Yoo, "Koreans," 883.

Chapter 6

1 Samuel Hugh Moffett, *A History of Christianity in Asia: Volume I, Beginnings to 1500* (New York: HarperCollins, 1992), 24–39.

2 Samuel Hugh Moffett, *A History of Christianity in Asia: Volume II, 1500 to 1900* (Maryknoll,NY: Orbis, 2005), 9–12.

3 Scott W. Sunquist, David Wu Chu Sing, and John Chew Hiang Chea, editors, *A Dictionary of Asian Christianity* (Grand Rapids, MI: Eerdmans, 2001), 796; P. R. W. Kendall, *The Sri Lankan Tamil Community in Toronto* (Toronto: City of Toronto Department of Public Health, 1989), 7.

4 Arul S. Aruliah, "The Sri Lankan Tamil Community," *Safe Haven: The Refugee Experience of Five Families*, edited by Elizabeth McLuhan (Toronto: Multicultural History Society of Ontario, 1995), 175–77.

5 Kendall, *The Sri Lankan Tamil Community in Toronto*, 6–7.

6 Norman Buchignani, Doreen M. Indra, and Ram Srivastava, *Continuous Journey: A Social History of South Asians in Canada* (Toronto: McClelland and Stewart, 1985), 143–44.

7 Ravindiran Vaitheespara, "Tamils," *Encyclopedia of Canada's Peoples*, edited by Paul Robert Magocsi (Toronto: University of Toronto Press, 1999), 1252.

8 Vaitheespara, "Tamils," 1248, 1251–3.

9 *International Edition: Thamilar Mathiyil (Amidst Tamils)—2000: The Business Directory.* "World's First Business Directory for Tamils." Toronto: Nanda Publications, 2000.

10 Interview, Anton Philip Sinnarasa, Tamil Eelam Centre, Toronto, on 29 January 2004; *Toronto Star*, 6 November 1998.

11   Interview, M. J. Augustine Jeyanathan, Mission of Our Lady of Good Health, Scarborough, 23 January 2005.

12   Interview, Father Christie Joachim Pillai OMI, St. Dunstan's parish, 24 April 2004.

13   Interview, Father Christie Joachim Pillai OMI, St. Dunstan's parish, 24 April 2004.

14   Interview, Joseph Andrews Arulappan and Nalini Daniel, Our Lady of Lourdes parish, Toronto, 3 February 2004.

15   Interview, Father Peter Gitendran's, Sick Children's Hospital, Toronto, 30 April 2004.

16   Interview, David Thomas and Jeyamani Victor, Our Lady of Lourdes parish, Toronto, 29 January 2004.

17   Interview, David Thomas and Jeyamani Victor, Our Lady of Lourdes parish, Toronto, 29 January 2004.

18   Interview, Philip S. and Merina Soosaithasan, St. Timothy's parish, Toronto, 29 January 2004.

19   Interview, George Antony and Regina Sinnathurai, Our Lady of Lourdes church, Toronto, 22 June 2004.

20   Interview, Francis and Mary Anne Joseph, St. Benedict church, Toronto, 20 May 2004.

21   Vaitheespara, "Tamils," 1248, 1252–53.

22   Kendall, *The Sri Lankan Tamil Community in Toronto*, 4.

23   Renu Khosla, "The Changing Familial Role of South-Asian Women in Canada: A Study in Identity Transformation," *Asian Canadian Regional Perspectives: Fifth Asian Canadian Symposium*, edited by K. Victor Ujimoto and Gordon Hirabayashi (Halifax: Mount Saint Vincent University, 1981), 178–83.

24   Susan S. Wadley, ed., *The Powers of Tamil Women* (Syracuse, NY: Syracuse University, 1980), 128–30.

25   Anita Beltran Chen, "Filipinos," in *Encyclopedia of Canada's Peoples*, edited by Paul Robert Magocsi (Toronto: University of Toronto Press, 1999), 503–05.

26   Professor Stanley J. Tambiah, in a talk at Tamil Studies Conference: Tropes, Territories, Competing Realities at the University of Toronto, on 12–14 May 2006.

27   According to Professor Stanley J. Tambiah, in a talk at Tamil Studies Conference: Tropes, Territories, Competing Realities at the University of Toronto on 12–14 May 2006, boys are given more freedom, are less studious, and end up at trade schools; but since the 1990s, the girls are determined to do better. Boys stay out late and join a gang; girls do not date, stay at home, and talk more with their mother but not about romance or sexuality. Romance for Tamils is only in films. Girls are more competent than boys across the board, secure places at university, and in the professional world.

28   Vaitheespara, "Tamils," 1252.

29   Interview with Philip S. and Merina Soosaithasan, St. Timothy's parish, Toronto, 26 May 2004.

30   Kendall, *The Sri Lankan Tamil Community in Toronto*, 7.

31   Buchignani, Indra, and Srivastiva, *Continuous Journey*, 221–26.

32   Interview, Francis and Mary Anne Joseph, St. Benedict church, Toronto, 20 May 2004.

33   Interview, Father Joseph Chandrakanthan, Annunciation parish, Toronto, 4 May 2004.
34   Notes from the Tamil Outreach, St. Lawrence church, Toronto, 22 November 2003.
35   Notes from the Tamil Outreach, Christi Joachim Pillai and Joseph Chandrakanthan, St. Lawrence church, Toronto, 22 November 2003.
36   Notes from the Tamil Outreach, Augustine Jeyanathan, St. Lawrence church, Toronto, 22 November 2003.
37   Notes from the Tamil Outreach, Paul Varghese Moonjely cmi, St. Lawrence church, Toronto, 22 November 2003.
38   Notes from the Tamil Outreach, Tony Chow, St. Lawrence church, Toronto, 22 November 2003.
39   Notes from the Tamil Outreach, Michele Meunier m afr, St. Lawrence church, Toronto, 22 November 2003; Visible Minority Population, census Metropolitan Areas, *Statistics Canada 2001.*
40   Notes from the Tamil Outreach, Terence J. Fay SJ, St. Lawrence church, Toronto, 22 November 2003.
41   Tamil Studies Conference: Tropes, Territories, and Competing Realities, University of Toronto, 12–14 May 2006, various lectures and interviews with participants.
42   Vaitheespara, "Tamils," 1253–4.
43   H. Billones and S. Wilson, "Understanding the Filipino Elderly," *Asian Canadians: Research on Current Issues: Eighth Asian Canadian Symposium,* 163–68.
44   Kendall, *The Sri Lankan Tamil Community in Toronto,* 14–15.
45   Nicholas Keung, "Footlights Shine on Tamil Life in Canada," *Toronto Star,* 17 July 2004.
46   Buchignani, Indra, and Srivastiva, *Continuous Journey,* 220–24.
47   Anita Beltran Chen, *From Sunbelt to Snowbelt: Filipinos in Canada* (Calgary: The Research Centre for Canadian Ethnic Studies, 1998), 57.

Chapter 7

1   Peter C. Phan, *Mission and Catechesis: Alexandre de Rhodes and Inculturation in Seventeenth-Century Vietnam* (Maryknoll, NY: Orbis Books, 1998), 45–68.
2   Louis-Jacques Dorais, "Defining the Overseas Vietnamese," *Diaspora* 10 (1) (2001), 8.
3   Phan, *Mission and Catechesis,* 45–68; Louis-Jacques Dorais, Lise Pilon-Lê, and Nguyên Huy, *Exile in a Cold Land: A Vietnamese Community in Canada* (Boston: University of Massachusetts and Yale Center for International and Area Studies, 1987), 152.
4   Samuel Hugh Moffett, *A History of Christianity in Asia: Volume II, 1500 to 1900* (New York: Orbis, 2005), 44.
5   Phan, *Mission and Catechesis,* 45–68; Dorais, Pilon-Lê, and Huy, *Exile in a Cold Land,* 152.
6   The Colombo Plan was founded in 1951 at the capital city of Ceylon, now Sri Lanka, as a framework for bi-lateral arrangements in the Asia-Pacific Region involving foreign aid and technical assistance for the economic and social development to raise the living standards of people in the region. Among its

benefits are scholarships for students studying drug advisory, the environment, private sector development, and public administration.

7   Dorais Pilon-Lê, and Huy, *Exile in a Cold Land*, 14–17.

8   Dorais, "Vietnamese," *Encyclopedia of Canada's Peoples*, edited by Paul Robert Magocsi (Toronto: University of Toronto Press, 1999), 1313–14.

9   Dorais, "Defining the Overseas Vietnamese," 17.

10   Dorais, "Vietnamese," 1315.

11   Interview, Father Dominic Bui, Pastor of the Vietnamese Martyrs Mission, and parishioner Jeanine Ho at St. Cecilia's church, Toronto, 14 July 2003.

12   Dorais, "Vietnamese," 1315.

13   Dorais, "Vietnamese," 1315–16.

14   Dorais, "Vietnamese," 1315–17.

15   Interview, Jasmine Nguyen (alias), Our Lady of Lourdes parish, 9 January 2004. Vietnamese come to North America with varied religious heritages which includes Confucian, Taoist, and Buddhist influence; Phan, *Christianity with an Asian Face: Asian American Theology in the Making* (Maryknoll, NY: Orbis, 2003), 234.

16   Interview, Bao Van Pham and Le Tham Huang Yen, St. Joan of Arc and Vietnamese Martyrs mission, Toronto, 8 October 2006.

17   Paul K. Leung and James K. Boehnlein, "Vietnamese Families," *Ethnicity and Family Therapy*, edited by Monica McGoldrick, Joe Giordano, and Nydia Garcia-Preto (New York: Guilford Press, 3rd ed. 2005), 367.

18   Interview, Bao Van Pham and Le Tham Huang Yen, St. Joan of Arc and Vietnamese Martyrs mission, Toronto, 8 October 2006.

19   Interview, John do Trong Chu, Transfiguration of Our Lord, Toronto, 11 September 2006.

20   Dorais, "Defining the Overseas Vietnamese," *Diaspora* 10 (1) (2001), 22.

21   Dorais, Defining the Overseas Vietnamese," 22, 9.

22   Interview, John do Trong Chu, Transfiguration of Our Lord, Toronto, 11 September 2006.

23   Phan, *Christianity with an Asian Face*, 233.

24   Interview, Archbishop Adam Exner, Vancouver, 22 August 2006.

25   Tan, *Introduction to Asian American Theologies*, 70.

26   Tan, *Introduction to Asian American Theologies*, 70.

27   Interview, Archbishop Adam Exner, Vancouver, 16 July 2003.

28   Phan, *Christianity with an Asian Face*, 230.

29   Http://www.edmontoncatholic-church.com (accessed 12 June 2009); http://www.rcdiocese-calgary.ab.ca (accessed 12 June 2009).

30   Dorais, "Vietnamese," 1320–21; Louis-Jacques Dorais, *The Cambodians, Laotians and Vietnamese in Canada* (Ottawa: Canadian Historical Association, 2000), 26.

31   Interview, Father John Te Nguyen, St. Philip Minh church, Saint-Boniface, Manitoba, 3 June 2004.

32   Interview, Father John Te Nguyen, St. Philip Minh church, Saint-Boniface, Manitoba, 3 June 2004.

33   Interview, Hien Duc Tran and Nguyet Nguyen, St. Philip Minh church, Saint-Boniface, Manitoba, 1 June 2004.

34   Interview, Kim Nguyen, St. Philip Minh church, Saint-Boniface, Manitoba, 1 June 2004.

35   Interview, Dao Lieu and Tia Pham, St. Philip Minh church, Saint-Boniface, Manitoba, 1 June 2004.
36   Interview, Father Dominic Bui, pastor of the Vietnamese Martyrs' mission, and parishioner Jasmine Nguyen (alias), St. Cecilia's church, Toronto, 14 July 2003.
37   Interview, Michael Huynh and Agnes H. Tran, Vietnamese Martyrs' mission, Toronto, 2 September 2006.
38   Louis-Jacques Dorais, "Defining the Overseas Vietnamese," 15–16.
39   Visible minority population, census metropolitan areas, 2001 Census, *Statistics Canada.*
40   Interview, Father J. B. Thanh Son Dinh, Vietnamese Martyrs' mission, Montreal, 11 September 2003.
41   Dorais, "Defining the Overseas Vietnamese," 21.
42   Interview, Father Dominic Bui, pastor of the Vietnamese Martyrs' mission, and parishioner Jasmine Nguyen (alias), St. Cecilia's church, Toronto, 14 July 2003.
43   Dorais, "Vietnamese," 1317.
44   Dorais, "Vietnamese," 1317–18; interview with Father Dominic Bui, pastor of the Vietnamese Martyrs' mission, 14 July 2003.
45   Interview, Jasmine Nguyen (alias), psychotherapist and Catholic parishioner, 15 July 2003.
46   Interview, Father Joseph Tap Tran, St. Cecilia's parish, Toronto, 22 August 2006.
47   Phan, *Christianity with an Asian Face,* 233.
48   Interview, Father Joseph Tap Tran, St. Cecilia's parish, Toronto, 22 August 2006.
49   Interview, Hien and Phuong Nguyen, Vietnamese Martyrs' mission, Toronto, 2 September 2006.
50   Interview, Kim Huynh, Vietnamese Martyrs' mission, Toronto, 2 September 2006.
51   Interview, Dac Dung Ho and Kim-Anh Vu, Vietnamese Martyrs' mission, Toronto, 2 September 2006.
52   Interview, Peter Tran, Vietnamese Martyrs' mission, Toronto, 12 September 2006.
53   Dorais, *Exile in a Cold Land,* 125–26.
54   Phan, *Christianity with an Asian Face,* 235, 237.
55   Dorais, "Vietnamese," 1322.

Conclusion

1   Grenz, *A Primer on Postmodernism,* 15–20, 41–53.
2   Grenz, *A Primer on Postmodernism,* 163–66.
3   Grenz, *A Primer on Postmodernism,* 35.
4   Jeong Mi Lee, Asian Minorities in Canada: Focusing on Chinese and Japanese People. Ottawa: National Library of Canada, 1991. M.A. Thesis, Microfiche, 53–55.
5   Peter S. Li, *The Chinese in Canada* (Toronto: Oxford University Press, 1988), 131–32.

Bibliography

Periodicals

Arevalo, Catalino G. "The Rebirth of the Local Church," *Teaching All Nations* (East Asian Pastoral Institute) 16 (1976), 249–52.

Billones, H. and S. Wilson, "Understanding the Filipino Elderly," *Asian Canadians: Research on Current Issues: Eighth Asian Canadian Symposium*, 163–68.

Couples for Christ. *CFC Newsletter* 1:1 (September 1995), 8–9, Couples for Christ Archives, Edmonton.

Dorais, Louis-Jacques. "Defining the Overseas Vietnamese," *Diaspora* 10 (1) (2001), 8-22.

"[The] Filipinos Colonized Psyche," *PN Magazine, The Philippine Star Life* (Manila), Week of 27 September – 3 October 1995.

Fung, Kenneth and Yuk-Lin Renita Wong, "Factors Influencing Attitudes towards Seeking Professional Help among East and Southeast Asian Immigrant and Refugee Women," *International Journal of Social Psychiatry* 53 (3): 226–27.

Gleason, Mona. "Psychology and the Construction of the 'Normal' Family in Postwar Canada, 1945–60," *Canadian Historical Review* 78, no. 3(Sept. 1997): 472–73.

Hwang, Wei-Chin. "Acculturative Family Distancing: Theory, Research, and Clinical Practice," *Psychotherapy: Theory, Research, Practice, Training* 43, 4 (2006), 397-400.

Jesena, Arsenio C. "The Sacadas of Sugarland," *Solidarity* VI, 5 (May 1971), 27–31.

Keung, Nicholas. "Footlights Shine on Tamil Life in Canada," *Toronto Star*, 17 July 2004.

Kim, Bok-Lim C. and Eunjung Ryu, "Korean Families," in *Ethnicity and Family Therapy*, 354.

Kim, Jung G. "Korean-Language Press in Ontario," *Polyphony. The Bulletin of the Multicultural Society of Ontario* 4: 1 (1982), 86.

Kirmayer, Laurence, J. Morton Weinfeld, Giovani Burgos, Guillaume Galbaud du Fort, Jean-Claude Lasry, Allan Young, "Use of Health Care Services for Psychological Distress by Immigrants in an Urban Multicultural Milieu," *The Canadian Journal of Psychiatry* 52 (5) (May 2007), 301–03.

"[How] Koreans Came to Call Toronto Their Home," *Polyphony: The Bulletin of the Multicultural Society of Ontario* 6: 1 (1984), 178.

Ley, David. "Explaining Variations in Business Performance Among Immigrant Entrepreneurs in Canada," *Journal of Ethnic and Migration Studies* 32 (5) (July 2006), 758–59.

Li, Peter S. "Ethnic Enterprise in Transition: Chinese Business in Richmond, B.C., 1980–1990," *Canadian Ethnic Studies* 24: 1 (1992), 131–38. Li, Peter S.

————. "The Consumer Market of the Enclave Economy: A Study of Advertisements in a Chinese Daily Newspaper in Toronto," *Canadian Ethnic Studies* 31:2 (1999), 49–51.

————. "Racial Supremacism under Social Democracy," 27: 1 (1995), 3–4 & 7 and "The Place of Immigrants: the Politics of Difference in Territorial and Social Space," 35:2 (2003), 3–5, *Canadian Ethnic Studies.*

Longtin, Pauline. "Mother May of the Holy Spirit and the Immigrants," *Precursor,* June 1977, 13.

Mission, Gina. *The Journal of History* (Winter 2003), http://truedemocrary. net/td-9/26.html, 12 November 2004.

Noh, Samuel et al. in the *Journal of Nervous and Mental Disease* 180: 9 (Sept 1992), 573–77.

Odem, Mary E. "Our Lady of Guadalupe in the New South: Latino Immigrants and the Politics of Integration in the Catholic Church," *Journal of American Ethnic History* 24: 1 (Fall 2004), 27–28.

Philippine Daily Inquirer, 20 October 2004.

The *Philippine Star,* 16 November 2004.

[The] Precursor (Montreal), March–April 1943, 80–81; November–December 1943, 337–38.

Sherman, Geraldine. "A Nanny"s Life," *Toronto Star,* September 1.

Turcotte, Huguette MIC, "Hospitals for Chinese in Canada: Montreal (1918) and Vancouver (1921)", CCHA *Historical Studies* 70 (2004), 131–42.

Books

Ahn, Chul Koo. *The History of Korean Catholics: Two Hundred Years.* Seoul: Seamoonsa Publishers, 1983.

Anderson, Kay J. *Vancouver's Chinatown: Racial Discourse in Canada, 1875–1980.* Montreal: McGill-Queen's University Press, 1991.

Arevalo, Catalino G. "Filipino Theology," *Dictionary of Mission: Theology, History, Perspectives,* eds. Karl Müller et al. (Maryknoll, NY: Orbis, 1997), 161–67.

Aruliah, Arul S. "The Sri Lankan Tamil Community," *Safe Haven: The Refugee Experience of Five Families,* edited by Elizabeth McLuhan. Toronto: Multicultural History Society of Ontario, 1995.

Blessed Chinese Martyrs' Catholic Church. *We Are the Church: Dedication of the New Church, October 15, 1994.* Toronto: Blessed Chinese Martyrs, c. 1994.

———. *We Are the Church: The Blessed Chinese Martyrs Catholic Mission.* Scarborough: Chinese Martyrs, c. 1994.

Billones, H. and S. Wilson, "Understanding the Filipino Elderly," *Asian Canadians: Research on Current Issues: Asian Canadian Symposium, The Eighth,* edited by K. Victor Ujimoto and Josephine C. Naidoo. Hamilton: McMaster University, 1987, 166–67.

Bramadat, Paul and David Seljak, eds. *Christianity and Ethnicity in Canada.* Toronto: University of Toronto Press, 2008.

———. *Religion and Ethnicity in Canada.* Toronto: Pearson Longman, 2005.

Brigham, Susan. "'I Want to Voice It Out!' Learning to Integrate in Canadian Multicultural Society," summary of her master's thesis at the University of Alberta, 1995, http://www.geog.queensu.ca/era21/papers/brigham.htm, 12 November 2004.

Buchignani, Norman, Doreen M. Indra, and Ram Srivastava, *Continuous Journey: A Social History of South Asians in Canada.* Toronto: McClelland and Stewart, 1985.

Canadian Catholic Church Directory /Annuaire de l'Église catholique au Canada 2008. Ottawa: Novalis, 2008.

Castagna, Maria and George J. Sefa Dei, "An Historical Overview of the Application of the Race Concept in Social Practice," in *Anti-Racist Feminism: Critical Race and Gender Studies.* Halifax: Fernwood, 2000, edited by Agnes Calliste and George J. Sefa Dei.

Catholic Korea: Yesterday and Today. Seoul: Catholic Korea Publishing Co., 1964.

Chan, Shun-hing and Beatrice Leung. *Changing Church and State Relations in Hong Kong, 1950–2000.* Hong Kong: Hong Kong University Press, 2003.

Chen, Anita Beltran. *From Sunbelt to Snowbelt: Filipinos in Canada.* Calgary: Canadian Ethnic Studies Association, ca.1998.

———. "Filipinos," *Encyclopedia of Canada's People,* edited by Paul Robert Magocsi. Toronto: University of Toronto Press, 1999.

———. "Kinship System and Chain Migration: Filipinos in Thunder Bay," *Asian Canadians Symposium V,* Mount Saint Vincent University, 1981, edited by K. Victor Ujimoto and Gordon Hirabayashi, 204.

Chinese Catholic Mission (Montreal). *50th Anniversary of the Priestly Ordination of Father Thomas Tou.* Montreal: Chinese Catholic Mission, ca.1998.

———. *Growing with God, 75 Years: The 75th Anniversary of the Montreal Chinese Catholic Church, 1917–1992.* Montreal: Private publication, ca.1992.

Clandinin, D. Jean and F. Michael Connelly, *Narrative Inquiry: Experience and Story in Qualitative Research*. San Francisco: Jossey-Bass, 2000.

Colayco, Francisco J. *Wealth within Your Reach: Pera Mo, Palaguin Mo!* Philippines, 2004.

Cusipag, Ruben J. and M.C. Buenafe, *Portrait of Filipino Canadians in Ontario, 1960–1990*. Toronto: Kababayan Community Centre and Kalayaan Media Ltd, 1993.

Denzin, N. K. and Y. S. Lincoln, eds., *Collecting and Interpreting Qualitative Materials*. Thousand Oaks, CA: Sage Publications, 1998.

————. *The Landscape of Qualitative Research: Theories and Issues*. Thousand Oaks, CA: Sage, 1998.

Directory of the Archdiocese of Toronto. 2000.

Dorais, Louis-Jacques. *The Cambodians, Laotians and Vietnamese in Canada*. Ottawa: Canadian Historical Association, 2000.

Dorais, Louis-Jacques, Lise Pilon-Lê, and Nguyên Huy, *Exile in a Cold Land: A Vietnamese Community in Canada*. Boston: University of Massachusetts and Yale Center for International and Area Studies, 1987.

Espiritu, Yen le. *Home Bound: Filipino American Lives across Cultures, Communities, and Countries*. Berkeley: University of California Press, 2003.

Fox, Thomas C., *Pentecost in Asia: A New Way of Being Church*. Maryknoll, NY: Orbis, 2003.

Grenz, Stanley J. *A Primer on Postmodernism*. Grand Rapids, MI: Wm B. Eerdmans Publishing Co., 1996.

Gresko, Jacqueline. *Traditions of Faith and Service: Archdiocese of Vancouver, 1908–2008*. Vancouver: Archdiocese of Vancouver, 2008.

Guidelines For House Expansion, De La Costa V. Manila, n.d.

Helly, Denise. *Les Chinois à Montréal, 1877–1951*. Montréal: Institute québécois de recherche sur la culture, 1987.

Hoe, Ban Sen. *Enduring Hardship: the Chinese Laundry in Canada*. Ottawa: Canadian Museum of Civilization, 2003.

The Homeowners Manual, Manila, ca. 2002.

Hong Kong Catholic Church Directory 2002. Hong Kong: Catholic Truth Society, 2001.

Houston, Cecil J. and W. J. Smyth, *Irish Emigration and Canadian Settlement: Patterns, Links, and Letters*. Toronto: University of Toronto Press, 1990.

International Edition: Thamilar Mathiyil (Amidst Tamils)–2000: The Business Directory. "World's First Business Directory for Tamils." Toronto: Nanda Publications, 2000.

Johnson-Bailey, Juanita. "Dancing between the Swords: My Foray into Constructing Narratives" in *Qualitative Research in Practice: Examples for Discussion and Analysis*, edited by Sharan B. Merriam and Associates. San Francisco: Jossey-Bass, 2002.

Kendall, P. R. W. *The Sri Lankan Tamil Community in Toronto*. Toronto: City of Toronto Department of Public Health, 1989.

Kim, Joseph Chang-mun and John Jae-sun Chung, eds., *Catholic Korea: Yesterday and Today*. Seoul: Catholic Korea Publishing Co., 1964.

Kim, Jung-Gun. Canadian Missionaries in Korea and the Beginnings of Korean Migration to Canada, Ed.D diss., University of Toronto, 1983.

Kim, Uichol and John W. Berry, "Acculturation Attitudes of Korean Immigrants in Toronto," in *From a Different Perspective: Studies of Behavior Across Cultures*, edited by Isabel Reyes Lagunes and Upe H. Poortinga. Lisse: Swets and Zeitlinger, 1985.

Lai, David Chuenyan, Jordan Paper, and Li Chuang Paper, "The Chinese in Canada: The Unrecognized Religion," in *Religion and Ethnicity in Canada* edited by Paul Bramadat and David Seljak. Toronto: Pearson Longman, 2005.

Laquian, Eleanor R. *A Study of Filipino Immigration to Canada, 1962–1972*. Ottawa: United Council of Filipino Associations in Canada, 1973.

Lee, Evelyn and Matthew R. Mock, "Chinese Families" in *Ethnicity and Family Therapy*, 3rd edition, edited by Monica McGoldrick et al. New York: Guilford Press, 2005.

Lee, Jeong Mi. Asian Minorities in Canada: Focusing on Chinese and Japanese People. Ottawa: National Library of Canada, 1991. M.A. Thesis, Microfiche.

Li, Peter S. *The Chinese in Canada*. Oxford: Oxford University Press, 1998.

———. "Chinese" in *Encyclopedia of Canada's Peoples*, edited by Paul Magocsi (Toronto: University of Toronto Press, 1999.

Ligo, Vivian. *Singing the Lord's Song in a Foreign Land: Reclaiming Faith in a New Culture*. Ottawa: Novalis, 2002.

Lo, Edmond. "Catechesis at the Chinese Martyrs Church from the Time of its Founding to the Present." Archives of Chinese Martyrs church, Toronto. Unpublished paper, 2002.

McNally, Vincent J. *The Lord's Distant Vineyard: A History of the Oblates and the Catholic Community in British Columbia*. Edmonton: University of Alberta Press and Western Canadian Publishers, 2000.

Moffett, Samuel Hugh. *A History of Christianity of in Asia: Volume I, Beginnings to 1500* .New York: HarperCollins, 1992.

————. *A History of Christianity of in Asia: Volume II, 1500 to 1900.* New York: Orbis, 2005.

Ng, Wing Chung.*The Chinese in Vancouver, 1945–80: The Pursuit of Identity and Power.* Vancouver: UBC Press, 1999.

Okamura, Jonathan Y. *Imagining the Filipino American Diaspora: Transnational Relations, Identities, and Communities,* New York: Garland, 1998.

Ooka, Emi. "Growing Up Canadian: Language, Culture, and Identity among Second-Generation Chinese Youths in Canada," Ph.D. diss., University of Toronto, 2002.

Padilla, Frank. *Facing the Future: The Vision and Mission of Couples for Christ in the Third Millennium.* Mandaluyong City, Philippines: Flame Ministries, 2003.

Phan, Peter C. *Christianity with an Asian Face: Asian American Theology in the Making.* Maryknoll. NY: Orbis Books, 2003.

————. *Mission and Catechesis: Alexandre de Rhodes and Inculturation in Seventeenth-Century Vietnam.* Maryknoll. NY: Orbis Books, 1998.

Pon, Madge. "Like A Chinese Puzzle: The Construction of Chinese Masculinity in *Jack Canuck,*" *Gender and History in Canada,* edited by Joy Parr and Mark Rosenfeld. Toronto: Copp Clark, 1996.

Renaud, Rosario. *Le Diocèse de Süchow (Chine): Champ apostolique des Jésuites canadiens de 1918 à 1954.* Montréal: Les Éditions Bellarmin, 1982.

Riessman, Catherine Kohler. *Narrative Analysis.* Thousand Oaks, CA: Sage Publications, 1993.

Rink, Deborah. *Spirited Women: A History of the Catholic Sisters in British Columbia.* Vancouver: Sisters' Association Archdiocese of Vancouver, 2000.

Root, Maria P. P. *Filipino Americans: Transformation and Identity.* Thousand Oaks, CA: Sage Publications Inc, 1997.

St Francis Xavier Parish, 1933–1983: The Golden Jubilee. Hong Kong, ca. 1983.

St Francis Xavier Parish, 1933–1988: Golden Jubilee. Vancouver, ca. 1988.

San Juan, E. Jr, *After Postcolonialism: Remapping Philippines–United States Confrontations* (Lantham, MD: Rowman & Littlefield, 2000.

Sharing the Harvest: The Tenth Anniversary of the Chinese Catholic Parish: Planning the Future, 1987–1997. Edmonton, ca. 1997.

Statistics Canada 2001. Religion (95) and Visible Minority Groups (15) for Population, for Canada, Provinces, Territories, Census Metropolitan Areas and Census Agglomerations, 2001 Census – 20% Sample Data, 97F0022XCB2001005.

Sugima, Momoye, ed. *Jin Guo: Voices of Chinese Women.* Toronto: Women's Press, 1992.

Summary Parish History, Korean Martyrs Catholic Mission, Montreal, n.d.

Sunquist, Scott W. et al. *A Dictionary of Asian Christianity*. Grand Rapids, MI: William B. Eerdmans Publishing Company, 2001

Taiwan Catholic Church Directory, 2001. Taipei: Catholic Archdiocese of Taipei, 2001.

Tan, Jin and Patricia Roy, *The Chinese in Canada*. Ottawa: Canadian Historical Association, Booklet 9, 1985.

Tan, Jonathan Y. *Introducing Asian American Theologies*. Maryknoll, NY: Orbis, 2008.

Tesoro, Dindo Rei M. and Joselito Alviar Jose, *The Rise of Filipino Theology*. Paasay City, Philippines: Paulines, 2004.

Toronto Our Lady of Mount Carmel Chinese Church. *Toronto Chinese Catholic Centre, 20th Anniversary, 1967–1987.*

Ujimoto, K. Victor and Gordon Hirabayash, eds. *Visible Minorities and Multiculturalism: Asian in Canada*. Toronto: Butterworths, 1980.

Wadley, Susan S. ed., *The Powers of Tamil Women*. Syracuse, NY: Syracuse University, 1980.

Wickberg, Edgar., ed. *From China to Canada: A History of the Chinese Communities in Canada*. Toronto: McClelland and Stewart, 1982.

Yu, Chai-Shin. "Koreans in Canada (in Toronto) and Korean Studies in Canada," *Korea-Canada in Emerging Asia-Pacific Community*. Seoul: Yonsei University, Institute of East and West Studies, 1988.

Zhu, Hong. Capital Transformation and Immigrant Integration: Chinese Independent Immigrants' Language and Social Practices in Canada. Ph. D. Diss., University of Toronto, 2005.

Zucchi, John. *A History of Ethnic Enclaves in Canada*, Ottawa: Canadian Historical Association, Booklet No. 31, 2007.

———. *Italians in Toronto: Development of a National Identity, 1875–1935*. Montreal: McGill-Queen's University Press, 1988.

Index

BIO GAS
ENERGY

This book has been printed on 100% post consumer
waste paper, certified Eco-logo and processed chlorine free.